The Hollywood Professionals

VOLUME 6

THE HOLLYWOOD PROFESSIONALS

Volume 1   Michael Curtiz
             Henry Hathaway
             Raoul Walsh
Volume 2   Henry King
             Lewis Milestone
             Sam Wood
Volume 3   Frank Borzage
             Howard Hawks
             Edgar G. Ulmer
Volume 4   Tod Browning
             Don Siegel
Volume 5   John Cromwell
             Mervyn LeRoy
             King Vidor
Volume 7   Leo McCarey
             Billy Wilder

The Hollywood Professionals

VOLUME 6

Capra, Cukor, Brown

Allen Estrin

South Brunswick and New York: A. S. Barnes and Company
London: The Tantivy Press

A.S. Barnes and Co., Inc.
Cranbury, New Jersey 08512

The Tantivy Press
Magdalen House
136-148 Tooley Street
London SE1 2TT, England

Library of Congress Cataloging in Publication Data (Revised)

Canham, Kingsley.
 The Hollywood professionals.

 CONTENTS: v. 1. Michael Curtiz. Raoul Walsh.
Henry Hathaway.—v. 2. Denton, C. Henry King.
Canham, K. Lewis Milestone. Thomas, T. Sam Wood.—
[etc.]—v. 6. Estrin, A. Frank Capra, George Cukor,
Clarence Brown.
 1. Moving-picture producers and directors—United
States—Biography. I. Denton, Clive. II. Thomas,
Tony, 1927-   III. Belton, John. IV. Rosenthal,
Stuart. V. Kass, Judith M. VI. Estrin, Allen.
VII. Title.
PN1998.A2C315   791.43'0233'0922 [B]   72-1786
ISBN 0-498-02237-4 (v. 6)

PRINTED IN THE UNITED STATES OF AMERICA

For my aunt, Lilian Gust

Contents

Acknowledgments
Author's Introduction

FRANK CAPRA   15
Frank Capra Filmography   78
GEORGE CUKOR   89
George Cukor Filmography   125
CLARENCE BROWN   139
Clarence Brown Filmography   180

Bibliographies   188
Index   191

Acknowledgments

Like film-making, a book written on film-makers, while the vision of one person, is largely a co-operative effort. I owe a great deal to the following people: my publisher, Peter Cowie, who maintained his enthusiasm for this book throughout thick and thin; Gail Runnfeldt, who provided the inspiration for the commencement of the project; Ingrid McCleod, whose wise counsel buoyed me throughout; John Frayne, Edwin Jahiel, Michael Mullin, John Stubbs, Steven P. Hill, and my editor, Allen Eyles, all of whom read and offered constructive criticism of various portions of the manuscript. I owe a profound thanks to Robert Carringer upon whose criticism and advice I relied heavily throughout the entire project, and Susan Chamberlin whose aid and encouragement were invaluable during the final stages. Douglas, J. Lemza who, while the director of Films Incorporated's National Theatrical Sales, generously provided many of the films I needed to see. Jeremy Boulton and Nicki North of the British Film Institute and Barbara Humphrys of the American Film Institute also gave unselfishly of their time to help me see films. The reference staffs of the BFI and the University of Illinois—Urbana libraries were most gracious in helping me to find important written materials. And others gave different, but equally important sorts of aid: my parents—Mildred and Donald Estrin, Edward Clancy, Billy Doroshow, Richard Reibman, Chris Kerr, Frank Hope, Lynne Bowkett and Kate McCauley.

Author's Introduction

To study the work of Frank Capra, George Cukor and Clarence Brown is to get an excellent composite picture of the so-called Golden Age of Hollywood. While each produced consistently fine work over several decades, taken together their respective cinemas offer an interesting insight into the development of American Film: Brown's brilliant silent work demonstrates how successfully the silent film director could communicate emotions and ideas through moving pictures; Capra's modern morality plays of the Thirties helped to shape the face of the industry in that decade and illustrated how accurately the cinema could reflect the hopes and aspirations of an entire society; Cukor's innovative social comedies of the late Forties and early Fifties provided an inspiration for the work of the French New Wave directors and that of American directors such as John Cassavetes. And while Capra, Cukor and Brown all had a complete command of their craft, each also excelled in one particular area: Capra in film editing and pacing, Cukor as a director of actors, and Brown in lighting and composition. Furthermore, while each placed a premium on the entertainment values of their films, each also pursued throughout their careers distinct and identifiable thematic preoccupations worthy of detailed study.

The Hollywood Professionals

VOLUME 6

FRANK CAPRA

For nearly half a century now critics have tried to identify exactly where Frank Capra's cinema stands politically. As Donald Willis notes, his films have been confidently labelled by different sources as communist and fascist propaganda.[1] He has been called a socialist, a marxist, a populist and an agrarian. *Mr. Deeds Goes to Town* (1936), to take a specific film, can be pro-New Deal or anti-New Deal depending on the critic. The reasons for the disparity of opinion is that Capra's work does not really fall into any political sphere. On the one hand, his criticism of society is so broad that it defies classification, while on the other, in its broadness, it touches a dozen political ideologies. The fact is that when Capra, a director who perhaps better understood the power of film to impress and influence than any of his contemporaries in Hollywood, attacks an idea or an institution he does so not from a particular political perspective, but from a moral one. He is not, for example, against big business *per se*. Grant Matthews in *State of the Union* (1948) owns a large airplane manufacturing company. Rather he is against monopolism, underhanded business practices—against greed. Capra does not despise politicians. Jefferson Smith's future is, after all, clearly in politics. He objects to corruption in government, deception of voters, easy compromise. Capra is not anti-intellectual. He is himself highly educated and a collector of rare books. He simply dislikes snobbery and elitism.

A limited, but useful parallel can be drawn here between Capra and Charles Dickens. Both raised themselves from youthful poverty to a position of great prominence in their art. Both retained an essentially middle-class view of life, and expressed this view in their work. Both established a unique rapport with a certain class of people, and, most importantly, both perceived social ills in moralistic terms. George Orwell, writing of Dickens generally and *Hard Times* specifically, draws some conclusions about the novelist's political vision which are equally appropriate to Capra:

> There is not a line in the book that can properly be called Socialistic; indeed, its tendency if anything is pro-capitalist, because its whole moral is that capitalists ought to be kind, not that workers ought to be rebellious. Bounderby is a bullying windbag and Gradgrind has

15

been morally blinded, but if they were better men, the system would work well enough—that, all through, is the implication. And so as social criticism goes, one can never extract much more from Dickens than this, unless one deliberately reads meaning into him. His whole 'message' is one that at first glance looks like an enormous platitude: If men would behave decently the world would be decent.[2]

For Capra then, as for Dickens, it is not specific errors in the social system that are of primary interest, but the manner in and degree to which the system has strayed from its proper moral base. Even in a setting as localised as that in *Mr. Smith Goes to Washington,* Capra's criticism is almost exclusively moral. For Capra, things begin to go wrong when people lose their moral centre, when they forget the common sense principles of moderation and fair play as Anthony Kirby does in *You Can't Take It with You* (1938), Senator Paine does in *Mr. Smith Goes to Washington* (1939) and the conventioneers do in *Meet John Doe* (1941). The only way to get things straight is to recover and hold firmly to a proper sense of morality. In other words, the reformation of the spirit is more important than specific changes in the social structure. Or better, changes in the spirit must occur before there can be positive changes in the structure. Hence, Capra offers no concrete solutions to the social ills he exposes. The seemingly detailed plans of Tom Dickson in *American Madness* (1932) and of Deeds in *Mr. Deeds Goes to Town* for economic recovery are really only important in so far as they highlight the exemplary character of the men who formulate them. Are we to believe, as Penelope Houston suggests, that Capra genuinely considered Deeds' plan for parcelling out an acre of land, some seed and a cow to dispossessed farmers to be the answer to the nation's agricultural problem?[3] I think not. But the scheme does tell us a lot about Deeds; that he is a dreamer (albeit a practical one) whose heart is in the right place. Whether his ambitious plan is executed as he intends is of little significance.

In the past several years Capra's critical "stock" has been rapidly rising. This is partly because critics have just begun to get a sense of the complexity of Capra's best films, and partly because the moral philosophy espoused in Capra's cinema has once again become acceptable. The director's most famous films were fashioned in a period of national self-doubt brought about initially by economic failures, and then later by the birth and rapid expansion of Fascism in Europe. These events threw into question the efficacy of the American system of democracy. The *raison d'être* of Capra's cinema was to reaffirm that system, and the director did so primarily by recalling the great principles on which the republic was founded, and the great men who formulated those principles—Washington, Jefferson, Lincoln—saints of American political history with whom Capra's own heroes are closely associated. So today, as the country once again re-evaluates itself and questions not only its political structure but its moral structure as well, Capra's glorification of individualism, his reverence for individual and institutional integrity and his plea for compassion have again found a sympathetic following.

★   ★   ★

It can be accurately stated that, as fantastic as the story lines of Capra's films sometimes are, none are as fantastic as the story of the director's own life. After learning Capra's personal history it is not difficult to see why he should have such an abiding faith in the individual's ability to triumph over great adversity; he overcame it himself not only in the course of his adult life, but from birth.

Capra was born in Sicily on May 18, 1897, the sixth of seven children. Like most of the residents of the island, his parents were poor farmers. They immigrated to the United States when Capra was six in order to join their eldest son, who had already settled in the Sicilian ghetto of Los Angeles. Being poor, they found life in America little better than it had been in Sicily. It was the painful knowledge that his family was illiterate, Capra says, that inspired him with a fierce desire for education. He pursued his goal with a vigour perhaps only a person of his background could. Earning money to give to his mother so that he could justify the time he spent in school proved more difficult than school itself. He breezed through high school, graduating at sixteen, and despite family objections, was determined to continue his education. He entered California Institute of Technology in February 1915.[4] He worked his way through school by labouring at a variety of odd-jobs including running a student laundry and waiting on tables in a campus fraternity. In June 1918 he was awarded a degree in chemical engineering.

In a nation embroiled in a world war, Capra's engineering skills were much in demand. But the new graduate had no intention of accepting civilian job offers. He had visions of fighting for democracy in the front lines, and so joined the Army. However, if Capra did not want to take immediate advantage of his education the Army did. Pvt. Capra was sent not to France but to San Francisco to teach mathematics to artillery officers. When the war ended he found himself caught in the post-war depression and could not find employment as an

engineer, so returned home to Los Angeles. There he became
seriously ill. After a slow recovery (more than a decade later this
illness was diagnosed as acute appendicitis), Capra left home physi-
cally battered and bitter over his recent personal failures. This phase
in his life, his aimless wandering throughout the American West to his
first encounter with film-making some three years later, comprises
one of the most interesting, but least detailed, chapters in Capra's
history.

During this interval, Capra does not seem to have had any
particular career ambition. Perhaps he was more interested in
self-discovery than anything else. After all, his life to this point had
left him little time for such reflection. Once again, he supported
himself by working a variety of odd jobs—hawking speculative
mining stocks and playing guitar in local bistros were among a few of
his occupations. Mostly, however, he sold photographs. Working
house to house in cities in California, Arizona, Utah and Nevada, he
peddled coupons for a major photographic chain. Capra's commission was the $1 deposit required for every sale. On a good day he
might make five or six dollars and, after a string of good days, he
could take the rest of the week off. He was independent and his time
was his own—personal freedoms which have always been of essential
importance to him.

It was during these years that Capra says he "fell in love with
America."[5] Contemporary critics of the director's early work found
his films so refreshing because he seemed to have a knack for
effectively characterising unique American types; it was during this
period of his life that he became familiar with such types—the Oscar
Shapleys of his cinema. *It Happened One Night* can be seen as an
homage to these years. The folksy roadside motels, the bus station
porter announcing stops in a high-pitched monotone, the sardonic
telegraph operator, the roadside thief who picks up Peter and Ellie,
Peter's happy salute to the bums on the freight train, his theories on
the science of hitch-hiking, were inspired by this free-wheeling and
fondly remembered period in Capra's life.

Capra's first job in motion pictures, like those of so many of his
contemporaries in Hollywood in the Twenties and Thirties, came
purely by chance. In the winter of 1921 Capra found himself in San
Francisco, unemployed. He read in a local newspaper that a small,
new film studio was just opening in town. He decided to investigate,
found the studio and its owner, a ham Shakespearian actor by the
name of Walter Montague, in a run-down gymnasium. Montague

wanted to make a film of Rudyard Kipling's poem "The Ballad of Fultah Fisher's Boarding House". Capra was intrigued. He told the actor that he was a director from Hollywood. Impressed more by his moxie than his bogus credentials, Montague gave Capra his commission.

Capra scoured the docks for real drunks and floozies to populate his film, and he hired a cameraman who could be trusted not to reveal how little he (Capra) really knew about film-making. Seeing the film, one can readily believe Capra's claim that he found most of his "actors" on the waterfront. The location, a waterfront drive, is also assuredly genuine and well-suited to Kipling's stark melodrama of jealousy among three wharfside low lifes. For a first attempt at film direction, Capra demonstrates an intuitive sense of the cinematic well worth noting. For example, he films most of the climactic struggle between the Dane and Salem Hardiecker in silhouette. At one point in the struggle, after the heroine, Anne, realises that her vanity has been responsible for the Dane's death, she rushes, her hair in disarray, her mascara streaked by tears, straight toward the camera, her face growing surrealistically larger and more grotesque as she approaches.

The film was released by Pathe. Critics were impressed by its realism. Their positive reaction to the film's apparent authenticity made a strong impression on the young director. After *Fultah's Boarding House,* Capra made a point of casting actors who were in real life as similar to their film characters as possible so that, in effect, they would need to do as little acting as necessary. He delayed the filming of *Mr. Deeds* for months, for instance, so that he could have Gary Cooper in the title role. His desire for authenticity extended to other phases of production, such as art direction and cinematography. Capra always preferred to shoot in the open air, and when he had to film in the studio, he fastidiously saw to it that every set came as close to the real thing as possible—such as when he had the Senate chamber reconstructed in detail on a Columbia sound stage for *Mr. Smith Goes to Washington.*

Capra says that the moment he gazed through the eyepiece of a camera his doubts about his future were resolved. Yet although his directing debut was auspicious, he really knew very little about the director's craft. He decided, therefore, to learn more about the mechanics of film-making before directing again. He got a job in a film lab processing and printing celluloid, worked as a prop man and then as an editor. He became a screenwriter when he was hired as a gag man for Hal Roach's "Our Gang" comedies. After six months with Roach he moved to Mack Sennett's studio, the hub of silent screen comedy throughout the Twenties. There Capra, along with another writer, Arthur Ripley, and a director, Harry Edwards, was assigned the seemingly unenviable task of developing a comic Sennett had recently discovered—Harry Langdon. In 1924 Langdon was touring tank towns as a second-rate vaudeville comedian. Sennett, legendary for spotting star potential where no one else could even imagine it, had seen Langdon's routine and had a hunch something could be done with him.

Capra, along with Ripley and Edwards, moulded Langdon into a screen comic who is fundamentally naive, a child-man whose most prominent trait is his innate child-like goodness. The key to the Langdon hero is that he is essentially a passive being, first a victim of circumstance, then finally triumphant over it. Capra describes him this way: ". . .he sees no evil, hears no evil, bears no evil to anybody. He is Mr. Good—he's the good little elf. And only his goodness wins out."[6] As Capra implies, the Langdon hero does not control his own destiny; it has already been mapped out by the providential force that looks after him.

The first comedy sequence in *The Strong Man* (1926), which Capra wrote and directed (Edwards having departed after Langdon's first feature, *Tramp, Tramp, Tramp* [1926]) is a crystallisation of this. The opening shots and subtitles set the action in a war-torn battlefield. During a lull in the fighting we find Harry alone in "no man's land" (certainly the most appropriate place for him) trying to hit a tin can with a machine gun. Having no success, he picks up a sling shot, which he happens to have handy, takes aim, and strikes the can on the first shot. Later when he is confronted by an enemy soldier his machine guns fails him once again. He turns to his trusty sling shot, and by slinging biscuits and mashed onions at the opponent drives him off (temporarily) in defeat. Had the biblical David been able to use a machine gun to slay Goliath he most assuredly would have, but it will not do for Harry. To him the machine gun is a toy, as are all such threatening and dangerous objects. When at the conclusion of the film he uses a cannon to triumph over a mob in a Cloverdale saloon he takes the same curious-child attitude toward the weapon. In *Long Pants* (1927), also directed by Capra, when Harry tries to murder his *fiancée* he proves hopelessly incapable of executing his plan. His all-encompassing innocence precludes him from being ruthless and

Harry Langdon in LONG PANTS (1927)

cunning enough to be able to effectively carry out a murder, just as it precludes his knowing how to use a machine gun.

The Langdon hero might be seen as a cherub (he certainly looks like one) whose mission on earth is, by his very presence, to throw into relief the moral corruption of the people who surround him: unscrupulous competitors, bootleggers, gangsters, gun molls. Capra defines Langdon's enemies as he defines the enemies of his heroes of the Thirties—in terms of their immorality. In *Long Pants,* for example, Harry rejects the dope-peddling *femme fatale* with whom he has become infatuated after he perceives her for what she really is. He has imagined her to be some sort of fairy princess and himself her white knight, but after he watches her behave in a manner very much unlike a princess (she gets into a brawl with another woman over the attentions of a gangster), he realises he has been sadly mistaken and returns home to his family and his *fiancée* for whom he is obviously much better suited.

Capra's heroes would come a long way from Langdon in the years ahead. They would demonstrate qualities of common sense, resourcefulness and determination which Harry woefully (but better for the comedy, of course) lacks. But Capra's heroes, particularly Long John in *Meet John Doe,* retain Harry's child-like moral purity; and their fundamental goodness serves to justify the timely intervention of Providence on their behalf, as it does for Harry. Capra's future films also retain many of the *motifs* established in these silent comedies. The director's affection for small towns and rural folk, his suspicion of big cities and distaste for city slickers, the "clothesline" plot on which to hang episodic, self-contained comedy sequences, all these features have their roots in the Langdon comedies. One can also trace to these films many of the sight gags found in Capra's later cinema. The gag in *Tramp, Tramp, Tramp,* for example, where Harry spits defiantly at the tornado he has just turned away, only to have this gesture come back and land on his own shoulder, appears again and again (though in different guises) throughout Capra's cinema.

Although Harry Edwards, not Capra, receives the directing credit for Langdon's first feature, Capra claims to have worked on nearly every phase of the production. "This was my first opportunity to become involved in all the mysteries of independent film-making. I became co-everything: co-producer with Langdon, co-director with Edwards, co-writing head with Ripley."[7] Edwards left Langdon because, according to Capra, he could not tolerate Langdon's "approval and disapproval of his every move."[8] Capra replaced Edwards. His ascension to the fast-changing sphere of Hollywood elite was nearly as remarkable as the star he was now to direct. Less than two years before he had been making $35 a week writing gags for Hal Roach; now he was directing "a rising star of compelling magnitude" commanding a salary of $650 a week.

The Strong Man is directed in essentially the same style as its predecessor, indicating—not surprisingly—that Capra at this state in his career relied primarily on what he had learned from Edwards. But the second Langdon feature is nevertheless clearly superior to the first. By the time Capra took control he understood all the nuances of his star's *persona,* and this knowledge enabled him to eliminate most of the inconsistencies that had weakened the first feature. In *The Strong Man* and *Long Pants* the comedy routines are more intricate and better paced; and the characterisation of the hero is purer Langdon and less imitative of Chaplin and Lloyd. Also the moral conflicts between Langdon and the villains are set off much more sharply in these two films than they are in *Tramp, Tramp, Tramp.* This is surely Capra's influence.

The Strong Man was a great success critically and financially. Langdon had now become a full-fledged super-star, ranked among the greats of silent screen comedy—Chaplin, Keaton and Lloyd—and consequently was exposed to all the trappings of stardom including an inflated sense of self-importance. He began to form his own ideas about his screen character, ideas that clashed with Capra's. This discord between star and director, which continued through the filming of *Long Pants,* ended when Langdon fired Capra sometime just before the final cut of this film was made. For Langdon, *Long Pants* was another hit. First National exercised its option for three more Langdon features. With Capra gone, Langdon decided to direct himself. Each successive effort proved a worse flop. By 1929 Langdon was a has-been. It remains an open question as to whether in dropping Capra, Langdon doomed himself to failure or whether he simply did not have enough time in three films to develop his own skills as a director. It would, however, be difficult to deny by any argument that Capra, through his deft fusing of Langdon's considerable talents as a comedian with his own carefully considered concept of the star's screen character, was in fact crucially responsible for the comic's phenomenal, though short-lived success, and by extension, responsible for some of the best moments of silent comedy.

After being sacked by Langdon, Capra had difficulty finding employment. Langdon, it seems, had spread the story that he had really been directing himself all along, that Capra was merely a gag man he kept around for laughs. It probably did not take much convincing to put this fiction over. After all, Chaplin, Keaton and Lloyd directed themselves and wrote their own material, so it might be readily assumed that Langdon had been doing the same. Nevertheless, after a few months Capra was hired by an independent producer, Robert Kane, to direct a sentimental comedy, *For the Love of Mike* (1927), starring Ben Lyon and Claudette Colbert. Shot in New York, the film was inadequately financed and Capra barely managed to put seven reels together. Although it received favourable reviews in the trade papers, the film was not a commercial success.

An unemployed director with a bleak future, Capra returned to Sennett's to work again as a screenwriter. The director does not hesitate to say that this period was the low point in his professional career. It is also another personal experience he has relived in his own cinema. Consistently, throughout his work, his heroes suffer a humiliating defeat at a key point in the drama. They must, as Capra himself had to do, struggle against the temptation to give up and go home, and reach within themselves to overcome the setback.

Capra's own chance to restore his lost dignity and confidence came after three long months in Sennett's writers' "tower". The mercurial Harry Cohn, production chief of Columbia Pictures, in 1928 a struggling minor studio, offered him a job as a director. Cohn had been battling to keep his studio solvent since he, his brother and another partner, Joe Brandt, had formed Columbia (then called CBC) in the early Twenties. Costs were kept down by cutting corners at every level of the studio's operation from making certain no one left the lights on in the studio offices to hiring actors and directors who could not find employment at the major studios. Somehow Cohn made it work. While most small studios were folding or being absorbed by bigger companies, Cohn kept his studio going. And despite its small production budgets and uncertain future, out of Columbia in the late Twenties and early Thirties came some of Hollywood's most gifted artists: cinematographer Joseph Walker who became "Capra's cameraman" was already there when the director arrived, as was Harrison Wiley, an ingenious, if unknown, art director, whose fine work can be seen in the early features Capra directed for Columbia; performers Roscoe Karns, Barbara Stanwyck and Jean Arthur, writers Jo Swerling and Robert Riskin, and art director Stephen Goosson all would make a name for themselves and Columbia a few years later.

Capra says that Cohn called him only because his name was the first on a list of unemployed directors. It seems more likely that Capra had the best credentials of those on the list. He had, after all, directed two popular comedies, *The Strong Man* and *Long Pants*, and Cohn would hardly have been one to pay much attention to the rumours about Capra's small contribution to Langdon's success, especially now that without Capra, Langdon was clearly on the way out. At any rate, Cohn and Capra struck up a unique bargain. Cohn would pay the director $1000 a film (considering that it took six weeks to make even these low budget features, this was far less than he had been earning while working for Langdon) and, as was Capra's wish, he would let Capra produce, direct and co-write each film. Even though the two men battled constantly over production questions, their bargain remained firm for thirteen years. Only the director's salary changed. It was the best deal Cohn ever made. In five years, primarily on the strength of Capra's successes, Columbia would move off "poverty row" to become recognised as a major American studio.

Of Capra's early years with Columbia, 1928-1932, a period in which he directed nineteen films, little has been written. In his autobiography Capra only skims this chapter of his life, often demeaning his work, claiming that it was an experimental phase in which he honed his technical skills and tried his hand at a variety of different genres. Yet an examination of some of these films proves that not only did Capra explore various genres and experiment with new camera techniques, but he also tested many of the thematic preoccupations which were later to dominate his cinema. These early films, beginning with *That Certain Thing* (1928), demonstrate that *Mr. Deeds* and the "message" films that follow—*Lost Horizon, You Can't Take It with You, Mr. Smith, Meet John Doe, It's a Wonderful Life* and *State of the Union*—are clearly part of a thematic chronology which begins not in the mid-Thirties but much earlier.

Like Capra's best comedies, *That Certain Thing* has an endearing, folksy charm and is expertly paced. Both of these qualities are evident in the film's first sequence which, in the manner of a Langdon comedy, is a series of gags that build upon each other toward a final "topper". The sequence begins with the film's heroine, Molly (Viola Dana), vainly attempting to get her two younger brothers to finish their bath. When the boys prove unruly, Molly pours cold water over their heads in order to get them moving. The water spills on the floor, leaking through it to the apartment below. A small dog watches the water drip from the ceiling to the floor. A woman walks into the room. She sees the water on the floor and the dog next to the water. She spanks the innocent canine and rubs his nose in the water, assuming, of course, that he has ruined her carpet. As is Capra's style, the comedy in this sequence is well endowed with pathos (in this case, literally dripping with it), but as in the best moments of the Langdon comedies, the pathos is unforced, flowing naturally from the carefully arranged events of the sequence. Although Capra recreates some of the best aspects of the Langdon comedies in this film, *That Certain Thing* also represents a sharp break from his past work. Freed from having to fit his thematic preoccupations to a specific, tightly prescribed screen personality, Capra began to explore new avenues.

Ralph Graves plays the hero, A.B. Charles Jr. the son of a wealthy restaurateur. Something of a Lost Generation dissolute, Junior spends his father's money impulsively and drinks heavily. Of course, he has never worked a day in his life, while Molly, like Capra's most famous heroines, is a working girl. As the opening sequence implies, she can be both fun-loving and kind-hearted, but spending much of her youth in a slum tenement (as the leaky roof also implies) supporting her mother and the two boys has left her frustrated and bitter. She does not disguise the fact that she desperately wants to get out. When she meets Junior by accident one afternoon, she sees her chance and grabs it. With a clear conscience she gold-digs Junior for all he is worth. Infatuated by her, he asks her to dinner that evening. Molly rushes through the tenement borrowing the best clothes she can find: shoes from one neighbour, a slip from another, a beautiful dress from the Jewish tailor. The building stirs with excitement over the news of Molly's good fortune. When Junior arrives in his chauffeured black limousine, Molly takes pains to be sure her fellow tenants get an "eye-full" of her prize.

Junior takes her to the best night club, and as the evening progresses grows steadily more drunk and more infatuated with Molly. When in a moment of caprice he proposes to her, she immediately accepts. They are married that night. The news of their whirlwind, six-hour courtship is splashed across the society pages of the morning papers. Junior's father sends his son an ultimatum— have the marriage annulled or face disinheritance. Junior refuses to obey his father's command. To his acute humiliation, the roomful of presents he has just purchased for Molly on his father's credit are immediately carted off. Molly, however, who has apparently fallen in love with Junior sometime during the night, overhears the conversation between Junior and his father's representative and leaves the honeymoon suite in order to give Junior the chance to return to his father. With distinctly Capra-like irony, then, her marriage—which Molly thought would put her on "easy street"—has left her worse off than she began.

In a driving rain Molly walks home. The clothes she has borrowed are ruined. The tenants, her friends, gather at the stairs as she enters. We might expect them to be sympathetic to her misfortune, but instead the opposite proves true. In a series of rapid crosscuts Capra juxtaposes the despondent heroine and the seemingly vengeful tenants (anticipating to a great degree the style in which he handles mob scenes in his later films) ridiculing Molly's adversity. This chilling sequence reveals that long before *Meet John Doe* Capra was aware of the paradox, a key one in his cinema, that your friends can become, if they believe you have abused their good faith, your worst enemies. Had Molly returned in great splendour, as her friends expected, she would have likely become a folk hero of the neighbourhood. But when she returns in disgrace—implying that she had been deceiving them all along; that she is, in effect, like Long John in *Meet John Doe*, a "fake"—they turn on her and take grim satisfaction in her downfall. She has proven to be no better than they. But it goes deeper than this. Just as they secretly had hoped she would fail and return to the tenement, they also had hoped she would escape, to prove that escape was possible. So not only has she ruined their best garments, she has also ruined their dreams.

Junior, however, does not desert her. Their marriage was built on morally unsound motives—Junior's flightiness and Molly's avarice—so in Capra's moralistic universe it was bound to lead them both to disaster. But now those motives have been purged. Their marriage begins anew, founded this time on their mutual love. They soon start to amass a fortune of their own after Junior gets the bright idea to sell hearty box lunches to labourers. Their firm, the Molly Box Lunch Company, does so well, in fact, that it threatens to drive Junior's father, who has made his fortune by selling flimsy sandwiches to workers ("Remember the secret of my success," he tells his aide. "Cut the ham thin!") out of business. The old man goes to visit his new competitors (he does not know his son and wife are behind it) with the intention of buying them out. He meets his son who pretends to be the company's bookkeeper. Junior bluffs his father into believing that the Molly Box Lunch Company is in excellent financial condition, when, in fact, because of his ambitious expansion plans it has over-extended itself. He and Molly then team up to hoodwink the frightened old man into buying the company for the inflated price of $100,000. When he learns that his son and new wife (once he has seen her as a practical businesswoman, he thoroughly approves of his son's choice) own the company, he is so delighted that he adds another $100,000 as a belated wedding present.

Consider, then, how neatly the film fits Capra's moral perspective.

It celebrates the benefits of hardwork, marriage, fair treatment of consumers (the secret of Junior and Molly's success is that they "cut the ham thick"),—and it scorns bogus class barriers. Each of the protagonists is punished for their most prominent fault—Molly for her false pride, Junior for his irresponsibility, his father for his miserliness. They each in turn are humiliated for their sins. But, once they accept their punishment, they are redeemed: Junior and Molly make a success of their marriage and their business, and the old man gets his son and daughter-in-law back. The family unit, a symbol of strength and harmony in Capra's cinema, is reaffirmed at the end of the film.

By the end of 1928, a year in which he directed seven full-length features, Capra had established himself as Columbia's ace director and overcome the Langdon stigma. As a reviewer of *Matinee Idol* noted in "Film Daily", "It looks as if Frank Capra has proved he doesn't need a Harry Langdon to prove he's a comedy director."[9] Yet as Capra shifted freely from comedy to straight drama, from aerial dog fights to Fifth Avenue drawing rooms, he never left any doubt as to who was "authoring" his films.[9] The same sort of preoccupations that can be identified in *That Certain Thing* also emerge in many of the other "unknown" films Capra directed between 1928 and 1933. There is unfortunately not space in this essay to examine these films in detail, but a survey will serve to demonstrate the point that Capra's thematic bent did not spontaneously generate during the production of *Mr. Deeds*, but developed surely and steadily from his earlier cinema.

The breakdown of the family unit and the consequence of such a disruption are the central concerns of *The Younger Generation,* Capra's first film to use sound (background music with some dialogue scenes). In the final sequence of the film, Capra depicts the fate of a man, Morris Goldfish (Ricardo Cortez), who has estranged himself from his family by his unconscionable pursuit of wealth and social position. In the beginning of the sequence Capra cross-cuts between three shots of Morris's mother, his sister and brother-in-law and their baby as they stand in the doorway of Morris's Fifth Avenue home, and single shots of Morris. The shot selection underlines Morris's sense that, after his life-long antagonism of his sister and her husband and the alienation of his mother, he has left himself alone without a refuge. Capra's innovative use of sound further highlights Morris's isolation: his mother and sister playfully argue off-camera as to the best way to hold the baby, while Morris (on camera) watches them silently in a single-shot.

Like Dombey in Dickens's "Dombey and Son", all Morris has to show for his successful, single-minded pursuit of money is an empty mansion. His father's remark early in the film that "money ain't good for nothing if it don't buy happiness" comes back in Dickensian fashion to haunt the unhappy millionaire. The truth of this platitude in Capra's moralistic universe is demonstrated throughout the director's work, reaching its fullest expression in *You Can't Take It with You* when multimillionaire industrialist Anthony Kirby learns that playing the harmonica (music for Capra signifies spiritual fulfillment) can be a great deal more rewarding than amassing a munitions monopoly. (The converse, however—giving away money—*can* bring happiness as Dave the Dude finds out in *Lady for a Day,* 1933.)

In *Ladies of Leisure* (1930), the film that made Barbara Stanwyck a star, the hero Jerry (Ralph Graves), a young playboy and artist, becomes very interested in painting a beautiful gold-digger, Kay Arnold (Stanwyck), when he sees hope (with a capital H) in her eyes, an inspirational contrast to the sordid lives both have been living. After several modelling sessions, artist and subject fall in love and make plans to escape the city together for the starlit skies of Arizona. Jerry's blueblooded mother, however, objects to the match and entreats Kay to break if off. Kay reluctantly agrees, but in her subsequent despair decides to take her own life (the first of many instances of a Capra protagonist considering suicide) and so, while on a steamer on her way to Havana, leaps overboard. She is saved, however, and reunited with her lover. Here, as it does in all of Capra's films, love acts as a purifying force that brings to light the best qualities of both lovers and lends meaning to their previously meaningless lives. Furthermore, the film provides another example of how Capra sees love in the best American tradition transcending all class barriers.

A spectacular fire, symbolically enough, climaxes *The Miracle Woman* (1931), a story of a fake evangelist whose show business-like revival meetings attract hundreds of "sinners" to her sermons. Barbara Stanwyck plays the spell-binding young orator, Florence "Faith" Fallon, who leads an evangelical extravaganza complete with phoney cripples, tranquillised lions and a musical chorus of apple-cheeked youths dressed in white sweaters and pants. Although Florence headlines the show, it is Hornsby (Sam Hardy), its unscrupulous promoter, who keeps it going. Hornsby, an opportunist and a cynic in the mould of Capra's more famous villains, Jim Taylor *(Mr. Smith)* and D.B. Norton *(Meet John Doe),* understands only too well how easily the masses can be manipulated. In his, the most didactic of cinemas, Capra was obsessed with the idea of warning his audience away from mountebanks—large and small. That Capra was himself a charlatan of sorts during his vagabond days might help explain why he pursued this concern so vigorously in so many of his films: he knew how easily people could be deceived. Hence, as his dedication to this film, he offers the following: "*The Miracle Woman* is offered as a rebuke to anyone who, under the cloak of religion, seeks to sell for gold God's choicest gift to Humanity—FAITH."

Florence, however, eventually sees the error of her ways through her love for a blinded aviator (David Manners). In the climactic scene, she intends to confess her sins to her following, but a fire (again looking ahead to *Meet John Doe*) started by Hornsby stops her. The temple goes up in flames and the reformed evangelist is saved from a fiery death by the aviator. The film ends with Florence marching down a city street as a soldier in the Salvation Army. Hornsby, who watches her march past, shakes his head in disbelief.

The Miracle Woman was adapted from a play written by Robert Riskin and John Meehan. Riskin came to Hollywood, as most successful playwrights did then, on a Columbia contract and he and Capra collaborated together on the director's next film, *Platinum Blonde* (1931). During the next decade they came to be regarded as Hollywood's most respected director-writer team, working on ten films together. Capra recognised in Riskin a screenwriter who could write the sort of forceful, witty, natural dialogue that suited his own dynamic cinematic style. The screenwriter in turn found a director who, because he did not send his work to a dozen other writers to be redone, preserved his integrity as an author.

Riskin's unique talents are clearly evident in *Platinum Blonde*, a film about a newspaper reporter who falls in love with a beautiful, but shallow, socialite (Jean Harlow). The film's statement, on the emptiness and sterility of inherited wealth as contrasted to the fulfilment to be derived from such middle-class virtues as hard-work and self-sufficiency, although not new to Capra's cinema, set a guideline for similar statements in other films. The wily, but misguided hero, ace newshound Stew Smith (Robert Williams) is the prototype for Peter Warne in *It Happened One Night* as well as for Babe Bennett in *Mr. Deeds*, Saunders in *Mr. Smith* and Ann in *Meet John Doe*. Capra liked to have newspaper people in his films firstly because their daily contact with the seamier side of life usually made them hardened cynics, and so good subjects for conversion to a more wholesome and optimistic view of life when it was convincingly offered to them, but secondly because they, as Capra himself has put it, "were where the action was".

Capra collaborated once again with Jo Swerling, whom he seemed to prefer when directing melodramas, on his next film, *Forbidden*, before reuniting with Riskin for *American Madness*. Ostensibly *Forbidden* (1932) is a film which seems uncharacteristic of Capra. Yet the fact that Capra wrote the story himself would suggest that it meant more to him than merely a routine attempt to cash in on the latest trend. Barbara Stanwyck plays a homely, small-town librarian who dreams of a life of romance and adventure (like Harry in *Long Pants*, her imagination finds inspiration in a florid painting that hangs on the wall across from her desk). She books passage on a luxury cruiser for Havana, and exchanges her plain dresses and rimless spectacles for elegant gowns and elaborate make-up. On the ship she falls deeply in love with an ambitious politician, Bob Grover (Adolphe Menjou). The two spend several idyllic weeks together but when they arrive back in New York, Grover returns to his crippled wife for the sake of his political career. Lulu nevertheless remains his faithful mistress. Their illicit romance spans a life-time and leads to an illegitimate child, frequent deceptions and finally murder.

Capra opens the film with a lengthy reverie to rural America—a farmer with a team of horses ploughs a field, beautiful flowers and snow capped mountains fill the screen—complete with sweet, pastoral mood music. "Variety" in its review of the film called this sequence "wasted footage" but clearly it serves an important purpose for Capra in light of what happens to Lulu, a one time denizen of this paradise who gives it up for a tragic life in the city.[10] Like a character in a Victorian novel, though our sympathies are always with her, Lulu has to pay a horrible price for her immorality. Not only does she give up her child but, in order to protect Grover's political career, also murders her husband (Ralph Bellamy) after he discovers her relationship with the politician and threatens to expose both her and Grover. Grover, who is torn between his love for Lulu and the practical need to stay with his wife, also suffers because of his adultery. Racked with remorse for the life he has consigned Lulu to, he dies before his time. "I'm rotting inside," he tells Lulu not long before he dies. At the conclusion of the film, Lulu, who is pardoned by Grover in his last act as governor, is seen walking down a city street, an old woman who has now lost everything. Her life might have been dull in the country but she would have been much better off there, Capra seems to suggest. Harry in *Long Pants* had the sense to come home when his dreams turned sour, but Lulu unfortunately does not.

This same Victorian moral outlook can also be observed in *The Bitter Tea of General Yen* (1932), another film that is usually and

mistakenly regarded as uncharacteristic of Capra. The director says
in his autobiography that the film was banned in the British Empire
because the Queen's censors did not approve of the frank way it dealt
with the idea of miscegenation between an American missionary,
Megan Davis (Barbara Stanwyck), and a Chinese warlord, the General Yen (Nils Asther).[11] The film, however, was favourably reviewed
by the London "Times" and there exists no evidence in the records of
the British Board of Censors that it was, in fact, banned. More likely
the singular nature of the story (one wonders how contemporary
audiences reacted to the film's remarkable Freudian dream sequence
in which we learn that Megan, despite her protestations to the
contrary, really loves the General) and its sobering theme that any
attempt to westernise oriental culture must be both futile and
hypocritical, reflecting the deficiences of our own culture, simply
closed out any possibility for popular success. Or as "Variety" put it:
"Seeing a Chinaman attempting to romance with a pretty and
supposedly decent young American white woman is bound to provoke adverse reaction."[12] Ultimately, however, Capra's view of miscegenation is as conservative as Conrad's or Kipling's. While western
civilisation is rife with serious imperfections, it is all the westerner has
and he should stick to it, this film (like Conrad's "Heart of Darkness"
or Kipling's "Without Benefit of Clergy") would seem to suggest. To
become entwined in a culture not one's own, Megan and Yen both
learn, is to invite disaster.

By 1932 the director's films were being advertised in the trade
papers as Special Frank Capra Productions, and if his name was not
yet above the title it was displayed prominently enough below it.
Although it was still four years before *Mr. Deeds*, Capra clearly knew
where he was headed. In an interview in "Variety" in February 1932,
he predicts his future cinema:

> Someone is going to evolve a great film out of the depression . . .
> Satirical treatment of a plutocrat insanely trying to conserve wealth
> and finding happiness only when he is reduced to the bread line,
> will strike a responsive note in the mass mind. When the picture is
> made, it will inaugurate the cycle that follows in the wake of any
> successful film.[13]

That someone, of course, was Capra himself. Perhaps he and Riskin
were working on a story along these lines when he gave this interview,
but although they never made a film that exactly fits this description,
Capra hints at ideas here that found expression in his later cinema,
and most immediately in *American Madness*.

American Madness does, in fact, deal directly with the Depression, but the hero is not a plutocrat who has lost his fortune, but a banker in danger of losing his bank. Tom Dickson (Walter Huston) must certainly be a *rara avis* among bank presidents—a shrewd businessman who has also retained a strong sense of idealism. His board of directors, who are less idealistic, want him to alter his policy of giving loans on the strength of his personal confidence in the borrower rather than on solid collateral. But Dickson refuses to go along. For him character has always been any borrower's most important asset, and, as he himself points out, his judgement has been right "one-hundred per cent." He tells a director who questions him on one particular loan, "Jones is no risk, nor are the thousand of other Joneses throughout the country. It's they who have built up this nation to be the richest in the world, and it's up to the banks to give them a break."

Dickson, however, has his faith in the "Joneses" of the community severely tested when a malicious rumour regarding the Union National's solvency starts a run on the bank. Dickson first attempts to convince the mob that the bank is in fine shape and in no danger of collapse, but the depositors are too worried about their savings to listen to reason. Then he tries to save the bank by raising money from the large corporations with which he has done business, but they refuse to help. His mistake is that he does not appeal to his friends, the small businessmen whom he has generously assisted. One of his tellers, Matt (Pat O'Brien), however, recognises Dickson's error and phones the people whom he knows will come to Dickson's aid, even at the risk of their own personal fortunes. Soon these trusted friends arrive and, while shouting their faith in the bank, break through the mob and make their deposits. Their inspiring demonstration convinces the board of directors to throw their support to Dickson and the bank is saved.

American Madness not only anticipates the thematic bent of Capra's later Thirties cinema—even if you can't rely on the masses, you can trust your close friends, for example—and the director's preference for dealing with contemporary social issues, it also marks a significant stylistic advance. Capra explains in his autobiography that the pace of his films seemed to slow down somewhere between the set and the movie theatre. In order to correct this problem the director, during the filming of *American Madness*, actively sought to increase the tempo of his film. He cut out long walks, pared transition scenes to a minimum, cut out dissolves and replaced them with straight cuts or fast wipes; he overlapped dialogue and most importantly speeded up the pace of the scenes to one-third faster than normal. Capra: "If a scene played normally in sixty seconds, I increased the actor's pace until it played in forty seconds."[14] Indeed, the film does exude that sense of urgency Capra sought. The new, faster pace also allowed him to deal with more material. In *American Madness*, for instance, in the first half-hour Capra introduces into the film not one or two key relationships but five—Dickson and the bank directors; Dickson and his neglected wife (Kay Johnson); Helen (Constance Cummings) and Matt; Cyril (Gavin Gordon) and Mrs. Dickson; and Cyril and the gangsters. And then while orchestrating the spectacular run on the bank, he neatly resolves the various conflicts that have sprung from each of these relationships.

In general, the films Capra directed between 1928 and 1933 reveal not only many of his thematic preoccupations but also many of his visual motifs and plot conceits. Rain, for example, an essential feature in nearly all of Capra's best-known films, which the director uses both to create an atmosphere for romance (*It Happened One Night*) and of foreboding (*Meet John Doe*), figures romantically in *Ladies of Leisure* and menacingly in *That Certain Thing*. Junior and Stew Smith are not only clever, but also demonstrate an excellent right-cross, one of the tell-tale qualities of the heroes of Capra's *Deeds, Smith* and *Doe* trilogy. In *The Miracle Woman* and *American Madness*, Capra evidences his knack for populating mob scenes with the most convincingly ordinary faces Central Casting had to offer. In *Dirigible* and *The Bitter Tea of General Yen* he displays his skill for staging large-scale action sequences of the sort found in *Lost Horizon* and *Meet John Doe,* and perhaps most tellingly as it relates to the way these sequences are edited, the "Why We Fight" documentary series.

For the most part, the quality of these early films improves as Capra gains experience, but generally they are both strong and weak where one would expect Capra's films to be. As with most of the director's work the comedy sequences are usually the most appreciated, and the courtship scenes such as the one set in the aviator's apartment in *The Miracle Woman* tend to go on too long. But there are other aspects of these films which are unlike later Capra and unexpectedly fine. The stories, certainly in part because they are less complicated than his later films, resolve themselves without raising as many questions as they answer, and as Capra demonstrates particularly in *The Younger Generation, Forbidden* and *The Bitter Tea of General Yen,* he does not feel compelled to end his films on an optimistic note. In fact, the final sequences of these three films are among the most honest and convincing Capra directed.

The financial failure of *The Bitter Tea of General Yen* (which actually follows *American Madness* chronologically) convinced Capra to return once again to a subject with a peculiarly American flavour and characters with whom he was familiar. *Lady for a Day*, adapted by Riskin from a short story by Damon Runyon, concerns an apple vendor (May Robson) who, with the help of her gangster friend, Dave the Dude (Warren William), becomes a "queen for a day" and fools her daughter and her daughter's seigneurial fiancé into thinking she is a grand lady. Like many of Capra's films, it is a variation on the Cinderella theme. The unabashed but adroitly handled sentiment proved enormously popular with Depression audiences. For Capra the film was the first in a string of successes which ran uninterrupted through *Meet John Doe*. It was thought during these eight years that anything he directed would necessarily be a smash hit. Directors in Hollywood were as a rule not known to the general public. People

May Robson as Apple Annie in LADY FOR A DAY (1933)

went to the movies to see a particular star, but in the films Capra directed during the second half of this decade, the director's name on the marquee was a prime attraction. He became a personality in his own right, the subject of articles in newspapers and magazines. In 1938 he appeared on the cover of "Time." "The New Yorker" did a profile on him. "The Ladies Home Journal" visited his home and interviewed his wife. In the Thirties, perhaps only Cecil B. De Mille's name was as readily recognised as Capra's. Suffice to say that during the second half of the decade Capra was generally thought to be the most admired and respected director in Hollywood.

In terms of the success it achieved, *Lady for a Day* sets itself off from Capra's earlier films for several reasons. Although the director's previous films had been profitable, it was his first whose box-office return equalled that of any film from one of the major studios. It was the first Capra work to appear on "Film Daily's" Ten Best List. Finally, it was his first film (and Columbia's, too) to receive an Academy Award nomination. It did not win in any of the four categories in which it was nominated; the Oscars would come next year, in bunches, for *It Happened One Night* (1934).[15]

It Happened One Night won all five major awards—Best Picture, Best Director, Best Screenplay, Best Actress and Best Actor. Forty-two years elapsed before another film, *One Flew over the Cuckoo's Nest,* repeated this feat. The success of the film allowed Capra to realise his own personal American Dream, established him as the premier director in Hollywood, and gave him the independence to make films on subjects that intrigued him, with a shooting schedule that suited him, the budget he needed, and the actors he desired. It made Columbia a major studio, Harry Cohn a full-fledged movie mogul, and Clark Gable and Claudette Colbert superstars. The film itself, perhaps Capra's best loved, stands as a quintessential expression of mid-Thirties humour. Like most of Capra's Depression films, it can be seen as an historical document, a reflection of the American psyche in the midst of a great economic crisis, as much as it can be viewed as a consummately entertaining film.

It is hard to believe that so much could have resulted from a film that began so modestly. From the first, Capra had serious difficulties with the script and in casting the leading roles. Because of contract obligations to Colbert, he had to shoot the film in one month and, as always, had only a small budget to work with. But, in fact, its modesty

Clark Gable and Claudette Colbert in IT HAPPENED ONE NIGHT (1934)

**Clark Gable and Claudette Colbert in IT HAPPENED
ONE NIGHT (1934)**

is one of the film's charms. Gable in his first comedy role plays Peter
Warne, a hard-pressed newspaper reporter who crosses paths with a
runaway heiress, Ellie Andrews (Colbert), on a cross-country bus trip
from Miami to New York. He recognises the news value of a
day-to-day account of her flight and so decides to stay with her
throughout the journey. She wants nothing to do with him, but soon
realises that he can help her reach her destination and so accepts his
aid. Together they outfox her father's private detectives and in the
process fall in love.

In the best tradition of the picaresque form, which this film
certainly follows, the two protagonists reinforce the strengths and
expose the weaknesses of each other. Although she is an heiress,
Ellie's money, as so often in Capra's cinema, has not brought her
happiness; only when Peter introduces her to certain working-class
pleasures such as doughnut dunking and hitchhiking does she begin
to find contentment. Concurrently, Ellie brings out the grace and
generosity that had lay dormant behind Peter's tough-guy veneer.
For Capra the film represents a synthesis of his silent and sound work.
If the laughter does not come from the dialogue, it comes from a sight
gag; often it comes from both, each enhancing the other. The scene

on the bus where Ellie is crushed by the dozing fat man would have fitted nicely into a Langdon comedy. The outrageous, sometimes nonsensical monologues of a character like Oscar Shapely (Roscoe Karns), on the other hand, no amount of pantomine could communicate. Appropriately, one of the film's best remembered scenes, Peter and Ellie hitchhiking down a country road, suceeds as a fine blend of witty dialogue and resourceful sight gags.

Following *It Happened One Night* Capra suffered what might best be described as a nervous collapse. The elation of having reached the top of his profession, and the simultaneous revelation that having reached there he had nowhere to go but down, understandably produced a great strain. During this period of illness, however, Capra seems to have grasped the true power of the medium over which he now reigned. He could see from *It Happened One Night* how strongly people reacted to his romantic comedy, how closely they identified with the characters in the film (an idea of how closely can perhaps be illustrated by the now well-known fact that as a result of Clark Gable's revelation that he did not wear an undershirt in the first motel scene, the sales for this particular garment plummeted by half). Significantly, the New York critics did not respond well to the film when it first opened. It was only after it moved out to towns like Topeka, Kansas, and Little Rock, Arkansas, that it began to receive popular support, and it grew into one of the biggest box-office hits of the year largely on the strength of word-of-mouth endorsement. Capra had established a unique rapport with middle-America, and he himself realised it. If he could reach these people through a romantic comedy, could he reach them with a story that more clearly carried a socially relevant theme? Capra was confident that he could. *Mr. Deeds* is the first of his films which might be described as a modern morality play. The ideas which Capra put forth in these films have their origins in earlier films, but *Deeds* definitely marks a turning point in the director's career. Whereas in films like the Langdon comedies or *Lady for a Day* Capra tended to communicate his personal philosophy through the comedy, beginning with Deeds this order was reversed; that is, the promulgation of his themes now became his first concern, and comedy, though vital, became secondary in importance, a means to make his audience receptive to the moral precept. Consequently, one might chart a steady drift away from the comic romances of the director's early period to a more ironic mode that reaches its apex at the beginning of the next decade with *Meet John Doe*. In short, *Deeds* marks Capra's self-conscious emergence as a critic of contemporary morality.

Riskin said that he applied the same concepts of play construction to the writing of his film scenarios. The application of these concepts can be clearly seen in *Mr. Deeds.* Here Riskin and Capra seem to have divided their screenplay into essentially five acts. The first introduces Deeds in his hometown of Mandrake Falls, the second chronicles his triumphant first day in New York City, the third the betrayal of his trust by the woman with whom he has fallen in love, the fourth the formulation and quashing of his plan to help needy farmers, and the final act, the climactic courtroom battle.

Opening sequences in Capra's films are almost always fast paced. One of the rules Capra learned while directing low budget "quickies" for Columbia in the late Twenties was that an action-packed opening was the surest way to capture the attention of the audience; he never forgot that rule. At the onset of *Mr. Deeds*, the dialogue and editing tempo proceed at a feverish rate as newspaper editor MacWade (George Bancroft), attorney John Cedar (Douglass Dumbrille) and press agent Corny Cobb (Lionel Stander) pursue their frantic nationwide search for the man who has just inherited the $20 million Semple fortune. Cedar and Cobb find their man, one Longfellow Deeds, a writer of sentimental greeting cards, a tuba player, and an owner of a small business, in a rural town in Vermont. As soon as they arrive in Mandrake Falls the pace of the film slows dramatically and the claustrophobic interiors of the city scenes suddenly give way to open-air shooting. Thus does Capra establish a key contrast between life in the city (frenzied) and life in the country (calm).

The director's depiction of rural communities generally fits the stereotype—unpretentious people going about their business in their own good time. The country, however, is not an untainted paradise for Capra: its denizens are not beyond falling easy prey to bogus evangelists (*The Miracle Woman*) or supporting, if unwittingly, machine politics (*Mr. Smith*). But for the most part the rural community exists for Capra as a living testament to the nineteenth century America in all its mythical moral soundness that he finds so attractive. Time, as Capra reveals in cinematic terms in the opening sequences, simply moves slower in the country, and therefore communities like Mandrake Falls and people like Deeds have drifted less further away from the America Capra wishes we might all recapture. The city, in contrast, represents the present, so to speak, the extent to which we as a nation have degenerated. It is in the city where we find the moochers, the con-men, the shysters, the racketeers, and the sob sisters of Capra's cinema.

When Deeds gets to town he is predictably besieged by people who wish to fleece him of his inheritance: Cedar wants to get the power of attorney from Deeds so that he can control Deeds' investments and milk the trust for his own purposes; a con-man who claims to represent the deceased Mr. Semple's "common law wife" tries to high pressure Deeds into settling a $1 million on her; the board of directors for the city opera expects him to finance their season and their $180,000 debt. These parasites assume that because of his rural background Deeds is a fool who can easily be separated from his money ("Like taking candy from a baby," Cedar tells his partners). But they sadly underestimate their adversary. Deeds quickly sees through their double talk. As he says: "All these people want to work for nothing. It just isn't natural." The moral rightness of Deeds' position is obvious but important: he wants to use his inheritance to do the most good for the most number of people; Cedar and the others want to use it for their own profit. Deeds has no difficulty foiling their plans. His straightforward, commonsense responses cut right through their schemes. He is not, then, as Graham Greene suggests, "manhandled in a deeply selfish and brutal world."[16] If anything, during this first day in New York, at any rate, the selfish and brutal world is manhandled by Deeds. The hero's strength, however, clearly resides in his moral perspective. As long as he retains that, he holds the upper-hand over the swindlers, but as soon as he begins to doubt himself, to lose faith in his ideals and his principles, he becomes vulnerable to their villainy. The manner in which he loses that all-important perspective and the consequences of his disillusionment are the primary concerns of the film's third and fourth "acts".

Deeds' romantic vision was accurately described back in Mandrake Falls by his housekeeper: "He has foolish notions about saving a damsel in distress." (Harry had a similar notion in *Long Pants*). Deeds thinks he has found his princess during his first evening in New York. As he steps outside his mansion into a downpour a young woman crosses his path and faints in his arms, ostensibly from hunger and exhaustion. In truth, she is the star reporter for the "Morning Mail", Babe Bennett (Jean Arthur), who, encouraged by her editor's promise of a month's paid vacation, stages the fainting spell and accepts Deeds' knightly offer to take her to dinner in order that she might get a first-hand account of his impression of New York. Babe's initial instinct is to believe that Deeds is just another phoney, and she has no compunction about making a fool out of him for the sake of her paper's circulation and her own profit, but her cynicism gradually melts in the face of Deeds' unswerving sincerity. Deeds, however, has no knowledge of Babe's transformation. He sees her as only the embodiment of all his romantic fantasies. When he suddenly learns that Babe, whom he has been led to believe is a lowly stenographer, is really the reporter who has been making a chump out of him in the newspaper, his dreams are shattered with such a force that he refuses to listen to any of her explanations. Her manipulation of his trust, unlike the machinations of those who wish to cheat him out of his money, is a manifestation of cynicism with which he simply cannot cope.

For Deeds, Babe's betrayal is reason enough to abandon his plans for the inheritance. "They can have the estate," he tells Cobb disdainfully as he prepares to leave New York and return to Mandrake Falls. He has become, as Leland Poague claims, a cynic himself.[17] But before he can take this pernicious urban debility back to Mandrake Falls, he is snapped out of his self-pity, significantly, by one of his own kind—a down-and-out farmer. Waving a gun and threatening to kill Deeds for squandering his fortune on meaningless expenditures when thousands stand in bread lines, the pathetic farmer with his heart-rending tale of his own sad fate (one of the perversities of the Depression that is not lost on Capra—farmers living in the city) inspires Deeds to take new action. He decides to use his fortune to buy land, cattle and seed and then parcel it out to needy farmers. Cedar, who needs desperately to get control of the Semple estate, sees in Deeds' plan his chance to seize the inheritance. He files suit (Deeds' greedy cousins are the plantiffs) declaring Deeds incapable of managing the Semple estate—his give-away scheme *proves* he is insane—and gets an injunction to halt the hero's philanthropy. While Deeds is processing the farmers' grant claims, the police arrive and escort him to the county hospital.

While at the hospital and during the first part of the trial when Cedar fabricates his flimsy case for his insanity, the defendant refuses to speak up in his own behalf. He has seen both his concepts of love and brotherhood called into question and ridiculed. In effect, his world has been turned upside down. Moral corruption—cynicism, greed, dishonesty—are now, he finds, pre-eminent. That Cedar uses the testimony of quacks to prove that the sane man is insane underlines the topsy-turvy situation in which Deeds discovers himself. And if there is no place for love and brotherhood, then there is no place for Deeds for whom these basic concepts mean so much. As Mark Van Doren writes: "Truly an innocent, truly a virtuous and rational young man, he is so empty of spiritual pride as in the end when it has been made clear to him that world is corrupt and crazy, to desire nothing save silence even in the court where his sanity is being

**Gary Cooper and Raymond Walburn in MR. DEEDS GOES
TO TOWN (1936)**

tried."[18] But if Deeds has lost faith in his principles, those to whose
lives he has brought a new sense of rightness—Babe, Cobb and the
farmers—have not, and they are determined to demonstrate their
faith in Deeds and the ideals he and now they stand for. When the
judge informs the defendant that he is to be committed to an
institution Babe leaps to her feet to protest the injustice of his action.
During her appeal she publicly confesses her part in Deeds' disillusionment and admits under cross-examination that she has fallen in
love with him. More than an admission of love, Babe's plea suggests
that Deeds' first impression of her as a damsel in distress was not
altogether a mistaken one. Babe is at heart a country girl whose better
instincts have been perverted into a hardened cynicism seemingly
necessary for survival in the city. She falls in love with Deeds when she
realises those principles she thought dead are alive in him, and her

courtroom confession is an admission of a wish that he take her away from the sordid, unnatural life she has been living. Soon after Babe finishes, the farmers who are depending on Deeds to give them a chance to regain their self-respect also encourage him to come to his own defence. For Deeds, these demonstrations set the world right side up again. He sees that his efforts to help others have not gone in vain, that Cedar and his kind do not represent the norm. Now that he has regained his moral perspective, he proves more than a match for Cedar. His clear-headed arguments annihilate the shyster's case. As the judge in rendering the final verdict says: "[Deeds] is not only sane, he's the sanest man in this courtroom."

Mr. Deeds did not cost very much money—approximately $600,000, only average by M-G-M standards. Somehow it seems inevitable that the budgets for Capra's film should increase with his own fame. It is difficult to think of a director who after making an important reputation for himself has not soon begun to direct films with a great deal of production value, and so it was with Capra. In retrospect, one looks upon this symbol of Capra's success—the big budget film—with some regret. Beginning with *Lost Horizon* (1937), on which Capra spent, according to "Variety", some $2,500,000, the director's films no longer exude to quite the same extent that close, personal sense of neighbourhood kin one finds in his earlier films for Columbia. It is difficult to explain why this should be so except to say that big, masterfully designed sets along with Capra's self-consciously projected themes somehow preclude the sort of easy intimacy—Capra was a genius at getting a lot out of next to nothing—that is such an attractive, though difficult to define, feature of his "inexpensive" films.

Of course, he did not spend money just for the sake of it. The exotic, oriental locations described in James Hilton's novel seem to call for elaborate sets; and elaborate sets are just what Capra bought for his multi-million dollar budget. *Lost Horizon* begins much like Capra's other film with an oriental setting, *The Bitter Tea of General Yen*, with the protagonists caught in the thick of a rebel uprising in China. On an airfield surrounded by the advancing insurgents, Robert Conway (Ronald Colman), a high-ranking British diplomat, organises the evacuation of foreign nationals from the strife-torn area. After seeing most of the foreigners off on the rescue planes, Conway boards the last plane with the few remaining occidentals: his brother George (John Howard); a scandalised businessman, Barnard (Thomas Mitchell); a palaeontologist, Lovett (Edward Everett Horton); and a prostitute, Gloria (Isabel Jewell). Again in this sequence Capra demonstrates his masterly skill of effectively organising and executing enormous crowd scenes. A hundred separate actions take place simultaneously here: soldiers fighting, civilians running in panic, Conway trying to marshall the foreigners onto the planes. Yet, all these varied elements are so precisely coordinated that one takes Capra's direction for granted.

Ironically, the director works the action to such a pitch in this opening sequence that all that follows seems strangely anticlimactic. The plane with Conway and the others is supposed to go to Shanghai, but after a night's flying the passengers realise that they are heading West toward the Himalayas—not East. No one knows where they are being taken or why. They refuel at an unknown Tibetan village (note here how the horsemen ride in a criss-cross pattern in front of the plane while it's being refuelled—it is a small touch, but it reveals how Capra even in transition scenes works diligently to keep our eyes glued to the screen) and then continue to head deeper into the unchartered wilderness. While still over the mountains, the plane runs out of fuel and crashes. The pilot is killed, but the others survive. Just when they have given up all hope of rescue they are discovered by a group of natives. After an arduous trek along treacherous mountain paths the party emerges through a small opening into the Valley of the Blue Moon, and gaze down upon a magnificent oriental paradise—Shangri-La.

Neither crime nor any other human foibles, for that matter, exist in this heaven on earth. The natives of the valley are passive, contented agrarians, and the few Europeans who have been lucky enough to stumble into this paradise engage in quiet contemplation and scholarly study for its own sake. Because they breathe only pure mountain air and are free from the tensions and pressures intrinsic to western society, denizens often live well beyond one hundred years. In short, Capra via Hilton has recast the Eden Myth. But somehow one might have expected Capra's utopian vision to be more secular, less ethereal: something more along the lines of King Vidor's commune in *Our Daily Bread* (1934). Shangri-La, after all, is an elitist society. Only a choice few outsiders ever get to this paradise—some, as in Conway's case, by purposeful design. There would appear to be little room for the masses here. Also unexpected in light of both Capra's previous and subsequent cinema are some of the conclusions to be drawn from this film. To accept civilisation as a lost cause, for example, as Conway and those in Shangri-La do, is also to separate

Ronald Colman and H. B. Warner in LOST HORIZON (1937)

oneself from all responsibility for the fate of mankind, an idea which sharply contradicts one of the most essential concepts of Capra's cinema—the individual's responsibility to his fellow man. Are these clashes simply holes in the story unperceived by Capra and Riskin, as the film's opponents often contend, or do they denote something else?

Viewed in relationship to the rest of his cinema, *Lost Horizon* can be seen as representing the dark side of the director's philosophy. He implies here, if subconsciously, that he feels the weight of his self-imposed responsibilities as a moralist film-maker. A crucial theme in Capra's cinema is that each individual possesses a capacity for goodness that, if given the chance, will emerge. Beginning with this film, Capra starts to qualify that theme. Under the surface of his subsequent cinema, though no more visible than in *Lost Horizon*, is the suggestion that while the individual is basically good, civilisation is rotten at the core. It is a paradox Capra never resolves. Maybe the best solution, as the High Lama suggests, is to forget the masses and save only the worthwhile elements of society. Conway finds the idea very tempting. Jefferson Smith, however, would not. It is interesting to note, though, that Capra personally could probably relate much more to Conway than to Smith. In fact, some interesting parallels between Conway and Capra can be drawn. For one, Conway writes highly regarded books which expound on the virtues of New Testament morality, just as Capra directs films on the same subject. Significantly, this feature of Conway's character is not to be found in the novel (which, for the most part, Capra followed faithfully), but is original to the film.

The only member of Conway's party not happy in Shangri-La is Conway's brother, George. Capra and Riskin created him from Hilton's character Mallinson who in the novel is merely a young associate of Conway's. By changing Mallinson into Conway's blood relation, Capra draws the two characters together spiritually, so much so in fact that George and Robert Conway can be seen as the two poles of one personality: Conway personifying that aspect which desires peace, solitude, logic; George that which is chaotic, restless, suspicious. Conway quickly adapts to Shangri-La, adopting native dress, finding satisfaction in the slow pace of the Valley, while George never changes out of his western garb and stirs anxiously, awaiting the chance to return home. Yet while George is a thoroughly detestable character, his hatred of Shangri-La and his ambition to leave it are no less genuine than Conway's love of the new life he has found here; that is, the self-destructive element of their mutual psyche (represented by George) is just as powerful as that element which longs for utopia (represented by Conway).

This dialectic between the will to regenerate and improve and the will to destroy becomes a dominating preoccupation in the last two films of the *Deeds/Smith/Doe* trilogy in which Capra sees contemporary American society pulled in opposite directions by competing and contradictory forces of self-destruction and self-renewal. In *Mr. Smith*, particularly, as here, Capra uses his hero and villain as personifications of these motivations. The hero, Jefferson Smith (James Stewart), represents self-renewal—that is, the impetus to establish the American utopia as envisioned by the founding fathers—and the villain, political boss Jim Taylor (Edward Arnold), the destructive force that works against the hero's vision. Like George and Robert Conway, they are symbolically disparate parts of the same psyche, at once Capra's own, the everyman's and society's as a whole.

In *Lost Horizon*, as in *Deeds*, the evil force nearly destroys its opposite when the hero loses faith in the efficacy of his own beliefs. When

Conway tries to convince George of the glory of Shangri-La, he fails: George never questions his own convictions; they are immutable. But when George seeks to persuade his brother to reject all he has come to believe about the paradise, he succeeds. George, for all his obtuseness, is clever enough to perceive that the way to topple his brother's faith is to offer tangible proof that the utopia is a hoax, and so relies on the young and beautiful Maria (Margo), the one discontented inhabitant of Shangri-La who, Conway has been told, is really by normal standards an old woman, youthful only because of the healthy environs of the valley, to make his point. Of course, when Conway tries to explain to his brother the secret of Maria's youth, George does not believe him. Maria laughs nervously at Conway's argument and dismisses it as just another trick by the rulers to keep her in the valley.

Conway, along with George and Maria, leaves Shangri-La; during their journey back to civilisation, Maria ages rapidly to death. The revelation drives George insane. He rushes madly over a cliff, nearly taking his brother along with him (they are tied together by a thick climbing rope), but Conway is saved when the rope fortuitously snaps just before he is about to follow his brother over the edge. Miraculously, he manages to make his way back to a Tibetan village. From there he makes repeated unsuccessful attempts to re-discover Shangri-La until finally, in a conclusion dictated by Capra's personal tenet that his films must end with a victory, he finds his way back to the Valley of the Blue Moon.

Lost Horizon did not do well in the provinces, those cities and towns in which Capra's films normally thrived. There are several possible explanations for this. For one, Capra appears to have all but ignored his own normally iron-clad rule that a director who wishes to communicate moral precepts to his audience must first work his way into their hearts through comedy. Given as this film is to sermonising, Capra's failure to trust his own rule was, commercially speaking at any rate, a costly error. For another, the director's phenomenal success in the Thirties can be traced primarily to his ability to create characters and situations with which people could closely identify. Clearly, a large portion of Capra's public found it difficult to focus on any character in this film. However, if Capra's public had difficulty relating to his characters, the director himself, as we have seen, did not. To this extent, *Lost Horizon* stands as perhaps Capra's most personal film of the decade, too personal in fact to be greatly popular. The central preoccupations which power his post-1935 cinema—the dichotomy between the self-destructive and self-renewing forces within the individual specifically and society in general, for instance—inhabit this film, and in a form so pure (no reaction shots here to undercut the High Lama's prophesies on the future of mankind) as not to be easily assimilable. There are few comic diversions in this film; Capra gives us his philosophy straight and undiluted.

The director, however, had not finished with utopias, as his next film, *You Can't Take It with You,* makes plain; but he did set his new Shangri-La in a more familiar locale—the U.S.A. And not only is the geography more familiar, but so are some of the themes—the importance of individualism, the melting of class distinctions through romance, the value of friendship, the spiritual emptiness of accumulating money for its own sake. Back also are the lovable eccentrics.

Utopia in *You Can't Take It with You,* as Otis Ferguson wryly observed, is the split-level home of the Vanderhofs, a family of harmless originals who spend their time doing what pleases them most: dancing, playing the xylophone, writing unproduceable plays, collecting stamps.[19] The High Lama of this Shangri-La is Grandpa Vanderhof (Lionel Barrymore), a former businessman who renounced his material ambitions one fine day when he realised he wasn't having any fun. Having fun, in fact, is finally what this film is all about. Certainly, if everyone did exactly as they pleased, our society would be hopelessly chaotic; to an extent it depends on the likes of Anthony Kirby (Edward Arnold) to keep it running smoothly, but here through comic overstatement Capra wants us to remember that too much efficiency is not healthy for the soul. For Capra, one of the glories of democracy is that it leaves room for eccentricity, whereas regimented totalitarian governments (such as the one Hitler was presiding over in Germany) do not, and the director in this film vigorously endorses the free man's privilege to do as he pleases.

The climax of the film occurs, as it does in *Mr. Deeds,* during a courtroom sequence. Tony Kirby (James Stewart), who wishes to marry his secretary, Grandpa Vanderhof's granddaughter Alice (Jean Arthur), brings his parents to his girlfriend's home for dinner. The strained meeting between the two families ends in disaster when the firecracker factory in the Vanderhofs' basement accidentally explodes. Everyone, including Mr. and Mrs. Kirby (Mary Forbes), is tossed into jail for disturbing the peace. A team of Kirby's lawyers appear on the scene to extricate their client from this most embarrassing and potentially scandalous position. With condescending magnanimity the multi-millionaire offers to pay the $100 fine imposed on Grandpa Vanderhof, but to the Vanderhof's neighbours who have gathered in the courtroom the penalty is strictly a "family matter". They band together, each contributing a few dollars, and raise the money. Indeed, it is a spirited demonstration of what Jeffrey Richards calls "good-neighbourliness".[20]

Kirby's condescension, however, incenses Alice who had made an honest effort to placate the industrialist and his pompous wife. With a portrait of George Washington behind her to lend credence to her words, she lambasts the Kirbys for their false pride and self-importance. In the midst of her tirade the newspaper reporters who have gotten wind of Kirby's arrest burst into the courtroom. Pandemonium errupts: in the space of fifty seconds Capra crams fifteen separate shots into the scene. All the judge's half-hearted efforts to restore order fall on deaf ears.

Alice breaks with Tony over the incident, condemning him, as it were, through guilt by association. Tony, in turn, breaks with his father. Tony's announcement and the concurrent death of a business competitor, whose demise Kirby's ruthless methods have been largely responsible for, affect the multi-millionaire deeply. He renounces (for a short while anyway) an important business deal to join Grandpa Vanderhof in a duet of PollyWollyDoodle. The action symbolises Kirby's renunciation of his unconscionable pursuit of wealth and power, as well as his understanding that there are far more important things in life than money and social position: like the love of his only son. His gesture clears the way for the re-unification of both the Vanderhof and Kirby families, and thus, by the end of the triumphant final sequence, Kirby and Vanderhof, along with Tony, Alice, the rest of the Vanderhofs and their neighbours, are dancing and singing together. Only the unredeemable Mrs. Kirby looks out of place.

You Can't Take It with You represents the last major film in which Capra with almost unqualified optimism endorses the possibilities of reformation and happiness for those who practise his New Testament morality. Perhaps the world situation—the persistent economic crisis and the frightening expansion of Fascism in Europe—precluded the sort of sudden positive epiphany Anthony Kirby experiences in this film. At any rate, beginning with *Mr. Smith* Capra's optimism gradually gives way to an ever-rising current of doubt and pessimism, and simultaneously his work becomes progressively more complex, less easy to fit into any simply defined social vision.

By the virtue of a freak coin toss, Jefferson Smith (James Stewart), a young, naive idealist, is appointed to the United States Senate to

James Stewart in MR. SMITH GOES TO WASHINGTON (1939)

complete the term of the elected representative who died in office. Although Smith does not realise it, his appointment has cast him into the midst of a powerful political machine single-handedly run by Boss Jim Taylor (Edward Arnold), a man who owns not only much of the state's industry and media but also its politicians, including the governor and senior senator, Smith's personal hero, Joseph Paine (Claude Rains). Taylor expects that one way or another Smith will fall in line with all the others, but he proves to be greatly mistaken. When Smith proposes a bill to establish a national boys camp on the site where Taylor plans to have a dam built, the neophyte and the seasoned politico clash. Taylor offers Smith a career in the senate for life if he will vote for the machine's graft-laden legislation, which authorises the construction of the dam, but the junior senator, shocked by

Taylor's offer, refuses to compromise his ideals. In ruthless fashion, Taylor moves to get Smith expelled from the august body to which he has just been admitted. Paine, at Taylor's behest, presents falsified evidence before the senate accusing Smith of the very thing the machine is guilty of: having bought the land for the proposed boys camp with the intention of selling it to the government for a windfall profit. In an Ethics Committee hearing, Smith watches helplessly as the full weight of the machine's treachery is brought down upon him. Perjured testimony is given by the machine's stooges, including Smith's now fallen idol, Senator Paine, and forged documents are presented as evidence against him. So dumbfounded is Smith by what he sees that, like Deeds, he refuses to testify in his own behalf at the hearing. The world appears to him, as it appeared to Deeds, to have lost its moral centre.

Before he leaves Washington, however, he visits the Lincoln

**Boss Jim talks to Smith: Edward Arnold and
James Stewart in MR. SMITH GOES TO WASHINGTON**

Memorial (now dark and immersed in shadow, in contrast to his first visit when it was cast in ethereal white light) for what he thinks will be the last time. As he sits there alone, broken and dejected, he is surprised by his senate aide, Saunders (Jean Arthur). Like the other heroines in Capra's trilogy, Saunders begins the film as a cynical mercenary who immediately brands the hero a phoney and plays her part in his eventual disillusionment. But gradually, like Babe, she converts wholeheartedly to supporting Smith and the ideals he expounds. She convinces him that to leave Washington without a struggle would represent a dangerous victory for machine-style politics; that he has a responsibility not only to himself and the boys who idolise him back in his state but also to the whole concept of American democracy to take on Taylor.

Guided by Saunders' shrewd counsel, Capra's paladin goes into battle. He filibusters against Taylor's graft bill, hoping that by

Smith and Senator Paine: James Stewart, Claude Rains and Astrid Allwyn in MR. SMITH GOES TO WASHINGTON

speaking from the senate floor he can inform his constituents of the political machine that is abusing their democratic freedoms. Taylor, however, chokes off the state's media and feeds them "doctored up junk" about Smith's efforts instead of the truth. When Saunders and her friend, newspaper reporter Diz Moore (Thomas Mitchell), succeed in getting the real story of Smith's filibuster to the electorate through Smith's own paper, "Boy's Stuff", a tabloid printed by the junior senator's young supporters, Taylor has his goons break up the presses and confiscate the paper. After speaking for nearly twenty-four hours, Smith finally collapses. But by this time Paine has been worn down by a deep remorse over what he has done to Smith and what his own life has become. After he watches his colleague faint from exhaustion, he makes a sudden, desperate attempt to commit suicide. When he fails, he rushes into the senate chamber and confesses that all Smith has said about Taylor and the machine is true.

Such a synopsis scarcely conveys the complexity of Capra's thematic vision in this film, or the extent to which it represents an ambitious advance over its predecessor, *Mr. Deeds*. Generally, *Mr. Smith* is regarded as a straightforward parable in which good triumphs over evil, but while this might be said of *Deeds* it cannot accurately be said of this film. For one, *Mr. Smith* ends ambiguously. Smith wins his filibuster, but has he really put a dent in the machine? Will his efforts alter the course of politics in his state? No answers are provided. For another, we are asked to question the nature of Capra's hero. What are we to make of this man-child so blissfully ignorant of the most basic political realities? Indeed, Capra goes to great lengths to illustrate the junior senator's naïveté. Smith's friends in his home state all seem to be boys half his own age; he brings homing pigeons with him to the capital to send messages back to his mother! And, in one superlative image, Capra depicts him placing nickels and dimes donated by the boys who want to go to his proposed camp into a makeshift piggy-bank as Paine's jaded daughter, Susan (Astrid Allwyn), and Saunders scheme to keep him out of the senate during the debate on Taylor's graft bill. But, seemingly in punishment for this ingenuousness, Smith's rite of initiation into the realities of political life is little short of brutal. He is made a fool of in the papers, branded a "Christmas tiger" by the press corps, and nearly railroaded out of the senate by the Taylor machine. His near expulsion, however, serves as a sort of purgatory which tempers him for the coming battle. Only when he learns that passive idealism is as worthless as abject cynicism, that his ideals must be constantly and viligantly defended, does he actually emerge as an unqualified hero.

Smith's collapse on the Senate floor:
MR. SMITH GOES TO WASHINGTON

Whether we accept Smith's triumph at the end of the film as something more than just elaborate wish-fulfilment depends on our willingness to accept Capra's multi-faceted characterisation of Paine as a man torn between Smith's seemingly suicidal idealism and Taylor's self-serving cynicism. The film is ultimately as much about Paine's identity crisis (his name itself suggests this crisis, just as Smith's name links him at once with one of the great figures of American history and the American everyman) as it is about Smith's. We know that Paine began adulthood with the same faith in democracy as he now finds in Smith. He and Smith's father, Clayton, once Paine's best friend, were known in fact as the "twin champions of lost causes". But when Clayton was murdered by a corrupt mining syndicate he had challenged, Paine became convinced that idealism and steadfastness were useless in an already immoral world dominated by powers no one individual could successfully hope to oppose. So he joined the machine and gave way to Taylor's rotten schemes in order to forward his own ambitions. Capra does not attempt to lessen or demean the sort of pressure brought to bear on the senator to become another wheel in Taylor's juggernaut. As Paine himself points out to Smith in an effort to rationalise his decision, he compromised his ideals so that he "might serve the state in a thousand honest ways". But, for Capra, Paine has done no less than sell his soul.

The senior senator, then, represents more than just a paradigm of what Smith might have become had he yielded to Taylor's generous offer to join the machine; he serves also as another example of the sort of people that Taylor and those like him depend on to gain power. The corrupt exploit passive idealists like Smith, who, in their unwillingness to face political realities, indirectly express the fear that their fantasies regarding the republic are nothing more than that, and the infirm of purpose like Paine, who willingly exchange their principles for more tangible rewards. That Capra sees Smith and Paine as the sort of men who are capable of defeating the likes of Taylor make their initial inaction all the more reprehensible. Their coming to terms with their responsibilities, each in his own way, is the crux of this film, as the idea of facing responsibility is the crux of the remainder of Capra's major cinema, including the "Why We Fight" series.

Smith's psychological struggle involves being able to deal with political realities while still maintaining his faith in his ideals. Paine is in turn involved in a struggle to wrench his identity away from Taylor. It is personal battle that is intense and complex enough to preclude the sort of lightning conversion taken for granted in Capra's previous films such as *Broadway Bill* (1934) and *You Can't Take It with You.* In one well-defined scene during the middle of the crisis surrounding Smith's unwillingness to go along with the machine, Capra crystallises the personal dilemma in which Paine is embroiled and the fateful extent to which he has permitted Taylor to master his moral judgement.

The political boss has flown to Washington to quash any attempt to disturb the smooth course of the Deficiency Bill. He meets Paine in his hotel room. Together the two men share the centre of the frame. Paine says that he will not go along with Taylor's steamroller methods. He tells Taylor that he does not want "any part in crucifying the boy [Smith]." Taylor then subtly threatens to ruin Paine's political career if he does not follow his wishes on the matter. It is now up to Paine to choose—Smith or Taylor. They are clearly poised as two mutually exclusive choices. When Paine makes no comment on his ultimatum, Taylor disdainfully assumes he has opted to join Smith and he walks toward the door at the top left of the frame. It is a crucial moment for Paine: his last chance to separate himself from Taylor and follow his own conscience even though it might cost him his political career (there are intriguing hints dropped all through the film to indicate that Paine has a good shot at the presidency in the next election). That he stands at the centre of the frame suggests that he is at this moment in control of his own destiny. Suddenly, as Taylor is just about to leave the room and, by extension, his life, Paine backs down. He calls Taylor back to the centre of the room (and the frame) and agrees to obey his master. Now Paine retreats to the door just as Taylor had done moments before. Taylor, then, is finally the dominant figure in the frame, and Paine recedes—a puppet, as it were, on Taylor's string.

The senator, however, is not oblivious to the consequences of his capitulation to Taylor. With each compromise he seems to move closer toward a nervous collapse. Compare, for example, his swaggering gait and bright, benevolent smiles at the beginning of the film to his troubled, frightened expressions and uncertain, jerky movements toward the end. Although he throws himself into the fight against Smith, playing the pivotal role in Taylor's plan to steamroll the junior senator out of government, he seems to function on a self-consuming neurotic energy. During the Ethics Committee hearing, he can no longer look Smith straight in the eye. Capra's last shot of him in this scene is of a man profiled in low key light, almost in silhouette—literally a shadow of his former self.

Whether or not Paine's confession at the conclusion of the film signifies that he has renounced Taylor in favour of Smith is left open to speculation as is just about every other conclusion one might draw from the sudden ending. Yet, because his confession comes at the end of a difficult psychological journey, an affirmation of sorts would seem to be suggested: that he has freed himself from Taylor and regained his own identity. Now, perhaps, he can begin anew and along with Smith take up the torch he dropped long ago. What can be claimed for Smith? What has he ultimately achieved at the end of his dramatic filibuster? Perhaps all that can be said confidently is that he survived—a victory, however, not as modest as it may sound. The machine has tried to smash him into a political nonentity, to steal his individuality and destroy his faith in his country and himself, but he foils their best efforts and in doing so emerges from the struggle toughened for the inevitable battles that lie ahead. Gone is the wide-eyed neophyte. In his place stands a canny, if still idealistic, politician.

Meet John Doe, Capra's next film, could, without stretching the imagination too far, be seen as a chronicle of what might have happened had Taylor won his battle over Smith. D. B. Norton (Edward Arnold again), a multi-millionaire, neo-Fascist industrialist, is a diabolical refinement of political boss Taylor. Whereas Taylor takes a risk with the Deficiency Bill because it ostensibly means more graft, Norton's only obsession is power. Whereas Taylor's steamroller methods lead him into a disastrous confrontation with Smith, Norton maniacally manipulates Long John Willoughby (Gary Cooper) and the John Doe movement to further his own Fascist ambitions. "These are daring times," he tells his yes-men at dinner before the giant John Doe convention. "We're coming to a new order of things. There's too much talk going on in this country, too many concessions have been made. What the American people need is an iron hand. Discipline!"

Capra suggests the coming of this "new order" with the opening shot of the film in which a workman with a pneumatic drill hammers off the following from the front of a building:

EST. 1862
THE BULLETIN
A FREE PRESS
MEANS
A FREE PEOPLE

This is replaced by a sleek new steel sign:

THE NEW BULLETIN
A STREAMLINED PAPER
FOR
A STREAMLINE ERA

The noble slogan of the old "Bulletin," a slogan carved in stone, significantly enough, during Abraham Lincoln's tenure as president, has given way to a new slogan which capsulises modern expediency and symbolises the death of once majestic values. Furthermore, it represents for Capra an obvious aggrandisement of the under-current of pessimism expressed in *Mr. Smith*. After spending the second half of the decade devoted to pointing the way to a better world only to see that world in which he once had so much faith embroil itself in a new, terrible conflict, is it possible that the director's once seemingly eternal spring of optimism had begun to run dry? After studying *Meet John Doe,* one is tempted to answer that question affirmatively.

The result of the clash between Capra's underlying pessimism and overt optimism can be seen in his treatment of the reactive character in this film, John's misanthropic travelling companion, the Colonel (Walter Brennan). As the hero's sidekick, the reactive character in Capra's cinema may serve to diffuse a sentimental scene in danger of becoming maudlin with a sour look, or highlight a particular triumph with a wisecrack or an approving smile. The Colonel works here as John's conscience. Like Lear's fool, he never loses his perspective. His biting retorts make so much sense that he seems to detail, as Corny Cobb did in *Mr. Deeds,* an aspect of Capra's own view. For the Colonel, a confirmed drifter, the world is full of "heelots" ("lots of heels") or people who make the acquisition of money and material possessions their first priority.[21] Deeds and Smith fought the worst of these "heelots" and sought to make their fellow men see that human kindness and brotherhood should be of fundamental importance, but the Colonel flatly rejects this as a delusion. Simple greed, he contends, has always been and will remain the foremost human ambition. "Tear down all the fences?" he asks John in his usual irreverent manner. "Why, if you tore down one picket of your neighbour's fence he'd sue ya."

As the reactive character goes, so goes the tone of the comedy. The acrid humour of *Meet John Doe* contrasts sharply with the wholesome humour of *Mr. Deeds.* Occasionally it borders on the bizarre, as during the scene just before the John Doe radio broadcast in which Capra hints at a striking self-parody. In order to cover himself in case the broadcast flops, the "New Bulletin" editor, Connell (James Gleason), arranges a couple of publicity stunts which he knows will sell at least a few papers. First, he has John pose with a beauty queen. Then one of Connell's assistants walks into the dressing room with the subjects for the next pose—male and female midgets. "There you are, boss," says the assistant, "symbols of the little people."

The John Doe movement begins, in fact, as something of a bizarre joke. When Norton buys the "Bulletin" sweeping new economies are made, and many of the staff of the old "Bulletin" are given the sack. Ann Mitchell (Barbara Stanwyck), who writes a daily column for the paper ("all lavender and no lace"), is among those fired. In her last instalment, she expresses her contempt for the new policies of the paper and her anger at having lost her job by fabricating a fictional

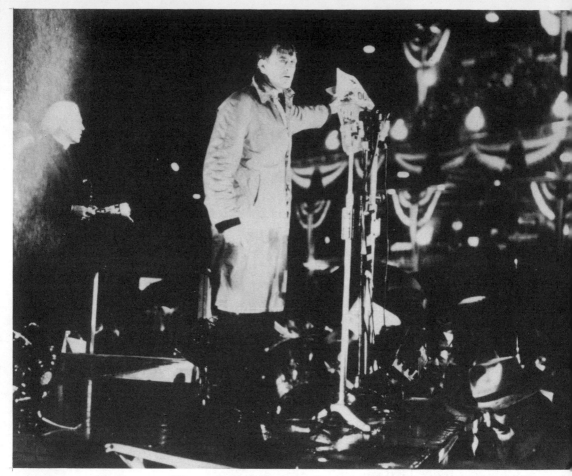

The convention: Gary Cooper in MEET JOHN DOE (1941)

character, John Doe, who, in a letter he allegedly has sent her, promises to jump off City Hall on Christmas Eve to protest social injustice. The column creates an immediate sensation. Connell's first instinct is to kill the story, but Ann, who cannot afford to lose her job, convinces him to continue it as a way to boost the paper's circulation. Out of a crowd of down-and-outs, Ann chooses John Willoughby, a bush-league baseball pitcher with a bad arm, to animate her fictional creation. As local interest in John Doe and his ideas continues to grow rapidly, Norton becomes interested in the possible political benefits of sponsoring a nationwide John Doe movement. After a nationally broadcast radio address in which John as Doe elaborates on the virtues of Christian charity, John Doe clubs spring up across the country. When John, who has come to believe in the ideas he has been espousing, learns that Norton intends to use the movement to expand his own power (Norton wants John to call for the formation of a third political party and endorse him as its presidential candidate), he decides to expose Norton before a giant John Doe convention. Norton, however, arrives at the convention before John can speak. Before the thousands gathered in the stadium Norton denounces John to be a fake and forces him to admit the original John Doe letter was a fraud. The John Doe movement comes to a sudden halt. The conventioneers who for weeks have been revelling in the glories of brotherhood and had minutes ago been singing hymns abruptly change into a vengeful mob. As in *That Certain Thing*, only here multiplied a thousand times, John's followers believe, upon learning the dubious origins of the movement, that he has violated their trust, and this revelation violently reawakens all their suspicions regarding the motives of any public figure. Disgraced, John decides to go through with Doe's original promise. On the top of City Hall he finds Norton and his crew, waiting for him (for reasons of their own they don't want him to jump—for one thing, it would discredit Norton), but their presence only makes John more determined to go through with his plan. "You killed the movement," he tells them. "Now you are going to see it reborn." A repentant Ann, however, arrives at the tower along with the Colonel and several members of the original John Doe club; she convinces John to live and fight for the principles of the movement, instead of dying for them: "John, look at me," Ann pleads. "You want to be honest, don't you? Well, you don't have to die to keep the John Doe idea alive. Somebody already died for that once, the first John Doe, and he's kept it alive for nearly 2000 years; he'll go on keeping it alive forever and always. For every John Doe movement these men kill, a new one will be born. That's why those bells are ringing: they're calling to us to keep on fighting."

Like *Mr. Smith*, this film primarily concerns the hero's coming to terms with both individual and political responsibility. John, whose mind at the outset might best be described as a blank slate, acquires his ideals as he tours the country talking to ordinary citizens and giving inspirational speeches. As with Deeds and Smith, his attainment of selfhood follows a process of ritual death, purgatory and re-birth: after he is rejected by his once faithful followers he begins to doubt all he has come to believe (death); then (as he wanders aimlessly through the city) through a painful process of self-questioning renews his faith in himself and his ideals (purgatory); and decides with the encouragement of trusted friends to fight the powers that oppose him (re-birth). Although Deeds and Smith can both be regarded as Christ figures (there are repeated references made in both films to the fact that the hero is being "crucified"), Capra takes the Christ imagery much further here as witness the fact that John is "re-born" at

midnight on Christmas Eve while Beethoven's "Ode to Joy" plays in the background. Capra seems to propose John as a new Messiah and in doing so suggests that the hope of the world rests with the John Does. But not only is this answer to Norton and his ambitions vague, it runs into a fascinating contradiction. In the baseball stadium as Norton denounces John, a scene of incredible power, the stylistics of which merit a separate analysis of their own, Capra cuts quickly to the crowd's reactions moving from face to face as expressions change from love to doubt to hate. The editing scheme reveals the sheep-like nature of the masses, these John Does; that they have no strong convictions, but will follow the strongest leader—first John, now Norton. Connell's dramatic epigram which closes the film after John has heeded Ann's plea—"There you are, Norton, the People. Try and lick that"—rings hollow. Norton has stopped the People and quite easily.

Capra had now moved from Deeds's undisputed triumph over the chisellers to Ann's desperate plea and the thin hope that a better world lies with the John Does, whoever they may be, living the Christmas spirit year round. It is the irony of this trilogy that although Capra's heroes fight the same battle for individual liberty, the outcome of each battle and the hope which may be taken from that battle becomes more nebulous with each succeeding film. It is a further source of irony that Capra's work in the second half of this decade, films so often regarded as mawkishly optimistic, should in fact reflect a society's and a world's expanding despair.

As a postscript to *Meet John Doe* and the other films of Capra's trilogy, I offer the following: in 1946, Aldous Huxley wrote in his forward to a new edition of "Brave New World," "Only a large-scale popular movement toward de-centralisation and self-help can arrest the present tendency toward statism. At present there is no sign that such a movement will take place."[22]

By 1940, the great holocaust predicted by the High Lama in *Lost Horizon* had arrived. When the United States became involved in the war, Capra volunteered his services. In 1942 after completing *Arsenic and Old Lace,* he was inducted into the Army. His commission came direct from General Marshall: to head the Army's effort to explain through film exactly why and what the United States was fighting. It seems unlikely that the choice of Capra for this important task could

On top of City Hall: Gary Cooper in MEET JOHN DOE

have been, as the director suggests in his autobiography, by chance. If Marshall had seen any of Capra's films of the last-half decade then he would have been aware of their strong anti-fascist content, their celebration of the finest American ideals, their passionate defence of individualism and their traditionalist moral stance. Indeed, as Robert Sklar has observed, "one might argue that it was precisely Capra's vision of American life that the government desired to enlist and present to its citizen soldiers as its own."[23] Nor would it have taken an esoteric knowledge of film to see that Capra's dynamic cinematic style would be just the sort required to hold the attention of the men who were to see the films. A little research into Capra's character and his reputation inside Hollywood would have further revealed a man possessing a considerable amount of *chutzpah,* an unswerving confidence in his own judgements and a knack for "infighting" (all aptly demonstrated during the fight he led for the legitimacy of the Director's Guild in the late Thirties)—qualities essential for anyone who would have to battle government bureaucracy. Yet still, the choice of Capra to direct and supervise a series of Army orientation films could not have been all that clear cut. For one thing, Capra had never directed a documentary film before. He had no experience in the *genre* and there were plenty around who did. But, not without good reason, people had always seemed willing to gamble on Capra: Sennett and Cohn, among others, and now Marshall. In each case their gamble paid off handsomely.

Of the documentary films Capra supervised for the Army by far the most important and influential was the *Why We Fight* series. These films have received nearly unanimous praise for their effective use of newsreel footage, hard-hitting narration and animation (produced by Disney). When analysing the series, commentators usually single out certain films. This method is quite appropriate in one sense because the series was produced over a period of three years, but inappropriate in another because it tends to lessen its full impact. In fact, only when the seven are viewed together, not as seven different films, but as seven parts to one film, can one fully appreciate the stunning depth and complexity of this work. Clearly Capra intended the series to exist as essentially a single opus, as the way in which he organised the films demonstrates. The first, *Prelude to War,* introduces the series with a general discussion of the motives behind Axis aggression; the second, *The Nazis Strike,* deals specifically with Hitler's conquest of Eastern Europe; the third, *Divide and Conquer,* with his conquests in the west, particularly France. The next three, *The Battle of Britain, The Battle of Russia,* and *The Battle of China,* as their titles suggest, deal with specific conflicts; and the last film, *War Comes to America,* capsulises the previous six and illustrates how the country's attitude toward the war has changed from isolationist to interventionist. But the bond between the seven films extends well beyond mere chronology. Generally, they all follow a similar organisational schemata: each opens with a stark depiction of the enemy's ruthlessness and savagery; an explanation of the history behind the specific conflict follows and, in the case of *The Battle of Russia* and *The Battle of China,* an attempt to familiarise the viewer with native history and culture. Then, the main battles and results are graphically delineated, and finally a concluding sequence summarises the situation. Key shots (the silhouette of a man swinging an axe, for example) are repeated in several films and so become emblems of Axis tyranny, and passages of music such as Rachmaninoff's "Isle of the Dead" resonate throughout the series. More general concepts—such as the characterisation of the Axis rulers as demigods, objects of fanatical, mindless pagan-like worship (Hitler at Nuremberg, for instance); unremitting Axis barbarism (the bombing of Rotterdam, Shanghai and London, the extermination of suspected insurgents, the murder of innocent civilians with a particular focus on small children); and contrasting examples of Allied courage and bravery (Warsaw, Dunkirk, Leningrad, over the skies of Britain and along the Burma road)—recur again and again throughout these films. In fact, as might already be clear, repetition of certain symbols and concepts is central to the emotional power of these films and gives the whole series a common rhythm.

In the introduction to his monograph on Capra, Richard Griffith states that Capra's most "salient talent" was film editing.[24] As Griffith recognised, nowhere was his incomparable skill more evident than in the *Why We Fight* series. Capra's idea for the series was to use captured newsreel footage to reveal exactly what sort of enemy the country was up against. But this is hardly as simple or innocent as it sounds for in order to get the desired effect Capra had to manipulate this footage in ways which it was obviously never intended to be used. Perhaps nowhere outside of Eisenstein and Capra's own films is the plastic power of film in better evidence than in these seven *Why We Fight* films. It is one of the hidden ironies of Capra's cinema that this, the most patriotic of film-makers, possessed the least democratic of *mise-en-scènes;* that is, while championing the rights of the individual to make free choices, he grants very little freedom to his audience. Our responses are very carefully guided by Capra's editing scheme. Case in point: the remarkable closing sequence to *Mr. Smith* in which Capra brilliantly cross-cuts between Taylor's massive, well-oiled machine and the bugles and basement printing press of Smith's Boy Rangers, a sequence about as subtle as the Odessa Steps sequence in *Potemkin*.

Sometimes simply the right selection of a single shot is enough to communicate the series' point of view. In *Prelude to War* our first look at Mussolini, for instance, is of him parading in top hat and tails before an adoring crowd. It is silent film footage, however, and Capra projects it here, of course, at sound speed thus making Mussolini look ridiculous. Certainly, Capra could have used sound film footage of Mussolini had he wished to, but throughout the series the dictator is slighted as Hitler's "stooge", referred to at various times as "Tarzan", and generally pictured as a buffoon, so the use of the silent film here is both appropriate and effective. Other examples of this sort of cinematic philippic are shots of an obese Field Marshall Goering rubbing his hands with glee over the signing of a surrender treaty, and a limp wrist gesture by Goebbels during an address to a Nazi assembly.

Capra's characterisation of Hitler is necessarily much more complex. Direct comparisons are made between the German dictator and Ghengis Khan in *Prelude to War* and John Dillinger in *The Nazis Strike*, but there is a more subtle and very effective effort to characterise him as an anti-Christ figure. The series makes much of the Nazis' religious persecutions, and there are many shots of churches and synagogues being destroyed. In *Prelude to War* one Nazi leader tells a party gathering that "Hitler is far too great to compare to one so petty as Christ." In *Divide and Conquer* the impression of Hitler as an anti-Christ is made dramatically during the sequence just preceding the Nazi blitzkrieg of France, when Capra jump-cuts from a church in which a congregation of people, primarily women (we have just seen their sons leave for the front), are praying (cut) to Hitler in a low angle shot, his head bobbing as he bombastically exhorts his audience into a frenzy. This characterisation allows Capra to establish obliquely the ultimate rightness of the allied cause: to reinforce the idea, no doubt a key one for Capra, that "God is on our side."

While aligning the enemy with an anti-Christ, Capra also recasts key stereotypes—the German proclivity for regimentation, for example—to further delineate the nature of the American soldiers' counterpart. Examples of the drone-like behavior of the German, Japanese and Italian masses appear throughout the series. Capra, as he does throughout, uses enemy-produced film to his own advantage, relying on the assumption that what would appeal to a German audience would repel an American one. The mass worship of Hitler at the Nuremberg Rally (excerpted from Leni Riefenstahl's *Triumph of the Will*), the Japanese Army shouting "Bonzai" to their emperor, and Italian crowds crying "Duce" are all employed to reinforce one of the central themes of the series: that these people willingly gave up their freedoms as individual human beings. This motif also takes the shape of a variety of powerful metaphors. Perhaps the most tell-tale can be found in *The Nazis Strike* where a montage of German factories producing weapons for the Nazi war machine (the dominant image is of a heavy industrial hammer producing hot, mouldable steel with precision regularity) becomes a metaphor for both the mindlessness of the German masses and the relentlessness of the war machine. Capra clinches this theme by illustrating what statism makes of children. In an ingeniously organised sequence in *Prelude to War*, Capra juxtaposes a number of shots of German, Japanese and Italian youngsters training to fight. As the sequence progresses the youths become younger and younger until we finally have a shot of a baby raising his hand in a Hitlerian salute with the help of his father. Then the process reverses itself: the children grow older with each progressive cut until they become an endless parade of goose-stepping Nazi soldiers. There is hardly any narration during this sequence, only the constant repetition of a percussion-heavy marching tune.

Yet, although Capra certainly wants to paint a repellent picture of the enemy while highlighting all that is ostensibly fine about American culture, he also takes pains to document our opponents' fighting skill; that this propensity for precision and regimentation are the very things that make Nazis and the Japanese such deadly foes. Even as Capra belittles the aggressors, he does not want his audience to take their ability as a military force for granted. In *The Nazis Strike* and *Divide and Conquer*, Capra demonstrates that the stunning Nazi victories in Eastern Europe and France came not merely as a result of treachery, but of ingenious military strategy. One example of such strategy can be found in *Divide and Conquer* in which the Nazis' brilliant conquest of the "impregnable" Belgium fortress, Fort Eden Emael, is described. The Nazis, the narrator informs us, had built an exact replica of the fortress in Czechoslovakia where they rehearsed their attack. Then, through captured Nazi footage, we see how the attack was executed exactly as planned.

Just as Capra seeks to strengthen certain stereotypes in regard to our adversaries, in other instances he seeks to break down or soften certain stereotypes in regard to our allies. This is done with great skill in both *The Battle of Russia* and *The Battle of China*. The idea behind both films is to establish a certain empathy for the people of these countries before dealing with the battles themselves, a task more difficult than it may first seem when one considers our long standing distrust of the Soviets, and our near total ignorance about the Chinese. In both films the history of the countries is summarised. In *The Battle of Russia*, Capra uses scenes from Eisenstein's *Alexander Nevsky*, among other films, to dramatise the fact that German aggression against Russia goes back centuries. In *The Battle of China*, we are informed that the Chinese, in sharp contrast to the Japanese, have "never waged a single war of conquest." For *The Battle of China*, Capra also has to overcome the additional difficulty that most occidentals tend to lump orientals together, drawing no distinctions between Chinese and Japanese. *The Battle of China* combats this by subtly anglicising certain aspects of Chinese culture: Confucius's philosophy is shown to parallel Christ's, and Dr. Sun Yat Sen, one of the leaders of the Chinese forces, is, like Jefferson Smith, directly compared to George Washington and Abraham Lincoln. Furthermore, in both *The Battle of China* and *The Battle of Russia*, Capra focuses on the cultural richness of the two nations. In the latter, for example, we are shown vignettes of the various diverse peoples of the country—the Ukrainians, the Moldavians, the Georgians, etc.—performing native dances, smiling, and laughing; images that form a vivid contrast to the gruesome battle scenes that soon follow.

Richard Barsam concludes his remarks about the *Why We Fight* series by observing that, "The *Why We Fight* series is not only the best group of films to come out of war, but also the best film record of the reasons behind that war, the most dramatic account of the battles in it, and the most eloquent tribute to the civilian and military men and women who fought and died in it."[25] For Capra himself, it may represent his most formidable achievement as a film director. As may already be clear, the *Why We Fight* series, though different in form from his fictional work, deals with essentially the same preoccupations: that the freedom of the individual is the country's greatest asset and most prized possession and needs to be defended at whatever cost. But never before had this and other ideas been conveyed so clearly and forcefully. All the standard objections to Capra's most famous films, those of the second half of the Thirties—that they are unsophisticated, overly sentimental and preachy, and that neither the hero nor the villain are convincing—hardly seem applicable to the *Why We Fight* series. Here, as he was not able to do in *Meet John Doe*,

Capra has constructed an epic elegy to the common man, the undisputed hero of this series.

In 1945, after having been awarded the Distinguished Service Medal for his work on the *Why We Fight* series and other Army films, Capra left the military and formed an independent production company with directors William Wyler and George Stevens and business manager Sam Briskin. RKO agreed to provide capital, the releasing apparatus, and the studio facilities under an agreement in which each of the three directors was expected to direct and produce at least one film a year. Capra's *It's a Wonderful Life* was the new company's first opus.

Having been out of the Hollywood mainstream now for three years and wondering whether perhaps he might have lost the "knack" of feature film-making, Capra assembled many of his old crew—cinematographer Joseph Walker, composer and musical arranger Dimitri Tiomkin, film editor William Hornbeck, assistant director Arthur S. Black, screenwriter Jo Swerling—a cast of actors, of which no less than nine had appeared in one or more of his previous films, and a story quintessentially Capra.[26] The animated Christmas card which precedes the credits makes it clear that the film is intended as the director's own "Christmas Carol", a fantasy certainly but one, like Dickens', as much about frustration and bitterness as about triumph.

The story spans the life of one George Bailey from his youth to middle age and the contemplation of suicide to his re-discovery of the glory of life. Born and raised in the small rural community of Bedford Falls, George develops a burning ambition to leave home for a bigger and better future. But destiny and his own subconscious work to keep him in Bedford Falls. He watches his school chums advance while he and his building and loan business go nowhere. On Christmas Eve his absent-minded uncle and partner, Billy (Thomas Mitchell), misplaces $8,000 while preparing to make a deposit. It also happens to be the day for the company's government audit. Without the $8,000 the books won't balance and so Capra's protagonist is suddenly faced with the prospect of scandal and jail. George has deftly handled financial crises before, and had he kept his composure during this one, he probably could have resolved it without much difficulty. But more than representing one more time that the building and loan is on the verge of bankruptcy, the incident represents the "last straw" in a life full of disappointments. It reawakens in George all the frustration that has been brewing inside him for the past twenty years. In a powerful scene which reveals how this film deals in emotions of a nature more deeply personal than those found in Capra's previous work, George returns home from the office and vents his anger on his wife and children. He storms out of the house to appeal to Potter (Lionel Barrymore), "the richest and meanest man in town," the man who ruined his father, and whose treachery is in fact responsbile for this crisis, for a loan. A Scrooge character who never reforms, Potter has made his fortune for the very reasons George has failed to do so: he is unremittingly selfish and ruthless. It is a trademark of Capra's cinema that the antagonist provides the most sobering description of the hero. Norton's assessment of Long John in the magnate's dining room after the hero has promised to expose Norton before the conventioneers, and Jerry Marks' (Keenan Wynn) incisive evaluation of Tony (Frank Sinatra) at the race track in *A Hole in the Head* (1959) are two examples. Potter's assessment of George may be the most brutally poignant of all:

> Look at you. You used to be so cocky. You were going to go out and conquer the world. You once called me a warped, frustrated old man. What are you but a warped frustrated young man: a miserable little clerk crawling in here on your hands and knees and begging for help. No securities, no stocks, no bonds, nothing but a little $500 equity in a life insurance policy. You're worth more dead than alive.

In his depressed state George takes Potter's words to heart and makes his way to the bridge outside of town with the intention of committing suicide.

Although George does not know it, his friends, realising that something is seriously wrong, have been praying for him. Heaven hears their prayers. All that described above actually occurs in flashback, part of the briefing for the angel (second-class) Clarence Oddbody (Henry Travers) who is being sent to earth to help George. Clarence immediately succeeds in saving George from suicide, but not in persuading him how mistaken his intention was. When George tells him that he wished he had never been born, Clarence, with help from Heaven, decides to grant him his wish, and George embarks on a classic psychological "night-journey" in which he learns what the world would have been like had he never existed: his brother Harry (Todd Karns) would have died in a tobogganing accident as a young boy because George was not there to save him, and the men on a World War Two transport ship would have died because Harry would not have been alive to shoot down the enemy plane that was heading straight for the vessel; Mr. Gower (H. B. Warner), the

**George the family man: James Stewart and
Donna Reed in IT'S A WONDERFUL LIFE (1946)**

chemist, would have gone to jail and then become a drunk because
George was not there to stop him from accidentally prescribing
poison to one of his customers; Uncle Billy would have been commit-
ted to an insane asylum without George to look after him; his wife
Mary (Donna Reed) would have become an old maid; and Bedford
Falls would be known as Pottersville, a seedy place full of whore-
houses, dive bars and gambling joints with its residents living in
Potter's "shacks" and spending what little money they earned on vice.

This privileged glimpse into the unknown instills George with a
new, fierce desire to live again. He recognises that he has not been a
failure and freely accepts his place in the scheme of things. He returns
home delirious with gratitude and happiness and discovers that his
friends have banded together to make up the lost $8000.

Leland Poague says that *It's a Wonderful Life* is a "mirror image of
Mr. Deeds Goes to Town."[27] To a point it is a mirror image of nearly all
of Capra's pre-war cinema. Like most of the director's work, the film

is very much concerned with the hero's moral perspective, but it approaches the issue from a different angle. In the trilogy, for instance, Capra's heroes have greatness thrust upon them, as it were. Deeds, Smith and John entertain no political ambitions at the outset, but are swept away by freak events to a fate they could have never predicted. George, on the other hand, is ambitious from the first, but events conspire to thwart him. Rather than soaring above the masses to a position of national prominence, he is forced to rationalise his own existence; the powers of darkness, so ominous in the trilogy, are here only within George himself. His ability to overcome disappoint-ment and despair spans not just one key sequence but the entire film; he achieves no spectacular triumphs, only a modest but crucially important realisation of self. Perhaps the realities of the war drained all the mythology out of the director's cinema. He suggests a certain divine justice in this film, but there are no traces here of the poetic justice so evident in his Thirties work. George, for instance, does not get the chance to punch any of the film's hateful characters in the nose as do Deeds, Smith and John. In fact, George is on the receiving end of a right cross.

Ultimately, *It's a Wonderful Life*, like all of Capra's films, is about faith: faith in oneself, faith in one's close friends, faith in God. Like that of Hitchcock and Ford, Capra's thematic bent was significantly influenced by his Catholic background. To lose faith is, for Capra, the greatest error one can make. Only when Deeds and Smith begin to doubt themselves and their ideals do they fail. George goes through the same process of ritual death (his leap into the river), purgatory (he sees a world unaffected by his presence) and resurrection. In this film an angel saves George from committing the one unforgivable sin by making him see all that he has contributed to the lives of others. But while divine intervention here is forceful and direct, Clarence's function does not differ significantly from that fulfilled by Babe in the courtroom, Saunders at the Lincoln Memorial or Ann on top of City Hall. In each case the hero is inspired to rediscover for himself the efficacy and rightness of his existence. That Capra uses a bumbling angel as the means to make George see that his life is very much worth living does not, as Richard Griffith contends, mar the final impact of the film. Capra clearly defines his terms even before the credits. Clarence finally only serves to highlight, as do the Ghosts in Dickens' "Christmas Carol", the director's central concerns.

Yet, however one regards Capra's story or the significance of his

James Stewart as George in IT'S A WONDERFUL LIFE

preoccupations, one cannot help but admire the director's mastery of the medium. To study this film is to understand how confidently Capra commanded all the nuances of his craft. His consummate editing skills and long-admired ability to manage crowd scenes are in full evidence here, but so are two other talents for which he has never been given his full due—his ability to get fine performances from actors and his aptitude for directing intimate scenes. It seems difficult to me, for instance, to dispute that James Stewart's finest perform-ance comes in this film where, in contrast to his usually unchallenging roles (*Mr. Smith* excepted), he is called upon to display convincingly a wide range of emotions from intense frustration to ecstatic joy. The brilliance of Stewart's performance, and the skilful way in which Capra modulated it, can perhaps best be illustrated in the scene where George and Mary are on the phone together to Sam Wainwright (Frank Albertson). George has just left his brother's wedding party despondent over the realisation that it will be difficult now, if not impossible, to leave Bedford Falls. He reluctantly makes his way to the home of his former girlfriend, Mary Hatch (Donna Reed). His disagreeable disposition makes for an unpleasant visit, but as he is about to leave Mary gets a call from Sam Wainwright, a boyhood chum of George's and now supposedly Mary's beau. The call draws George to the phone, and George and Mary are brought face to face for the first time in four years (Mary has been away at college). She has always loved George, and George her, since the night of the senior prom, but he has never chosen to admit his feelings for her because she symbolises a life bound to Bedford Falls. But now, as this exquisite scene develops, both his love for her and the agony of his own realisation of what the consummation of that love will mean, painfully emerge. Capra plays it primarily in one shot, the camera moving in as emotions build. In its basically static movement, the straightforward-ness of the lighting scheme and the length of the take, some two minutes, the scene contrasts sharply with the more spectacular moments in Capra's cinema. This scene depends solely on the actors and the camera's ability to chart their emotions with force and accuracy. So superbly does Capra control both these elements that the contrast between the scope of this scene and, say, the stadium scene in *Meet John Doe* only serves to point out how completely the director had mastered the aesthetics of his art.

It's a Wonderful Life* was produced at the cost of some $2 million, an enormous sum for 1946. The film attracted a large audience, but not large enough to turn a profit; *State of the Union* (1948), which was released through M-G-M, cost nearly $3 million and suffered essentially the same fate at the box office. All along Capra and his partners continued to pour money into their company to cover expenses; Capra even sold his collection of rare books, but the project proved to be a losing one from a financial standpoint despite everyone's best efforts. Independent film-making is difficult because it depends on the producing company to release films often and profitably to cover day-to-day overhead and expenses for future projects. Unfortunately, the formation of Liberty Films coincided with the great Hollywood bust of the late Forties and so, after only two years, it, like many similar ventures, was swallowed up by a major studio.

The effect of Liberty's failure on Capra is vividly described in the director's autobiography. Capra saw his company as the great hope of the independent film-maker, the liberator of the artist from the suffocating influences of the studios. A less subjective observer than Capra would have to question the director's bold claim that Hollywood's slide in the late Forties and early Fifties was directly related to the fall of Liberty Films, but in any case, when the company failed, Capra seems to have considered himself a failure: he had let down himself, his colleagues and his friends. Liberty Films was sold to Paramount, and Capra, as he saw it himself, sold his artistic freedom (his "soul") to Barney Balaban for a one million dollar contract. Capra: "And so, the one man, one film apostle became, for the first time, an employed contract director taking orders. I was tempted by a million dollars—and fell; never to rise to be the same man again, either as a person or as a talent. For once, I had lost (or sold) control of the content of my films and of my artistic liberty to express myself in my own way—it was the beginning of my end as a social force in films."[28]

Yet, while Capra remains convinced that his fall is linked to the dissolution of Liberty Films, it might be argued (as William Pechter has done) that Capra simply reached the culmination of his career in *It's a Wonderful Life* and so afterwards experienced, as many artists do after producing the piece that crystallises all that their previous work has been trying to say, a falling-off in the quality of his output.[29] This can be seen immediately in *State of the Union*, a long, often ponderous film which seem to lack the usual breathless pace of Capra's best work. Subsequent to *State of the Union*, Capra made two amusing musical comedies for Paramount—*Riding High* (1950), a remake of *Broadway Bill*, and *Here Comes the Groom* (1951) from a story by Riskin. After completing the latter he retired from feature film-making and supervised a series of highly regarded animated science documentaries for television which are still regularly shown to school children.

In 1959 he returned to the film capital after nearly a decade's absence to make *A Hole in the Head* with Frank Sinatra. Certainly the best of the films Capra made after *It's a Wonderful Life,* it concerns a small-time hotel owner, Tony Manetta (Sinatra), who has great ambitions but lacks the money and the acumen to realise them. The sequence at the dog races in which Tony's boyhood friend, Jerry Marks (Keenan Wynn), now a multi-million dollar entrepreneur, lays it on the line for Tony and brands him a loser remains one of the most compelling moments in Capra's cinema.

For his last film, *A Pocketful of Miracles,* Capra, perhaps appropriately, returned to pure fantasy to remake the film that first established him as a major director, *Lady for a Day.* It remains, however, in sharp contrast to the original and Capra's other comedies of the early Thirties, an uninspired, sometimes unconsciously sad effort to recapture a glorious past. All through the production of the film, Capra suffered severe "cluster" headaches, and it was primarily this ailment that convinced the director, after thirty-seven years in "pictures", to retire.

In *Mr. Smith Goes to Washington*, Smith, who, like all of Capra's heroes, is really a poet at heart, explains to Saunders that his father had an idea that one should try to see life "as if you have just come out of a tunnel." One might interpret this bit of philosophy thus: "use your intellect and your senses to the fullest so as not to take the smallest of life's glories for granted." It is one of those hokey but endearing sentiments that echo all through the director's work, an intrinsic part of the tapestry of ideas and images that comprise his cinema. And while some may find this sentiment and others of his maudlin and out of place in the contemporary world, one must admire Capra for the fact that in the midst of the assembly production methods that pre-dominated Hollywood Thirties' cinema, his films were, in essence, hand-crafted, the product (as near as possible in the collaborative effort of film-making) of one man's genius. It is this distinctiveness, the originality of his work, that will uphold Capra's status, after all the arguments regarding the efficacy of his thematic preoccupations have been made, as a major and enduring figure of the American cinema.

NOTES

[1]Donald Willis, *The Films of Frank Capra* (Metuchen, New Jersey: Scarecrow Press, 1974), p. 8, 9.

[2]George Orwell, *Critical Essays,* "Charles Dickens" (London: Secker and Warburg, 1946), p. 10.

[3]Penelope Houston, "Mr. Deeds and Willis Stark," *Sight and Sound*, November 1950, p. 278.

[4]As Capra notes in his autobiography, Caltech was in 1915 known as Throop Polytechnic Institute, and in the process of being reorganised as California Institute of Technology.

[5]My interview with the director on March 3, 1976 at the University of Illinois.

[6]Richard Schickel, *The Men Who Made the Movies* (New York: Atheneum, 1975), p. 65.

[7]Frank Capra, *The Name Above the Title* (New York: Macmillan, 1971), p. 64.

[8]Capra, p. 66.

[9]*Film Daily*, "Matinee Idol," 29 April 1928, p. 5.

[10]*Variety*, "Forbidden," 12 January 1932, p. 24.

[11]Capra, p. 141, 142.

[12]*Variety*, "The Bitter Tea of General Yen," 17 January 1933, p. 14.

[13]Ruth Morris, *Variety*, "Capra Foresees Satirical Cycle; Many Subjects 'Ripe for Ridicule!' " 2 February 1932, p. 2.

[14]Capra, p. 140.

[15]*Lady for a Day* was nominated for Best Film, Best Direction, Best Screenplay and Best Actress (May Robson).

[16]Graham Greene, *Graham Greene on Film: Collected Film Criticism, 1935-1939*, "Mr. Deeds Goes to Town" (New York: Simon and Schuster, 1972), p. 96. British title: *The Pleasure-Dome* (London: Secker and Warburg, 1972).

[17]Leland Poague, *The Cinema of Frank Capra: An Approach to Film Comedy* (New York: Barnes; London: Tantivy, 1975), p. 175.

[18]Mark Van Doren, *The Private Reader: Selected Articles and Reviews*. "Second Comings," (New York: Henry Holt, 1942), p. 332.

[19]Otis Feguson, *New Republic*, 21 September 1938, p. 188.

[20]Jeffrey Richards, *Visions of Yesterday* (London: Routledge and Kegan Paul, 1973) p. 250-252.

[21]"Lots of heels" is the Colonel's definition of "Heelots," but perhaps Capra and Riskin had the Greek term "Helot" meaning slave or peasant in mind.

[22]Aldous Huxley, *Brave New World* (New York: Harper and Row, 1946 ed.), p. xv.

[23]Robert Sklar, *Frank Capra: The Man and His Film*, eds. Richard Glatzer and John Raeburn, "The Imagination of Stability: The Depression Films of Frank Capra," (Ann Arbor: University of Michigan, 1975), p. 122.

[24]Richard Griffith, *Frank Capra*, New Index Series No. 3 (London: The British Film Institute, 1951), p. 5.

[25]Richard Barsam, *Non-Fiction Film: A Critical History* (New York: Dutton, 1973), p. 000.

[26]Capra also wanted Riskin's help, but the screenwriter had formed his own production company (also releasing through RKO) and was busy on his company's first effort, *Magic Town;* and so he declined Capra's invitation to renew their collaboration.

[27]Poague, p. 205.

[28]Capra, p. 402.

[29]William Pechter, *Twenty-Four Times a Second: Films and Film-makers* (New York: Harper and Row, 1971), p. 132.

Frank Capra Filmography

Capra wrote and directed a series of live action/animation science films for the American Telephone and Telegraph Company:

OUR MR. SUN (1956). *With* Dr. F. C. Baxter, Eddie Albert.

HEMO, THE MAGNIFICENT (1957). *With* Dr. F. C. Baxter, Richard Carlson.

THE STRANGE CASE OF THE COSMIC RAYS (1957). *With* Dr. F. C. Baxter, Richard Carlson.

THE UNCHAINED GODDESS (1958). *Dir:* Richard Carlson *Sc:* Frank Capra, Jonathan Latimer. *With* Dr. F. C. Baxter. *Prod:* Frank Capra.

SHORT FILMS

BALLAD OF FULTAH FISHER'S BOARDING HOUSE (1921). *Ph:* Roy Wiggins. *With* Mildred Ownes (*Anne of Austria*), Olaf Skavlan (*Hans*), Ethan Allen (*Salem Hardieker*), Gerald Griffin (*British sailor*), Oreste Seragnoli (*Luz*). *Prod:* Fireside Productions for Pathe. 12m.

THE CAVALCADE OF ACADEMY AWARDS (1940). *Dir:* Ira Genet. *Supervision:* Frank Capra. 31m.

REACHING FOR THE STARS (1964). *Prod:* Martin Marietta Corp. for the New York World's Fair. 20m.

SCREENWRITER

Capra worked on the following films as a screenwriter while primarily employed at Mack Sennett Studios:

PICKING PEACHES (1924). *With* Harry Langdon.

SMILE PLEASE (1924). *With* Harry Langdon.

SHANGHAIED LOVERS (1924). *With* Harry Langdon.

FLICKERING YOUTH (1924). *With* Harry Langdon.

THE CAT'S MEOW (1924). *With* Harry Langdon.

HIS NEW MAMA (1924). *With* Harry Langdon.

THE LUCK O' THE FOOLISH (1924). *With* Harry Langdon.

THE HANSOM CABMAN (1924). *With* Harry Langdon.

ALL NIGHT LONG (1924), *With* Harry Langdon.

THE WILD GOOSE CHASE (1925). *With* Ben Turpin.

THE FIRST FLAME (1925). *With* Harry Langdon. (Not released until 1927.)

SEA SQUAK (1925). *With* Harry Langdon.

HIS MARRIAGE VOW (1925). *With* Harry Langdon.

BOOB IN THE WOODS (1925). *With* Harry Landgon.

PLAIN CLOTHES (1925). *With* Harry Langdon.

THE MARRIAGE CIRCUS (1925). *With* Ben Turpin.

SUPER-HOOPER-DYNE LIZZIES (1925). *With* Billy Bevan.

GOOD MORNING NURSE (1925). *With* Ralph Graves.

REMEMBER WHEN? (1925). *With* Harry Langdon.

CUPID'S BOOTS (1925). *With* Ralph Graves.

HORACE GREELY, JR. (1925). *With* Ralph Graves.

THE WHITE WING'S BRIDE (1925). *With* Harry Langdon.

LUCKY STARS (1925). *With* Harry Langdon.

THERE HE GOES (1925). *With* Harry Langdon.

SATURDAY AFTERNOON (1925). *With* Harry Langdon.

FIDDLESTICKS (1925). *With* Harry Langdon.

THE SOLDIER MAN (1926). *With* Harry Langdon.

THE SWIM PRINCESS (1928). *With* Daphne Pollard.

THE BURGLAR (1928). *With* Raymond McKee.

OTHERS (excluding films also directed)

TRAMP, TRAMP, TRAMP (1926). *With* Harry Langdon. *Prod:* Harry Langdon for First National. 62m.

WESTWARD THE WOMEN (1950). *Dir:* William Wellman. *Sc:* Charles Schnee (a story by Frank Capra). *Prod:* Dore Schary for M-G-M. 116m.

DIRECTOR

THE STRONG MAN (1926). Harry straightens out a crooked small town. *Sc:* Arthur Ripley. *Ph:* Elgin Lessley, Glenn Kershner. *Ed:* Harold Young. *With* Harry Langdon (*Paul Bergot*), Priscilla Bonner (*Mary Brown*), Gertrude Astor (*Lily*), William V. Mung (*Parson Brown*), Robert McKim (*Roy McDevitt*), Arthur Thalassa (*Zandow the Great*). *Prod:* Harry Langdon for First National. 60m.

LONG PANTS (1927). Harry falls in love with a gangster's moll. *Sc:* Arthur Ripley. *Adaptation:* Robert Eddy. *Ph:* Elgin Lessley, Glenn Kershner. *With* Harry Langdon (*Harry*), Priscilla Bonner (*Priscilla*), Alan Roscoe (*Harry's father*), Gladys Brockwell (*Harry's mother*), Alma Bennett (*Bebe Blair*). *Prod:* Harry Langdon for First National. 60m.

FOR THE LOVE OF MIKE (1927). A delicatessen dealer, a tailor and a street cleaner raise an abandoned child. *Sc:* J. Clarkson Miller (story "Hell's Kitchen" by John Moroso). *Ph:* Ernest Haller. *With* Claudette Colbert (*Mary*), Ben Lyon ("*Mike*"), George Sidney (*Abraham Katz*), Ford Sterling (*Herman Schultz*), Hugh Cameron (*Patrick O'Malley*), Skeets Gallagher ("*Coxey*" *Pendleton*), Rudolph Cameron (*Henry Sharp*), Mabel Swor (*Evelyn Joyce*). *Prod:* Robert Kane for First National. 75m.

THAT CERTAIN THING (1928). Romance between profligate and working girl. *Sc:* Elmer Harris (titles by Al Boasberg). *Ph:* Joseph Walker. *Art dir:* Robert E. Lee *Ed:* Arthur Roberts *With* Viola Dana (*Molly*), Ralph Graves (*A.B.Charles Jr.*), Burr McIntosh (*A.B.Charles Sr.*), Aggie Herring (*Mrs. Kelly*), Carl Gerard (*Brooks*), Syd Crossley (*valet*). *Prod:* Harry Cohn for Columbia. 69m. (In his autobiography, Capra says that he wrote the story. Harris, however, receives the screen credit.)

SO THIS IS LOVE (1928). Romantic triangle involving flaxen-haired waif, dress designer and pugilist. *Sc:* Norman Springer. *Adaptation:* Elmer Harris. *Ph:* Ray June. *Art dir:* Robert E. Lee. *Ed:* Arthur Roberts. *With* Shirley Mason (*Hilda Jensen*), Buster Collier (*Jerry McGuire*), Johnnie Walker ("*Spike*" *Mullins*), Ernie Adams ("*Flash*" *Tracy*), Carl Gerard (*Otto*), William H. Strauss ("*Maison*" *Katz*), Jean Laverty (*Mary Malone*). *Prod:* Harry Cohn for Columbia. 60m.

THE MATINEE IDOL (1928). Sophisticated New York actor falls in love with country girl. *Sc:* Elmer Harris (story "Come Back to Aaron" by Robert Lord). *Continuity:* Peter Milne. *Ph:* Philip Tannura. *Art dir:* Robert E. Lee. *Ed:* Arthur Roberts. *With* Bessie Love (*Ginger Bolivar*), Johnnie Walker (*Don Wilson/Harry Mann*), Lionel Belmore (*Col. Jasper Bolivar*), Ernest Hilliard (*Wingate*), Sidney D'Albrook (*J. Madison Wilberforce*), David Mir (*Eric Barrymaine*). *Prod:* Harry Cohn for Columbia. 66m.

THE WAY OF THE STRONG (1928). Badly-scarred gang leader falls in love with a blind violinist. *Sc:* William Counselman. *Continuity:* Peter Milne. *Ph:* Ben Reynolds. *With* Mitchell Lewis ("*Hand-*

some" Williams), Alice Day (*Nora*), Margaret Livingston (*Marie*), Theodor von Eltz (*Dan*), William Norton Bailey (*Louie*). *Prod:* Harry Cohn for Columbia. 61m.

SAY IT WITH SABLES (1928). Father tries to protect son from former mistress—a gold-digger who guns for big game and usually gets it. *Sc:* Frank Capra, Peter Milne. *Continuity:* Dorothy Howell. *Ph:* Joseph Walker. *Art dir:* Harrison Wiley. *Ed:* Arthur Roberts. *With* Francis X. Bushman (*John Caswell*), Helene Chadwick (*Helen Caswell*), Margaret Livingson (*Irene Gordon*), Arthur Rankin (*Doug Caswell*), June Nash (*Marie Caswell*), Alphonse Ethier (*Mitchell*), Edna Mae Cooper (*maid*). *Prod:* Harry Cohn for Columbia. 70m.

SUBMARINE (1928). Action and adventure in the China Seas. *Sc:* Winifred Dunn. *Ph:* Joseph Walker. *Art dir:* Harrison Wiley. *Ed:* Ben Pivar. *With* Jack Holt (*Jack*), Dorothy Revier (*Bessie*), Ralph Graves (*Bob*), Clarence Burton (*submarine commander*). *Prod:* Harry Cohn for Columbia. 93m.

THE POWER OF THE PRESS (1928). Cub reporter breaks big story. *Sc:* Frederick A. Thompson. *Adaptation and continuity:* Sonya Levien. *Ph:* Chet Lyons. *Art dir:* Harrison Wiley. *Ed:* Ben Pivar. *With* Douglas Fairbanks Jr. (*Clem Robers*), Jobyna Ralston (*Jane Atwill*), Mildred Harris (*Marie*), Philo McCullough (*Blake*), Wheeler Oakman (*Van*), Robert Edeson (*city editor*), Edward Davis (*Mr. Atwill*), Del Henderson (*Johnson*), Charles Clary (*district attorney*). *Prod:* Jack Cohn for Columbia. 62m.

THE YOUNGER GENERATION (1929). Jewish family moves from lower East Side to Fifth Avenue. *Sc:* Sonya Levien (a story by Fanny Hurst). *Dialogue:* Howard J. Green. *Ph:* Ted Tetzlaff. *Art dir:* Harrison Wiley. *Ed:* Arthur Roberts. *With* Jean Hersholt (*Julius Goldfish*), Lina Basquette (*Birdie Goldfish*), Ricardo Cortez (*Morris*), Rex Lease (*Eddie Lesser*), Martha Franklin (*Mrs. Lesser*), Julanne Johnson (*Irma Striker*), Rosa Rosanova (*Tildie Goldfish*). *Prod:* Jack Cohn for Columbia and F.B.O. 75m.

THE DONOVAN AFFAIR (1929). A "whodunit." *Sc:* Howard J. Green, Dorothy Howell (a play by Owen Davis). *Dialogue:* Howard J. Green. *Ph:* Ted Tetzlaff. *Art dir:* Harrison Wiley. *Ed:* Arthur Roberts. *With* Jack Holt (*Inspector Killian*), Dorothy Revier (*Jean Rankin*), William Collier Jr. (*Cornish*), Agnes Ayres (*Lydia Rankin*), John Roche (*Jack Donovan*), Fred Kelsey (*Carney*), Hank Mann (*Dr. Lindsey*), Wheeler Oakman (*Porter*), Virginia Brown Faire (*Mary Mills*), Alphonse Ethier (*Capt. Peter Rankin*), Edward Hearn (*Nelson*), Ethel Wales (*Mrs. Lindsey*), John Wallace (*Dobbs*). *Prod:* Harry Cohn for Columbia. 80m.

FLIGHT (1929). Action, adventure and romance when two aviators move to crush a rebel uprising in Central America. *Sc:* Howard J. Green (a story by Ralph Graves). *Dialogue:* Frank Capra. *Ph:* Joseph Walker, Joe Novak. *Aerial ph:* Elmer Dyer, Paul Perry. *Art dir:* Harrison Wiley. *Ed:* Ben Pivar, Maurice Wright, Gene Milford. *With* Jack Holt ("*Panama*" *Williams*), Lila Lee (*Elinor*), Ralph Graves ("*Lefty*" *Phelps*), Alan Roscoe (*Major*), Harold Goodwin (*Steve Roberts*), Jimmy De LaCruze (*Lobo*). *Prod:* Harry Cohn for Columbia. 110m.

LADIES OF LEISURE (1930). Wealthy artist finds inspiration in the eyes of a beautiful gold-digger. *Sc:* Jo Swerling (play "Ladies of the Evening" by Milton Herbert Gropper). *Ph:* Joseph Walker. *Art dir:* Harrison Wiley. *Ed:* Maurice Wright. *With* Barbara Stanwyck (*Kay Arnold*), Ralph Graves (*Jerry*), Lowell Sherman (*Standish*), Marie Prevost (*Dot*), Nance O'Neill (*Mrs. Strange*), George Fawcett (*Mr. Strange*), Johnnie Walker (*Charlie*), Juliette Compton (*Claire Collins*). *Prod:* Harry Cohn for Columbia. 98m.

RAIN OR SHINE (1930). When circus performers strike, acrobat puts on one man show. *Dialogue and continuity:* Dorothy Howell and Jo Swerling (the play by James Gleason). *Ph:* Joseph Walker. *Art dir:* Harrison Wiley. *Ed:* Maurice Wright. *Songs:* "Happy Days Are Here Again", "Rain or Shine" by Jack Yellen and Milton Ager; "Sitting on

Barbara Stanwyck, Johnnie Walker and Marie Prevost in LADIES OF LEISURE

a Rainbow" by Jack Yellen and Dan Dougherty. *With* Joe Cook *(Smiley)*, Louise Fazenda *(Frankie)*, Joan Peers *(Mary)*, William Collier Jr. *(Bud)*, Tom Howard *(Amos)*, David Chasen *(Dave)*, Alan Roscoe *(Dalton)*, Adolph Milar *(Foltz)*, Clarence Muse *(Nero)*, Ed Martindale *(Mr. Conway)*, Tyrrell Davis *(Lord Gwynne)*. *Prod:* Harry Cohn for Columbia. 90m.

DIRIGIBLE (1931). Action and adventure during an expedition to the South Pole. *Sc:* Jo Swerling (a story by Commander Frank Wilber Wead, U.S.N.). *Continuity:* Dorothy Howell. *Ph:* Joseph Walker. *Aerial ph:* Elmer Dyer. *Ed:* Maurice Wright. *With* Jack Holt *(Bradon)*, Ralph Graves *(Frisky Pierce)*, Fay Wray *(Helen Pierce)*, Hobart Bosworth *(Rondelle)*, Roscoe Karns *(Sock McGuire)*, Harold Goodwin *(Hansen)*, Clarence Muse *(Clarence)*, Emmett Corrigan *(Admiral Martin)*, Alan Roscoe *(commander of the Lexington)*, Selmar Jackson *(Lt. Rowland)*. *Prod:* Harry Cohn for Columbia. 102m.

THE MIRACLE WOMAN (1931). Bogus evangelist walks the straight and narrow path after falling in love with blind aviator. *Sc:* Jo Swerling (the play "Bless You Sister" by John Meehan and Robert Riskin). *Continuity:* Dorothy Howell. *Ph:* Joseph Walker. *Ed:* Maurice Wright. *With* Barbara Stanwyck *(Florence "Faith" Fallon)*, David Manners *(John Carson)*, Sam Hardy *(Hornsby)*, Beryl Mercer

(Mrs. Higgins), Russell Hopton *(Welford)*, Charles Middleton *(Simpson)*, Eddie Boland *(Collins)*, Thelma Hill *(Gussie)*, Aileen Carlyle *(Violet)*, Al Stewart *(Brown)*, Harry Todd *(Briggs)*. *Prod:* Harry Cohn for Columbia. 90m.

PLATINUM BLONDE (1931). Ace newshound falls in love with shallow socialite and lives to regret it. *Sc:* Jo Swerling (a story by Harry Chandler and Douglas W. Churchill). *Dialogue:* Robert Riskin. *Continuity:* Dorothy Howell. *Ph:* Joseph Walker. *Art dir:* Stephen Goosson. *Ed:* Gene Milford. *With* Loretta Young *(Gallagher)*, Robert Williams *(Stew Smith)*, Jean Harlow *(Anne Schuyler)*, Reginald Owen *(Grayson)*, Louise Closser Hale *(Mrs. Schuyler)*, Edmund Breese *(Conroy)*, Walter Catlett *(Bingy Baker)*, Donald Dillaway *(Michael)*, Halliwell Hobbes *(Smythe)*, Claude Allister *(Dawson)*. *Prod:* Harry Cohn for Columbia. 98m.

FORBIDDEN (1932). Small-town girl finds unhappiness in the big city. *Sc:* Jo Swerling (a story by Frank Capra). *Ph:* Joseph Walker. *Ed:* Maurice Wright. *With* Barbara Stanwyck *(Lulu)*, Adolphe Menjou *(Bob)*, Ralph Bellamy *(Holland)*, Dorothy Peterson *(Helen)*, Thomas Jefferson *(Wilkinson)*, Myrna Fresholt *(Roberta as a child)*, Charlotte V. Henry *(Roberta)*, Oliver Eckhardt *(Briggs)*. *Prod:* Harry Cohn for Columbia. 83m.

AMERICAN MADNESS (1932). Exaggerated rumour starts a run on a major bank. *Sc:* Robert Riskin. *Ph:* Joseph Walker. *Art dir:* Stephen Goosson. *Ed:* Maurice Wright. *With* Walter Huston *(Dickson)*, Pat O'Brien *(Matt)*, Kay Johnson *(Mrs. Dickson)*, Constance Cummings *(Helen)*, Gavin Gordon *(Cluett)*, Arthur Hoyt *(Ives)*, Robert E. O'Conner *(Inspector)*. *Prod:* Harry Cohn for Columbia. 76m.

BITTER TEA OF GENERAL YEN (1932). American missionary falls in love with Chinese warlord. *Sc:* Edward Paramore (the novel by Grace Zaring Stone). *Ph:* Joseph Walker. *Ed:* Edward Curtiss. *Mus:* W. Franke Harling. *With* Barbara Stanwyck *(Megan Davis)*, Nils Asther

(*General Yen*), Gavin Gordon (*Robert Strike*), Walter Connolly (*Jones*), Lucien Littlefield (*Mr. Jackson*), Toshia Mori (*Mah-Li*), Richard Loo (*Captain Li*), Clara Blandick *(Mrs. Jackson)*, Moy Ming *(Dr. Lin*), Robert Wayne (*Rev. Bostwick*), Knute Erickson (*Dr. Hansen*), Ella Hall (*Mrs. Hansen*), Arthur Millette (*Mr. Pettis*), Helen Jerome Eddy (*Miss Reed*), Martha Mattox (*Miss Avery*), Jessie Arnold (*Mrs. Blake*), Emmett Corrigan (*Bishop Harkness*). *Prod:* Walter Wanger for Columbia. 89m.

LADY FOR A DAY (1933). Apple vendor becomes "queen for a day." *Sc:* Robert Riskin (story "Madame LaGimp" by Damon Runyon). *Ph:* Joseph Walker. *Art dir:* Steve Goosson. *Ed:* Gene Havlick. *With* Warren William (*Dave the Dude*), May Robson (*Apple Annie*), Glenda Farrell ("*Missouri*" *Martin*), Guy Kibbee (*Judge Blake*), Ned Sparks (*Happy*), Jean Parker (*Louise*), Walter Connolly (*Count Romero*), Barry Norton (*Carlos*), Nat Pendleton (*Shakespeare*), Hobart Bosworth (*the governor*). *Prod:* Columbia. 88m.

IT HAPPENED ONE NIGHT (1934). Hard-nosed journalist and unhappy heiress fall in love on a cross-country bus trip. *Sc:* Robert Riskin (story "Night Bus" by Samuel Hopkins Adams). *Ph:* Joseph Walker. *Art dir:* Stephen Goosson. *Ed:* Gene Havlick. *Mus:* Louis Silvers. *With* Clark Gable (*Peter Warne*), Claudette Colbert (*Ellie Andrews*), Walter Connolly (*Alexander Andrews*), Roscoe Karns (*Shapely*), Jameson Thomas (*King Westley*), Alan Hale (*Danker*), Ward Bond (*bus driver*), Eddie Chandler (*chauffeur*), Wallis Clark (*Lovington*), Harry Bradley (*Henderson*), Charlie Brown (*reporter*), Harry Holman (*owner of motel*), Maidel Turner (*owner's wife*), Arthur Hoyt (*Zeke*), Irving Bacon (*station attendant*), Charles C. Wilson (*Gordon*), Harry Todd (*Flag Man*), Blanche Frederici (*Zeke's wife*). *Prod:* Frank Capra for Columbia. 105m.

BROADWAY BILL (1934). Unhappy business man stakes all he has on a race horse. *Sc:* Robert Riskin (the story by Mark Hellinger). *Ph:* Joseph Walker. *Ed:*

Gene Havlick. *With* Warner Baxter (*Dan Brooks*), Myrna Loy (*Alice*), Walter Connolly (*J. L. Higgins*), Helen Vinson (*Margaret*), Douglass Dumbrille (*Eddie Morgan*), Raymond Walburn (*Colonel Pettigrew*), Lynne Overman (*Happy McGuire*), Clarence Muse (*Whitey*), Margaret Hamilton (*Edna*), Frankie Darro (*Ted Williams*), Charles C. Wilson (*Collins*), Harry Todd (*Pop Jones*), Jason Robards (*Arthur Winslow*). *Prod:* Frank Capra for Columbia. 90m.

MR. DEEDS GOES TO TOWN (1936). Small town poet inherits large fortune and goes to New York. *Sc:* Robert Riskin (story "Opera Hat" by Clarence Budington Kelland). *Ph:* Joseph Walker. *Art dir:* Stephen Goosson. *Ed:* Gene Havlick. *Mus:* Harold Jackson. *With* Gary Cooper (*Longfellow Deeds*), Jean Arthur ("*Babe*" *Bennett*), George Bancroft (*McWade*), Lionel Stander ("*Corny*" *Cobb*), Douglass Dumbrille (*John Cedar*), Raymond Walburn (*valet*), H. B. Warner (*Judge Walker*), Margaret Matzenauer (*Pomponi*), Warren Hymer (*bodyguard*), Muriel Evans (*Theresa*), Ruth Donnelly (*Mabel Dawson*), Spencer Charters (*Mal*), Emma Dunn *(Mrs. Meredith)*, Wryley Birch (*Psychiatrist*), Arthur Hoyt (*Budington*), John Wray (*farmer*), Jameson Thomas (*Mr. Semple*), Mayo Methot (*Mrs. Semple*), Gene Morgan (*servant*), Walter Catlett (*Morrow*), Margaret Seddon (*Jane Faulkner*), Pierre Watkin (*Arthur Cedar*), Christian Rub (*Swenson*), Margaret McWade (*Amy Faulkner*), Russell Hicks (*Dr. Malcolm*), Gustav von Seyffertitz (*Dr. Frazier*), Edward Le Saint (*Dr. Fosdick*), Charles Lane (*Hallor*), Irving Bacon (*Frank*), George Cooper (*Bob*). *Prod:* Frank Capra for Columbia. 115m.

LOST HORIZON (1937). Diplomat finds a paradise in the Himalayas. *Sc:* Robert Riskin (the novel by James Hilton). *Ph:* Joseph Walker. *Aerial ph:* Elmer Dyer. *Special effects:* E. Roy Davidson, Ganahl Carson. *Art dir:* Stephen Goosson. *Ed:* Gene Havlick. *Mus:* Dimitri Tiomkin. *With* Ronald Colman (*Robert Conway*), Jane Wyatt (*Sondra*), Edward Everett Horton (*Lovett*), John Howard (*George Conway*), Thomas Mitchell (*Bar-*

Capra (right) conferring with cameraman Joseph Walker

MR. SMITH GOES TO WASHING-TON (1939). Idealist has to come to grips with political realities when he becomes a senator. *Sc*: Sidney Buchman (story "The Gentleman from Montana" by Lewis R. Foster). *Ph:* Joseph Walker. *Art dir:* Lionel Banks. *Ed:* Gene Havlick, Al Clark. *Montage:* Slavko Vorkapich. *Mus:* Dimitri Tiomkin. *With* James Stewart (*Jefferson Smith*), Claude Rains (*Sen. Joseph Paine*), Edward Arnold (*Jim Taylor*), Jean Arthur (*Saunders*), Thomas Mitchell (*Diz Moore*), Guy Kibbee (*Gov. Hopper*), Eugene Pallette (*Chick McGann*), Beulah Bondi (*Mrs. Smith*), Harry Carey (*Vice President*), H. B. Warner (*majority leader*), Astrid Allwyn (*Susan Paine*), Ruth Donnelly (*Mrs. Hopper*), Grant Mitchell (*Sen. MacPherson*), Porter Hall (*Sen. Monroe*), Pierre Watkin (*leader of the minority*), Charles Lane (*Nosey*), William. Demarest (*Bill Griffith*), Dick Elliot (*Carl Cook*), Billy Watson, Delmar Watson, John Russell, Harry Watson, Gary Watson, Baby Dumpling (*Hopper boys*), H. V.

nard), Margo (*Maria*), Isobel Jewell (*Gloria*), H. B. Warner (*Chang*), Sam Jaffe *(High Lama)*, Hugh Buckler *(Lord Gainsford)*, John T. Murray (*valet*). *Prod:* Frank Capra for Columbia. 132m.

YOU CAN'T TAKE IT WITH YOU (1938). Industrialist finds there is more to life than money and social position. *Sc:* Robert Riskin (the play by George S. Kaufman and Moss Hart). *Ph:* Joseph Walker. *Art dir:* Stephen Goosson. *Ed:* Gene Havlick. *Mus:* Dimitri Tiomkin. *With* James Stewart (*Tony Kirby*), Jean Arthur (*Alice Sycamore*), Lionel Barrymore (*Martin Vanderhof*), Edward Arnold (*Anthony P. Kirby*), Mischa Auer (*Kolenkhov*), Ann Miller (*Essie*), Spring Byington (*Penny*), Samuel S. Hinds (*Paul Sycamore*), Donald Meek (*Poppins*), H. B. Warner (*Ramsay*), Halliwell Hobbes (*De Pinna*), Dub Taylor (*Ed*), Mary Forbes (*Mrs. Anthony Kirby*), Lillian Yarbo (*Rheba*), Eddie Anderson (*Donald*), Clarence Wilson (*John Blakely*), Joseph Swickard (*Professor*), Ann Doran (*Maggie O'Neill*), Christian Rub (*Schmidt*), Charles Lane (*Henderson*), Harry Davenport (*Judge*). *Prod:* Frank Capra for Columbia. 127m.

James Stewart in MR. SMITH GOES TO WASHINGTON

Kaltenborn (*announcer*), Jack Carson (*Sweeney*), Allan Cavan (*Ragner*), Maurice Costello (*Diggs*), Lloyd Whitlock (*Schultz*). *Prod:* Frank Capra for Columbia. 127m.

MEET JOHN DOE (1941). Sore-armed, bush-league baseball pitcher becomes a national hero. *Sc:* Robert Riskin (story "The Life and Death of John Doe" by Richard Connell and Robert Presnell). *Ph:* George Barnes. *Art Dir:* Stephen Goosson. *Ed:* Daniel Mandell. *Montage*: Slavko Vorkapich. *Mus:* Dimitri Tiomkin. *With* Gary Cooper (*Long John Willoughby*), Barbara Stanwyck (*Ann Mitchell*), Edward Arnold (*D. B. Norton*), Walter Brennan (*The Colonel*), James Gleason (*Connell*), Regis Toomey (*Bert*), Ann Doran (*Mrs. Hansen*), Spring Byington (*Mrs. Mitchell*), Gene Lockhart (*Mayor Lovett*), Rod La Rocque (*Ted Sheldon*), Irving Bacon (*Beany*), J. Farrell McDonald (*Sourpuss*), Warren Hymer (*Angelface*), Harry Holman (*Mayor Hawkins*), Andrew Tombes (*Spencer*), Pierre Watkin (*Hammett*), Stanley Andrews (*Weston*), Mitchell Lewis (*Bennett*), Charles Wilson (*Charlie Dawson*), Vaughn Glaser (*Governor*), Sterling Holloway (*Dan*), Mike Frankovich, Knox Manning, John B. Hughes (*radio announcers*). *Prod:* Frank Capra for Warner Bors. 135m.

ARSENIC AND OLD LACE (1941). Two innocent-looking old ladies prove to be diabolical murderers. *Sc:* Julius J. Epstein, Philip G. Epstein (the play by Joseph Kesselring). *Ph:* Sol Polito. *Art dir:* Max Parker. *Ed:* Daniel Mandell. *Mus:* Max Steiner. *With* Cary Grant (*Mortimer Brewster*), Priscilla Lane (*Elaine Harper*), Raymond Massey (*Jonathan Brewster*), Peter Lorre (*Dr. Einstein*), Jack Carson (*O'Hara*), Josephine Hull (*Abby Brewster*), Jean Adair (*Martha Brewster*), Edward Everette Horton (*Mr. Witherspoon*), James Gleason (*police lieutenant*), Grant Mitchell (*Rev. Harper*). John Alexander (*Teddy Brewster*), Charles Lane (*reporter*). *Prod:* Frank Capra for Warner Bros. 118m. (Although Capra made the film in 1941, it was not released until 1944 due to an agreement that the film would not be shown until after the play had finished its run).

THE WHY WE FIGHT SERIES (1942-1945)

PRELUDE TO WAR (1942). *Dir:* Frank Capra, Anatole Litvak. *Sc:* Eric Knight, *Narr:* Walter Huston. *Mus:* Dimitri Tiomkin. *Ed:* William Hornbeck. *Prod:* U.S. War Department. 52m.

THE NAZIS STRIKE (1942). *Dir:* Frank Capra, Anatole Litvak. *Sc:* Eric Knight, Anthony Veiller, Robert Heller. *Narr:* Walter Huston. *Mus:* Dimitri Tiomkin. *Ed:* William Hornbeck. *Prod:* U.S. War Department. 40m.

DIVIDE AND CONQUER (1943). *Dir:* Frank Capra, Anatole Litvak. *Sc:* Anthony Veiller, Robert Heller. *Narr:* Walter Huston, Anthony Veiller. *Mus:*

**Left, filming MEET JOHN DOE
Right, Cary Grant, Raymond Massey and Peter Lorre in
ARSENIC AND OLD LACE**

Dimitri Tiomkin. *Ed:* William Hornbeck. *Prod:* U.S. War Department. 58m.

THE BATTLE OF BRITAIN (1943). *Supervisor:* Frank Capra. *Dir:* Anthony Veiller. *Sc:* Anthony Veiller. *Narr:* Walter Huston, Anthony Veiller. *Mus:* Dimitri Tiomkin. *Ed:* William Hornbeck. *Prod:* U.S. War Department. 55m.

THE BATTLE OF RUSSIA (1943). *Supervisor:* Frank Capra. *Dir:* Anatole Litvak. *Sc:* Anatole Litvak, Anthony Veiller, Robert Heller. *Narr:* Walter Huston, Anthony Veiller. *Mus:* Dimitri Tiomkin. *Ed:* William Hornbeck. *Prod:* U.S. War Department. 80m.

THE BATTLE OF CHINA (1944). *Dir:* Frank Capra, Anatole Litvak. *Sc:* Anthony Veiller, Robert Heller. *Narr:* Walter Huston, Anthony Veiller. *Mus:* Dimitri Tiomkin. *Ed:* William Hornbeck. *Prod:* Army Pictorial Service. 64m.

WAR COMES TO AMERICA (1945). *Supervisor:* Frank Capra. *Dir:* Col. Anatole Litvak, Anthony Veiller. *Narr:* Walter Huston, Anthony Veiller. *Mus:* Dimitri Tiomkin. *Ed:* William Hornbeck. *Prod:* Army Pictorial Service. 70m.

Other propaganda which Capra supervised:
KNOW YOUR ALLY: BRITAIN (1943)
THE NEGRO SOLDIER (1944)
TUNISIAN VICTORY (1944)
KNOW YOUR ENEMY: JAPAN (1945)
KNOW YOUR ENEMY: GERMANY (1945)
TWO DOWN, ONE TO GO (1945)

IT'S A WONDERFUL LIFE (1946). Frustrated middle-aged man rediscovers the glory of life. *Sc:* Frances Goodrich, Albert Hackett, Frank Capra. *Additional scenes:* Jo Swerling. *Ph:* Joseph Walker, Joseph Biroc. *Special effects:* Russell Cully. *Art dir:* Jack Okey. *Ed:* William Hornbeck. *Mus:* Dimitri Tiomkin. *With* James Stewart (*George Bailey*), Donna Reed (*Mary Hatch*), Lionel Barrymore (*Henry Potter*), Thomas Mitchell (*Uncle Billy*), Beulah Bondi (*Mrs. Bailey*), Frank Faylen (*Ernie*), Henry Travers (*Clarence*), Ward Bond (*Bert*), Gloria Grahame (*Violet*), H. B. Warner (*Mr. Gower*), Frank Albertson (*Sam Wainwright*), Samuel S. Hinds (*Pa Bailey*), Mary Treen (*Cousin Tilly*), Virginia Patton (*Ruth*), Charles Williams (*Cousin Eustace*), Sara Edwards (*Mrs. Hatch*), Bill Edmunds (*Martini*), Lillian Randolph (*Annie*), Bobbie Anderson (*Little George*), Ronnie Ralph (*Little Sam*), Jean Gale (*Little Mary*), Jeanine Ann Roose (*Little Violet*), Danny Mummert (*Little Marty Hatch*), George Nokes (*Little Harry Bailey*), Sheldon Leonard (*Nick*), Frank Hagney (*Potter's bodyguard*), Ray Walker (*Joe*), Charles Lane (*real estate salesman*), Edward Kean (*Tom*), Carol Coomes (*Janie*), Karolyn Grimes (*Zuzu*), Larry Sims (*Pete*), Jimmy Hawkins (*Tommy*). *Prod:* Frank Capra for Liberty/RKO. 130m.

STATE OF THE UNION (G.B: THE WORLD AND HIS WIFE) (1948). Industrialist decides to run for President. *Sc:* Anthony Veiller, Myles Connolly (the play by Howard Lindsay and Russell Crouse). *Ph:* George J. Folsey. *Art dir:* Cedric Gibbons, Urie McCleary. *Ed:* William Hornbeck. *Mus:* Victor Young. *With* Spencer Tracy (*Grant Matthews*), Katharine Hepburn (*Mary Matthews*), Van Johnson (*Spike MacManus*), Angela Lansbury (*Kay Thorndyke*), Adolphe Menjou (*Jim Conover*), Lewis Stone (*Sam Thorndyke*), Howard Smith (*Sam Parrish*), Charles Dingle (*Bill Hardy*), Maidel Turner (*Lulubelle Alexander*), Raymond Walburn (*Judge Alexander*), Margaret Hamilton (*Norah*), Art Baker (*radio announcer*), Pierre Watkin (*Sen. Lauterback*), Florence Auer (*Grace Draper*), Irving Bacon (*Buck*), Charles Lane (*Blink Moran*). *Prod:* Frank Capra for M-G-M. 124m.

RIDING HIGH (1950). Remake of *Broadway Bill*. *Sc:* Robert Riskin (story "Broadway Bill" by Mark Hellinger). *Additional dialogue:* Melville Shavelson, Jack Rose. *Ph:* George Barnes. *Art dir:* Hans Dreier, Walter Tyler. *Ed:* William Hornbeck. *Mus:* Victor Young. *Songs:* "Sunshine Cake", "The Horse Told Me To", "Sure Thing", "Someplace on Anywhere Road" by Johnny Burke and

James Van Heusen. *With* Bing Crosby (*Dan Brooks*), Coleen Gray (*Alice Higgins*), Charles Bickford (*J. L. Higgins*), Frances Gifford (*Margaret Higgins*), William Demarest (*Happy*), Raymond Walburn (*Prof. Pettigrew*), James Gleason (*racing secretary*), Ward Bond (*Lee*), Clarence Muse (*Whitey*), Percy Kilbride (*Pop Jones*), Harry Davenport (*Johnson*), Margaret Hamilton (*Edna*), Paul Harvey (*Whitehall*), Douglass Dumbrille (*Eddie Howard*), Gene Lockhart (*J. P. Chase*). *Prod:* Frank Capra for Paramount. 112m.

HERE COMES THE GROOM (1951). Reporter and millionaire compete for the same woman. *Sc:* Virginia Van Upp, Liam O'Brien, Myles Connolly (story by Robert Riskin and Liam O'Brien) *Ph:* George Barnes. *Art dir:* Hal Pereira, Earl Hedrick. *Ed:* Ellsworth Hoagland. *Mus dir:* Joseph L. Lilley. *New Songs:* Jay Livingston and Ray Evans, "In the Cool, Cool of the Evening" by Johnny Mercer and Hoagy Carmichael. *With* Bing Crosby *(Pete Garvey)*, Jane Wyman *(Emmadel Jones)*, Franchot Tone *(Wilbur Stanley)*, Alexis Smith *(Winifred Stanley)*, James Barton *(Pa Jones)*, Connie Gilchrist *(Ma Jones)*, Robert Keith *(George Degnan)*, Jacky Gencel *(Bobby)*, Beverly Washburn *(Suzi)*, Anna Maria Alberghetti *(Theresa)*, Alan Reed *(Walter Godfrey)*, Minna Gombell *(Mrs. Godfrey)*, Walter Catlett *(Mr. McGonigle)*, Maidel Turner *(Aunt Abby)*, H. B. Warner *(Uncle Elihu)*, Charles Lane *(Burchard)*. *Prod:* Frank Capra for Paramount. 113m.

A HOLE IN THE HEAD (1959). Florida hotel owner struggles to keep his establishment afloat. *Sc:* Arnold Schulman (his play). *Ph:* William Daniels. *Art dir:* Eddie Imazu. *Ed:* William Hornbeck. *Mus:* Nelson Riddle. *Songs:* "All My Tomorrows", "High Hopes" by Sammy Cahn and James Van Heusen. *With* Frank Sinatra (*Tony Manetta*), Edward G. Robinson (*Mario*), Eleanor Parker (*Mrs. Rogers*), Eddie Hodges (*Ally*), Carolyn Jones (*Shirl*), Thelma Ritter (*Sophie*),

Keenan Wynn (*Jerry Marks*), Joi Lansing (*Dorine*), George De Witt (*Mendy*), Jimmy Komack (*Julius*), Dub Taylor (*Fred*), Connie Sawyer (*Miss Wexler*), Benny Rubin (*Mr. Diamond*). *Prod:* Frank Capra for Sincap/United Artists. 120m. De Luxe Colour. CinemaScope.

POCKETFUL OF MIRACLES (1961). Re-make of *Lady for a Day*. *Sc:* Hal Kanter, Harry Tugend, Jimmy Cannon [uncredited] (the original screenplay by Robert Riskin from the story "Madame La Gimp" by Damon Runyon). *Ph:* Robert Bronner. *Art dir:* Hal Pereira, Roland Anderson. *Ed:* Frank P. Keller. *Mus:* Walter Scharf. *Songs*: "Pocketful of Miracles" by Sammy Cahn and James Van Heusen. *With* Glenn Ford (*Dave the Dude*), Bette Davis (*Apple Annie*), Hope Lange (*Queenie Martin*), Arthur O'Connell (*Count Romero*), Peter Falk (*Joy Boy*), Thomas Mitchell (*Judge Henry Blake*), Edward Everett Horton (*Hudgins*), Mickey Shaughnessy (*Junior*), David Brian (*governor*), Sheldon Leonard (*Steve Darcey*), Peter Mann (*Carlos*), Ann-Margret (*Louise*), Barton MacLane (*police commissioner*). *Prod:* Frank Capra for Franton/United Artists. 136m. Panavision. Technicolor.

Uncompleted Projects. Capra worked on the following films, but for a variety of reasons never completed them:

SOVIET (1934). An adventure film which Capra was to make during a loanout to MGM. Cancelled by Louis B. Mayer after its mentor, Irving Thalberg, became ill.

THE JIMMY DURANTE STORY (1959). The film was to star and be co-produced by Frank Sinatra and Dean Martin. After production questions could not be resolved, Capra left the project.

THE BEST MAN (1960). Capra had plans to film an adaptation of Gore Vidal's novel, but after disagreements with the author, abandoned the project. The novel was, however, made into a film by Franklin J. Schaffner in 1964.

CIRCUS WORLD (1962). The film was to star John Wayne, but when it became clear that he (Capra) would not have complete control over the project, he left it. Henry Hathaway finally directed the film which was released in 1964 (in Britain as *The Magnificent Showman*).

MAROONED (1964). Capra did pre-production work on this film, but was eventually replaced by John Sturges who completed the film in 1969.

Sources for Capra filmography:

Leland Poague, *The Cinema of Frank Capra* (New York: A.S. Barnes, 1975); *Positif* no. 133, December 1971; Victor Scherle and William Turner Levy, *The Films of Frank Capra* (Secaucus, N. J.: Citadel, 1977); Donald Willis, *The Films of Frank Capra* (Metuchen, N. J.: Scarecrow, 1974); and the credits from the films themselves.

GEORGE CUKOR

George Cukor modestly refers to himself as "an interpretative director," one who sees as his principal function the translation of pre-existing material—a play, a novel, a short story—into cinematic terms. Furthermore, once the script is completed he admits that he rarely tampers with the dialogue. If a line strikes a sour note on the set, he asks the screenwriter to re-write it. This self-effacing approach to film directing has led Richard Schickel to observe that: "Perhaps his [Cukor's] major contribution is the creation of a salubrious climate for creative work—an air of confidence, trust, focused energies, an atmosphere in which everyone feels free to chance his or her instincts, knowing that the director will encourage what seems interesting and valid in the explorations, but squelch notions that are unsound."[1] Some may be reluctant to ascribe much importance to a director who works in such a manner. Even Schickel, who has great admiration for Cukor, seems uncertain as to just what the director contributes to his films in the way of his own personality. Schickel's uncertainty is shared by many; it is easy enough to characterise Cukor as a consummate craftsman whose films, though entertaining, do not express a personal outlook. But this contention (which has dominated critical evaluations of Cukor's career) is fundamentally incomplete because, in calling so much attention to his selfless method of directing, critics forget to chart that vast expanse between the finished screenplay and what the director finally puts on film. Once a script becomes Cukor's instrument it yields to his interpretation of it. For all its fidelity to the original, his *David Copperfield* is.as Cukorian as it is Dickensian. Though perhaps a dozen different writers were involved in *A Woman's Face*, this film is distinctively stamped by Cukor's direction. No matter what the original source or who the screenwriter, each of his films possesses his personal imprint, not only visually but in the ideas they express. In fact, the body of his work, some forty-eight features, is as individualistic as that of a writer-producer-director like Frank Capra. Cukor even pursues certain thematic preoccupations as relentlessly as his counterpart, but without Capra's thematic self-consciousness. This does not make Cukor's work any less personal; what it does mean is that the richer tones and meanings in his work exist somewhere below the surface. Whereas most directors' films tend to fall apart under close scrutiny, Cukor's only really begin to come to life once one starts to probe beneath that finely polished style for which he is so justly admired.

Seeing past the gloss is perhaps more difficult with Cukor's work than with that of some other directors. Although he exerts a profound influence on all aspects of any film he directs, that influence manifests itself in ways which do not always immediately draw attention to themselves. For example, although Cukor did not write the screenplay for *David Copperfield*, he did influence what was written by insisting that the screen adaptation stay as close to the original as possible. The extensive research he does before each production— visiting locations, looking at photographs and paintings, reading library materials—also influences both his treatment of the subject matter and the visual scheme of the film. Cukor himself provides a descriptive example:

> This is what we did for *Les Girls*. The set was not an exact slice of reality, but a combination of things. We came to Paris and climbed up six and seven flights of stairs and took stills of this room and that room. The set was a composite of all sorts of elements . . . there was a scene where the girls are eating. Usually the food in a scene is left to the last minute to the property man who rushes off to the studio commissary to get a few pieces of ham, some bread . . . and spreads it all over the table. But in *Les Girls* we had the most wonderful real French food . . . down to the smallest details. We even looked at Cézanne still lifes. On the table were wine and cheeses and with the girls all around, it was pure Cézanne. There was quite a bit of loving thought put into it and it paid off—scenes must be done this way, and with no slapdash about them. I do them with a great deal of affection and detail.[2]

Although Cukor's films are noteworthy for the accuracy of their visual details, Cukor does not depend on these details to convey his point of view. Rather he makes himself felt mainly through his actors. His use of the camera and his editing scheme are planned to allow the actors the fullest means of expression. As Charles Higham writes: "Cukor, like Lean in England, believes that the actor is the expressive centre of a film, that the cinema's great virtue lies in its ability to explore human beings in depth through the selective use of images and sound."[3] The way in which he influences the actor's reading of the screenplay shapes the form and content of a film as surely as any dialogue he might have written.

As Higham suggests, Cukor is unusual among his fellow directors in the value he assigns to his actors. His particular approach can be explained in part by his background. He came to Hollywood during the advent of sound after extensive experience as a stage manager and director. Through his theatre experience he acquired a reverence for what he calls "the acting gift". One might expect that he would have been disheartened with the discontinuous shooting schedules and fabricated screen personalities of films. But the director was quick to sense that the cinema offered unique possibilities for him to shape and modulate the work of his actors. Cukor has remarked:

> There are some wonderful directors who are not terribly interested in performances—who are much more intrigued by the picture as a whole. They build up an effect of a door knob turning rather than concentrating on the actor's face. I think human values are more important. Human behaviour, to me, is what makes things go[4] . . . I accomplish things sometimes through the actor—through the acting gift . . .[5]

The movies did not shake his belief in the power of this gift—they only affirmed it—and it has seemingly become his "mission" to enlighten those who possess it. That the likes of Katharine Hepburn, Cary Grant, Rosalind Russell, Joan Fontaine, Jack Lemmon and Aldo Ray all first became aware of the extent of their acting gifts while working with Cukor springs from this ambition to make each actor cognisant of his full potential. Even more impressive perhaps than his work with rising actors is the consistency with which he has been able to direct established stars, male and female, to some of their best performances. Spencer Tracy, John Barrymore and James Mason have never been better than when under Cukor's direction. James Stewart, Ronald Colman and Rex Harrison each won Academy Awards for performances directed by Cukor. His special *métier*, however, is with actresses. Why, for instance, is Garbo's work in *Camille* so clearly superior to that in *Grand Hotel* or *The Painted Veil*? I would suggest that Cukor, in persuading his star to abandon the routine selling of her screen personality in favour of a close identification with her role, provided the key. In *Camille*, Garbo is involved in a process of self-definition, rather than (as is usually the case) just projecting her stereotyped screen personality. In order to clarify this contention, the rather tricky question of what an actor finally hopes to achieve through his craft must be explored. As murky as one might expect the answer to be, an attempt has to be made if we are to get closer to the essence of Cukor's unique talent.

In her novel, "The Garrick Year", Margaret Drabble suggests that the answer to the puzzle lies in the actor's search for a personal sense of clarity. This observation is made by the novels protagonist as she watches her husband, a professional actor, perform on stage:

> All he wanted from life was to be able to express, like this, in public, to a mass of quiet people, what he felt himself to be. It was not merely pleasure that he had there on the stage: it was a sense of clarity, a feeling of being, by words and situations not of his own making, defined and confined, so that his power and his energy could meet together in one great explanatory moment. It was not enough for David that I should try to understand him or that his friends and employers should understand him, for we subjected him by the pressure of our needs and opinions to amorphous confusion: what he wanted was nothing less than total public clarity.[6]

Was it the possibility of achieving this sort of clarity, the chance to reveal an aspect of herself so long denied her by the demands of her screen image, that charged Garbo's performance in *Camille*? Her close identification with her character, Marguerite Gautier, needs to be emphasised. Specifically in *Camille* Garbo seems to express her dissatisfaction with her life in Hollywood; her sense that she had to maintain a pose foreign to her own nature. Who, after all, was Garbo but another simple, beautiful girl who sold herself, as it were, in exchange for a life of luxury and glamour? Also like Marguerite, she was never finally happy with her decision and, although she wished to return to the life she had once known, she realised that this part of her past was forever behind her.

A similar liberation from a stereotyped screen image seems to be the key behind Judy Garland's phenomenal performance in *A Star Is Born*. In Cukor's film she was able, perhaps for the first time, to release all those anxieties and frustrations she had to repress while making the cheery musicals for which her fans loved her. The result is a grippingly personal portrayal in which, as Penelope Houston says, "she seems to be playing on her nerves."[7] The situation has been more positive for Katharine Hepburn, whose development as an actress and a woman can be traced through the eight films she has made with Cukor over a forty year period. Her best work also comes in roles which reflect her own attitudes: *Little Women, The Philadelphia Story, Adam's Rib, Love Among the Ruins*. Her remarkable performances in these films seem to originate in the fact that all the things her

Making CAMILLE: Cukor, Greta Garbo and Robert Taylor

On the set of A STAR IS BORN: James Mason, Judy Garland and Cukor

characters stand for (love of family in *Little Women*, equal rights for women in *Adam's Rib*, for example), Hepburn stands for as well.

It is facile to assume, as some have done, that the exquisite performances of these actresses are the result of merely a perfect meeting between actress and part. A much better answer, though still incomplete, would be that Cukor introduced these women to the possibilities intrinsic in the roles they were to play. In a profession in which most directors only feel comfortable dealing with *machismo* themes, women sense in Cukor a rare capacity for understanding their fears and aspirations. That they let down their defences while working with him attests to the trust and confidence they have in him. Garbo clearly felt this while working with Cukor on *Camille*. In the movies she made before this one, she would usually retire to her dressing room after each take, but during *Camille* she remained on the set. Irving Thalberg also noted a difference in Garbo's performance when he watched the first rushes of the film. "She has never been quite this good," he told the director. "She's unguarded for the first time."[8]

I have dwelt on this particular skill of Cukor's because it is, I believe, the most noteworthy of his many talents. But, as with most of the director's talents (the acknowledgement of which is hardly unique to this essay), it has never been fully explored for what it might say about Cukor as a film director. Like most directors with considerable experience in Hollywood, Cukor is a master of cinematic technique. His use of the camera, of lightning, and his editing schemes, for those who care to delve into them (and unfortunately, the limits of this essay prevent me from doing so here), are complex as well as expert. But it is the skill with which he directs his players which finally sets him apart from his colleagues. Cukor is the master of the nuances of the fine art of emoting, as Professor Higgins of *My Fair Lady* is of the fine art of language. There are as many variations of a gesture for Cukor as there are dialects for Higgins. And what better example of Cukor's own Pygmalion myth than his work with Katharine Hepburn, his Galatea, who became, largely as the result of his sagacious instruction, one of the world's finest actresses.

Yet as nicely as this Pygmalion myth might fit as an explanation for Cukor's success with actresses, it does not quite explain the totality of his skill. How does one account for his success with actors and bit players? The answer, and this may be as close as one can get to the secret of his special talent, is that Cukor simply treats his players equally, without prejudice and without regard to their sex, and actors like Spencer Tracy react as positively to the director's approach as actresses like Hepburn. As probably one of the few directors in Hollywood without *macho* preoccupations, Cukor reaches his performers—actors and actresses alike—through his mastery of acting technique. The crucial fact is that he treats them with honest respect as actors and not merely movie stars. This idea that only by stripping away the false and limiting stereotyped notions of masculinity and feminity can true and lasting communication between the sexes be established, be it a director-actress or husband-wife relationship, is not only Cukor's attitude on the set, but the primary preoccupation of his cinema.

★ ★ ★

Cukor's attitude toward his screenplays and actors is traceable to his pre-Hollywood background which is much different from those of most of his colleagues. Typically they came from some background (flying or cattle-herding or engineering) unrelated to film-making. Cukor, on the other hand, is one of the few directors of the Thirties and Forties whose first serious adolescent ambition was to be what he in fact became. He was born July 7, 1899, to upper middle-class Jewish parents who had immigrated to America from Hungary as young adults. His father and uncle were both prominent lawyers in New York City and George was expected to follow in their footsteps. While watching the Barrymores, Laurette Taylor, and other great stage stars of the period from the second balconies of Broadway theatres, he nurtured a different ambition. Although his mother was an avid theatre-goer, his parents were far from pleased when he announced his rather bizarre intention of becoming a stage director. (Cukor says that it would be a bit like telling one's parents today that one wanted to be a drug pusher.) Nevertheless, they eventually gave way, probably because it had become obvious that their son, who demonstrated no particular aptitude for his studies, was not cut out for the legal profession.

Like so many others who grew up during the first part of the century, Cukor had to postpone his ambitions because of war. After graduating from high school, he joined the Students' Training Corps in 1917; when the Armistice was signed he became one of the post-war army of job-seekers.[9] Luckily, he was able to find the sort of employment he sought simply by answering an advertisement in a newspaper. His first job was an assistant stage manager for the Chicago company of a play entitled "The Better 'Ole". He soon advanced to the position of stage manager, and in this capacity worked for several years for the Selwyns and other important producers. In 1920 he took charge of a summer stock company in Rochester, New York. It was here Cukor began his career as a director. In the eight years he managed the company, it came to be regarded as one of the best of its kind in the country, and Cukor as one of the theatre's most promising and innovative young talents. It was noted in "Theatre" (October 1925) that, "His [Cukor's] summer stock company this past year set new records in a town commonly designated as 'dead' theatrically."[10]

At the end of each summer season, Cukor would move back to New York where he continued to work as a stage manager. In the fall of 1925 he was given the opportunity to direct his first Broadway play, a comedy written by noted Hungarian playwright, Melchior Lengyel, and adapted by Arthur Richman—"Antonia". The critics liked leading lady Marjorie Rambeau, but response to the play itself was tepid. Cukor had much more success with his next effort, an adaptation of F. Scott Fitzgerald's novel, "The Great Gatsby", which opened in February, 1926. The following season Cukor directed four more plays, including "The Furies" by Zoë Akins, with whom he would soon again successfully collaborate in Hollywood. Even at this early stage in his career Cukor was known for his ability to bring out the best in highly-strung but very talented actresses. Samson Raphaelson remembers that Dorothy Gish would appear in his play "Young Love" (1928) only if Cukor directed it. Gish, in her thirties, was cast in the role of a nineteen-year-old girl. She was very nervous about the part, Raphaelson recalls, and would only trust herself to the director in whom she had the greatest confidence.[11] Cukor continued to direct steadily for the next two seasons the works of (among others) W. Somerset Maugham and Maxwell Anderson. He explored a variety of *genres* while guiding the brightest headliners of Broadway, including his own personal idol, Laurette Taylor.

In 1929, when it had become clear that the future of the movies was in talkies, persons with a stage background became very valuable commodities in Hollywood. The studios scoured the east coast for talent and Cukor, like countless others, migrated west. He had been signed by Paramount and soon after his arrival in Hollywood was put to work as a dialogue director coaching actors in a southern accent for a minor melodrama, *River of Romance* (1929).[12] Following this assignment the studio apparently did not quite know what they wanted to do with Cukor, and the young director might have returned to New York had it not been for the aid of a new friend, David Selznick, then an ambitious young executive assistant to Ben Schulberg, Paramount's west coast production chief. Selznick could see that the studio was wasting Cukor's talent, and on his own initiative convinced Universal's Lewis Milestone, a veteran of the silent screen, to engage Cukor as his dialogue director for *All Quiet on the Western Front* (1930). After completing the assignment with Milestone, Cukor (again with Selznick's backing) was given his first directing job for Paramount: *Grumpy* (1930), based on a moribund 1913 stage play that had previously been filmed in 1923 by Cecil B. De Mille. The studio was reluctant to give Cukor complete control because he had so little experience, so a camera-wise editor, Cyril Gardner, was assigned as co-director to insure that everything Cukor shot would cut smoothly.[13] Intended as nothing more than a programmer to be sold in an overall studio package, *Grumpy* is nonetheless not without interest as a first film. Intriguingly, for a director who would later be accused of confining his stage adaptations to interiors, Cukor begins this film with an open-air shot. *Virtuous Sin* (1930), a melodrama with Kay Francis and Walter Huston, and *The Royal Family of Broadway* (1930), an adaptation of a hit Broadway stage play by George S. Kaufman and Edna Ferber and a thinly disguised portrait of the Barrymores, followed. Both were also co-directed. The latter, notable for a rousing performance by Fredric March as a young John Barrymore, was favourably compared to the stage version and convinced Paramount that Cukor was ready to direct on his own. *Tarnished Lady* (1931) is a movie of curious firsts: Cukor's first solo directing effort, Donald Ogden Stewart's first screenplay (adapted from his own story, "New York Lady"), and Tallulah Bankhead's first appearance in a sound film. But for all the project had going for it, it was still a failure.[14] Cukor's next film, *Girls About Town* (1931), a romantic comedy about two gold-diggers, was less curious and more successful.

Now seemingly on his way to a happy relationship with Paramount, Cukor must have considered his next directing assignment a plum: *One Hour with You*, a musical comedy to star two of Paramount's hottest properties, Maurice Chevalier and Jeanette MacDonald, and to be produced by its ace director, Ernst Lubitsch. In fact, *One Hour with You* turned out to be one of the most sour experiences of his whole career. The script for the film had been prepared by Samson Raphaelson, Lubitsch's favourite screenwriter; they had carefully laid everything out, as was their custom, and all Cukor had to do was follow the numbers, so to speak. But he had his own ideas, which clashed with Lubitsch's. Cukor was removed after two weeks of filming and Lubitsch himself took over. Cukor remained on the set and watched the great director shape what turned out to be one of his most engaging sound films. Although Cukor's involvement had been brief and minor, he would not allow his name to be removed from the credits; he felt that neither Lubitsch nor Paramount had treated him fairly, and he did not want to suffer any further humiliation. When B.P. Schulberg went ahead with his plans to remove Cukor's name from the credits, Cukor sued. In the meantime, Selznick had left Paramount in order to become production chief for RKO. Before he had gone to RKO, however, and while Schulberg was in Europe, he was offered Schulberg's job. Although he turned down the offer because he did not want to replace the man who had been responsible for bringing him into the studio, when Schulberg learned of the offer he was convinced that Selznick had been dealing behind his back. When, in the midst of the controversy surrounding the credits of *One Hour with You*, Cukor asked to be released from his Paramount contract so that he could join Selznick, Schulberg, who still had a grudge against his former assistant, refused. The litigation over *One Hour with You* proved to be Cukor's ticket out of the studio. As a result of an out-of-court settlement Cukor was credited as the dialogue director, but more importantly was released from his contract with the studio.

Selznick put Cukor in charge of RKO's most popular star, Constance Bennett. He directed her in three films. The first of the three, *What Price Hollywood?* (1932), provided the story line for a later, more famous movie about life in the film colony, *A Star Is Born* (1937), which Cukor himself re-made in 1954. But it was with *A Bill of Divorcement* (1932), the film he made just after *What Price Hollywood?*, that the young director began to attract serious critical attention. Norma

Henry Stephenson, John Barrymore, Katharine Hepburn and Billie Burke in A BILL OF DIVORCEMENT (1932)

Shearer (along with several other prominent actresses) wanted the part of Sydney Fairchild, but Cukor saw a ten-minute screen test of Katharine Hepburn, then a minor talent with limited stage experience, and was convinced that only she was right for the part. Not surprisingly RKO executives objected to this choice, but Cukor stuck to his guns and with Selznick's support won his battle.

A Bill of Divorcement was the first in a string of hits that would soon establish Cukor as one of the premier directors in Hollywood. In 1933 Selznick left RKO to work for his father-in-law, Louis B. Mayer, at M-G-M. Cukor came with him to direct the first movie Selznick produced there, *Dinner at Eight*. Upon completing this project Cukor returned to RKO to make *Little Women* (1933), a commitment Selznick still had at that studio. He then returned once more to M-G-M to direct *David Copperfield* (1934), again with Selznick producing. On the strength of the box-office and critical response to these three films, Cukor rose to the top of his profession. *Dinner at Eight* and *Little Women* comprised one-fifth of the "Film Daily" Ten Best Pictures list for 1934 and *David Copperfield* topped that same list in 1935. By 1936 "Motion Picture" could say of Cukor, now one of M-G-M's leading contract directors:[15]

> His list of film successes including *Little Women, David Copperfield, The Royal Family, Dinner at Eight,* and the forthcoming *Romeo and Juliet,* reads like a list of banner attractions of the past five years. Certainly no director can point with greater pride over what he has accomplished since he set foot in Hollywood. Making five such distinctive pictures almost on top of each other is an accomplishment closely allied with genius.[16]

One major setback in Cukor's otherwise remarkably successful first decade of film-making needs, however, to be noted.[17] In February 1939, after months of preparation and two and a half weeks of shooting, he was fired as the director of *Gone with the Wind* by his close friend, David Selznick. No one has ever been able to pinpoint the exact reasons for Cukor's dismissal from one of the most prestigious assignments in the history of film. Cukor does not know himself. The most intriguing theory is that Clark Gable, an actor noted for his masculine insecurities, felt that Cukor was emphasising the female roles of Scarlett (Vivien Leigh) and Melanie (Olivia de Havilland) at his expense. Perhaps Selznick, who had secured Gable's services at great cost, felt that this investment was his top priority. At any rate, the director and producer signed a joint statement declaring that, as a result of disagreements between them, they both believed a new director to be in the best interests of the production. Cukor has indeed reported that his relationship with Selznick during his participation in the film was not as harmonious as it had been in the past. Selznick, according to Cukor, began to visit the set during shooting offering him "hot tips"—something he had never done before. If the producer had continued to interfere, it seems fair to suggest that Cukor might have left on his own.[18] His involvement with the film did not end, however, with the termination of his contract. Vivien Leigh and Olivia de Havilland, both of whom cherished Cukor's direction, were horrified when they learned of his dismissal. They pleaded with Selznick to retain him, but to no avail. Although, of course, Cukor could not be with them on the set, he continued, at the request of the two actresses, to coach them at his home.[19]

Cukor quickly plunged himself into a new work, an adaptation of Claire Booth Luce's *The Women* (1939), which proved to be one of the big hits of the year. *The Women* is one of several so-called comedies of manners Cukor directed in the late Thirties. These films (*Holiday*, 1938, and *Susan and God*, 1939, are two others), which concern the emotional trials of wealthy female protagonists, are notable for their dry wit and high society elegance. It was primarily for his smooth direction of these films that Cukor earned the reputation as a director of incomparable style and unquestionable good taste. After taking the comedy of manners, of which he had been the cinema's most articulate observer, to its summit in *The Philadelphia Story*, Cukor demonstrated both his sense of timing and his versatility by shifting to straight drama. During the Forties he made some of the most impressive *films noir*, another *genre* he helped to pioneer with films like *A Woman's Face* (1941), *Keeper of the Flame* (1942) and *Gaslight* (1944). Cukor's films during this decade almost invariably rotate around a protagonist's perverse obsession. In *Gaslight*, Gregory (Charles Boyer) murders one woman and almost drives another insane for the sake of a self-consuming passion for a particular set of jewels; in *Edward, My Son*, Arnold Boult (Spencer Tracy) carries a desire to see that his son has the best of everything to a ruinous and unconscionable mania for money; in *A Double Life*, actor Tony John (Ronald Colman) becomes so engrossed in his own renditon of Othello that he nearly murders his Desdemona on stage one night and does in fact murder a waitress with whom he has been having an indifferent affair, out of a misdirected sense of jealousy. It is also in these *films noir* that Cukor's cinematic talents are perhaps most clearly evident.

Almost all the action in these works takes place at night and/or indoors. These settings effectively carry the sense that the protagonists are imprisoned by their own self-destructive obsessions. Consider, for example, the scene in the producer's office in *A Double Life*. Here the film's protagonist, Tony John, relates his life story in the space of several minutes. He roams about the small, dark office like a caged panther as he speaks. The room is cluttered with papers and other items just as John's mind is cluttered with disturbing memories. The key to the scene, however, is that Cukor gives Colman the chance to build a sort of emotional momentum by staying with the actor as he reminisces, filming this part of the scene in a single take with one mobile camera.

The post-war years represent a transition period for Hollywood rivalled only by the advent of sound. As the Forties drew to a close, the "fantasy factory" glow of the major studios began to dim as anti-trust action threatened to break up the studios' profitable distribution network, and television began its assault on film attendance. Unlike many of his contemporaries, those with whom he had shared the limelight in the Thirties, Cukor made the transition not through retrospection, but through innovation. Though the style and tone of his work in the early Fifties (I include *Adam's Rib,* 1949) is clearly linked to earlier work, the films of this period represent in various respects a new approach to his art: lavish production values give way to open-air shooting; wealthy protagonists are replaced by middle-class ones. Instrumental in this development was Cukor's association with the husband and wife screen-writing team of Garson Kanin and Ruth Gordon. Of the ten films Cukor made between 1947 and 1954, the Kanins together or separately wrote seven of them. Kanin, like Cukor, came to films via the theatre, where he had also worked as a stage manager and director. As a contract director for RKO in the late Thirties he directed several excellent comedies, including *Bachelor Mother* (1939) with Ginger Rogers. He preferred writing to directing, however, and during the war collaborated on a number of screenplays, including George Stevens' *The More the Merrier* (1943). In 1947 with his wife, actress Ruth Gordon, he wrote *A Double Life* for Cukor. Their collaboration with the director continued to produce six more films.

These six—*Adam's Rib* (1949), *Born Yesterday* (1950), *The Marrying Kind* (1951), *Pat and Mike* (1952), *The Actress* (1953), and *It Should Happen to You* (1954)—all have a similar look and feel about them. In contrast to his Thirties comedies, these films were usually shot on

**Ruth Gordon and
Garson Kanin**

location: on city streets, in subways, in parks. The director proves
particularly adept at catching the right atmosphere of these locations:
the harsh contrasts of New York City, the antiseptic impersonality of a
jail, or the dullness of a giant post office. Such insights into daily
routine as New Yorkers boarding a subway train during rush hour or
spending a hot summer's day in Central Park almost anticipate *cinéma
verité*. Clearly, the director's approach was influenced by the Kanins'
screenplays, which allow their story and humour to build organically
through the characters and contain a great deal of colloquial
dialogue. After *It Should Happen to You,* this remarkable partnership
between Cukor and the Kanins came to an end. The reasons for the
split have never been made clear. Perhaps it was simply that they all
felt they had exploited their mutual talents to the fullest and that it
was time to go their separate professional ways. At any rate, the
Kanins returned to the theatre and Cukor went on to direct his first
colour film, *A Star Is Born* (1954).

By the mid-Fifties the studios were impressed with the idea that in
order to bring people into movie theatres, films would have to show
them things they could not see on television; hence the advent of
big-budget spectaculars like *A Star Is Born. Star* was months in
production due to a variety of difficulties. Not the least of Cukor's
problems was having to deal with the studio's latest gimmick,
CinemaScope, a new, larger, and hard-to-manage screen size. But

once again he demonstrated his versatility and adaptability. He had been told of all the taboos regarding CinemaScope—no depth of focus, everything to be shot on a level plain, deliberate cutting—but soon broke all the rules and in doing so set a new standard for others working in this so-called "mailslot" form. He gave his actors the freedom to roam about the screen by using long, intricate travelling shots and he cut rapidly during the première and funeral scenes to develop tension and excitement. His work in colour also set new standards. Collaborating with renowned photographer George Hoyningen-Huene, Cukor eliminated the bright, garish reds, greens and yellows which dominated most Technicolor productions of the time and replaced them with softer hues like brown, light blues and pinks to give the film a much more realistic, "natural" look.

When his contract with M-G-M expired in the early Fifties Cukor was free to work as and for whom he pleased. Over the next two decades he continued to direct primarily big-budget films: *Bhowani Junction* (1955), *Les Girls* (1957), *Heller in Pink Tights* (1959), *My Fair Lady* (1964), *Travels with My Aunt* (1972), and *The Blue Bird* (1976). With big budgets, however, came some big headaches. Among others, Cukor encountered a problem he rarely had to deal with during his contract years with M-G-M—producer interference. Scenes he felt to be crucial to *A Star Is Born,* for instance, were axed when the producers thought the movie ran too long.[20] Incredibly, though they cut a half hour of Cukor's material, they added an extraneous (albeit entertaining) twenty minute song and dance sequence (shot while Cukor was vacationing in Europe and without his knowledge). Producer interference continued during *Heller in Pink Tights* and *The Chapman Report* (1962), two movies which he now all but disowns because of cuts made against his wishes.

In 1964 Cukor won his first Academy Award as the director of *My Fair Lady,* the biggest box-office hit of his career. Perhaps because of his decade-long battle with producers and the strain of directing *My Fair Lady,* Cukor was inactive for a time. He did not direct again until 1969 when he was called in to complete the ill-fated *Justine,* which had been started by Joseph Strick. In 1972 he made *Travels with My Aunt,* adapted from Graham Greene's best seller, for an ailing M-G-M. Cukor wanted Katharine Hepburn to play the lead. At first M-G-M went along, then reneged for reasons that remain unclear. But this time, unlike forty years before, Cukor's efforts to keep her were unsuccessful, and he had to settle for Maggie Smith.

In the last few years, Cukor has worked steadily. *Love Among the*

Ruins (1975) with Hepburn and Laurence Olivier, made for American television, brought him an Emmy Award. Olivier plays a barrister who defends the woman he has worshipped for decades from a breach of promise suit brought by her young suitor. Like *Travels with My Aunt,* it deals in part with the perils of living in and for the past. Cukor lends the film that air of mannered elegance which graces so many of his pictures. Neither Hepburn or Olivier has been used to better advantage recently than here. Marred by countless production delays, *The Blue Bird* (1976) proved, despite some intriguing moments, to be a disappointing effort overall. The director's latest film, *The Corn is Green* (1979), starring the incomparable Hepburn as an indefatigable schoolteacher determined to bring the benefits of education to a Welsh mining town, is much more successful. Cukor is now involved in the pre-production stage of several new projects. Retirement is one subject he will not discuss.

★　　★　　★

Having completed a survey of Cukor's career we can now deal with some of the recurring preoccupations of his cinema. In order to get at these ideas, it is necessary to push to the heart of the director's cinema, though thereby bypassing some of his legitimate, but less central, concerns. Only rarely has Cukor had the benefit of this sort of study—perhaps the most illuminating can be found in Molly Haskell's book, *From Reverence to Rape: The Treatment of Women in the Movies.* Essentially what Haskell says is that, in a national cinema which has been and still is dominated by a *machismo* philosophy, Cukor remains the only American director who has consistently represented the female point of view. In her discussion of the American cinema's attitude toward women she compares, for example, the most important distinction between a *macho* director, such as Howard Hawks, and Cukor. "In quite different ways, Hawks and Cukor were concerned throughout their careers with the tension and possibilities of a heterosexual relationship between equals: Hawks from a male point of view, always tempted back into the enveloping womb of male camaraderie, but evolving and resisting; Cukor, from the female point of view, championing the most intelligent side of a woman's personality."[21] Put this way Cukor becomes, in fact, a "woman's director", but no one has yet explored what this hackneyed label really means. Dealing honestly with adult relationships is perhaps the artist's most difficult task. That Cukor approaches the problem from the female's viewpoint certainly does not make his investigation of male-female interaction any less important. On the contrary, considering how infrequently the female point of view is intelligently represented (in film and literature), Cukor's work is all the more significant for what it achieves.

It must now be clear that, in order to understand Cukor's cinema, we must first understand not so much his heroes as his heroines. As Haskell implies, Cukor's heroine may generally be described as intelligent and clever; she is also high-spirited, usually more than a little neurotic, and most importantly fiercely independent. Although the manner in which these characteristics are expressed differs from heroine to heroine, the impulse behind them is similar. The characters played by Katharine Hepburn and Judy Holliday (both actresses whose careers are closely linked to Cukor's), for example, represent ostensible opposites: Hepburn—svelte, well-educated, aristocratic; Holliday—graceless, scatter-brained, middle-class. Yet for all the surface differences that separate the screen personalities of these two women, they are both after the same thing: both are involved in a personal struggle to prove to themselves and the world their worth as human beings. Only the way they go about achieving their goal separates them. This struggle links not only Hepburn and Holliday but most of Cukor's heroines.

In their quest for a distinct identity, the efforts of these women are significantly affected by the fundamental fact that they are female. Certainly the process of coming to terms with oneself is difficult under any circumstances, but for the women in Cukor's films it is exacerbated by the truism that, in seeking to establish their independence, they must overcome traditional social beliefs as basic as the one that insists that women are inferior to men ("the Big Lie," Haskell calls it). Not surprisingly, the men in Cukor's films frequently cannot understand the need of their women to establish an identity of their own, and consequently remain oblivious to their trials. As far as they are concerned, the female's place in the male-female relationship specifically, and in society generally, is not open to question. The reaction to this obliviousness might be said to generate the energy that drives Cukor's women. Again, although the ways in which this energy is expressed varies from woman to woman, the factor which motivates them—their desire to establish themselves and their independence— proves to be very similar for heroines as seemingly diverse as Anna (Joan Crawford) in *A Woman's Face* and Victoria (Ava Gardner) in *Bhowani Junction*.

Obviously, in order to liberate herself from a traditionally subser-

Charles Boyer and Ingrid Bergman in GASLIGHT (1944)

vient role a woman must be able to fend for herself. The women of
Cukor's comedies of manners of the Thirties are usually indepen-
dently wealthy. The others support themselves through a variety of
professions which range from acting to practising law. Yet for these
women achieving financial independence despite all the difficulties
involved is a fairly straightforward proposition—literally a matter of
dollars and cents. Achieving a spiritual independence is another
matter entirely. Here Cukor is not suggesting a colony of misanthropic feminists who will have nothing to do with the male sex.
Rather, he fears male-female relationships in which the woman's
function is to serve her man, relying totally on his kindness simply to
survive. Financial independence is the first step his heroines take to
free themselves from this situation; the ability to sustain themselves
emotionally is the next step. As we shall see, only with this sort of
balance—when male and female are equal—can a marriage truly be
successful in Cukor's world. A relationship where one partner

attempts to dominate the other (male or female) inevitably leads to disaster. In the one film in which a woman allows herself to be managed by a man, *Gaslight,* she is nearly destroyed by him. The protagonist, Paula (Ingrid Bergman), whose childhood was marred by tragedy and who has since spent her life sheltered from pain, unconditionally surrenders herself to her husband (Charles Boyer), whom she sees as both a lover and father-figure. In return for her innocent devotion he cruelly manipulates her so as to obtain the precious jewels he knows are hidden without her knowledge somewhere in her London home. He schemes diabolically to drive her insane, and Paula, who lacks the qualities usually found in Cukor's women, is powerless to prevent him. Though somewhat obliquely, the movie demonstrates a woman's essential need for spiritual self-sufficiency if she wishes to preserve and develop her sense of self. The point is made more explicitly in *Pat and Mike.* Pat (Hepburn) finally rejects her *fiancé* because she does not want to become his "little woman". In *The Actress,* Ruth (Jean Simmons), with only her own self-confidence to guide her, leaves a comfortable future as the housewife of a well-to-do and handsome young man because she feels the pressing need to prove to herself that she can succeed by her own resources.

The fact that Ruth chooses to be an actress is not without significance. First, by choosing this profession (hardly a respectable one for a girl growing up during the beginning of this century), she expresses both her individuality and her spirit. She might have chosen to become a physical instructress, as her father wishes, but for a girl of Ruth's ambition and temperament this choice is unacceptable. As an actress there always exists the possibility, however slim, of becoming a famous star. What better way to prove her worth to the doubting world than by getting her name up in lights across a marquee? Ruth shares both her ambition and her profession, the portrayal of which is the one most popular in Cukor's cinema, with other of his heroines: Julie Cavendish (Ina Claire) is a member of a renowned stage family and one of Broadway's leading actresses in *Royal Family of Broadway*; Amanda (Marilyn Monroe) works Off-Broadway in *Let's Make Love*; Angela (Sophia Loren) belongs to a travelling troupe of actors who tour the Old West in *Heller in Pink Tights*; Claudette Colbert in *Zaza* and the girls (Kay Kendall, Mitzi Gaynor and Tania Elg) in *Les Girls* are cabaret stars; Mary Evans (Constance Bennett) in *What Price Hollywood?* and Esther Blodgett (Judy Garland) in *A Star Is Born* are film stars. The longing for

Above, Constance Bennett and Lowell Sherman in
WHAT PRICE HOLLYWOOD? (1932)
Below, Jean Simmons (left) in THE ACTRESS (1953)

notoriety, a tell-tale ambition of the Cukor heroine, is not confined to his actresses. Amanda's (Hepburn) clever courtroom tactics which make her page-one news in *Adam's Rib,* Gladys' (Holliday) scheme to have her name written in giant letters across a billboard in Columbus Circle in *It Should Happen to You,* and Lily's (Lana Turner) ambition in *A Life of Her Own* to become a top model, her face adorning the covers of fashion magazines, are all expressions of this need to "advertise" self-importance. It is simply not always enough for these women that they have the love and respect of their friends and spouses; they are looking to have their triumphs (which subconsciously they may question) confirmed by a fuller, public acceptance. There is still more. With fame, after all, comes a certain degree of power, and with it an implied sense of superiority. When Lily, for example, reaches the peak of her profession, the men in the profession must come to her.

In *A Life of Her Own* (one of the more maligned of Cukor's repertoire, yet, I think, one of the most powerful *films noirs*), Cukor deals specifically with the dangers that can befall a woman who seeks to live her own life. Lana Turner plays a mid-western girl who arrives in New York determined to become a leading fashion model. Soon after she enters the trade she meets another model, Mary (Ann Dvorak), who was once at the top of the profession, but who has lost the beauty and grace that put her there. Sometime before her fall Mary began to drink to avoid the reality of the day when she would lose the qualities necessary to maintain her status as a top model. Finally, she commits suicide just about the time Lily begins her climb to the top. By the end of the film Lily's life has deteriorated much as Mary's had. The original story idea held that Lily was also to have committed suicide, but the filmed ending leaves her fate in doubt. She finds herself alone—her lover, Steve (Ray Milland), has returned to his crippled wife—her world in collapse. The attributes which will pull her through this crisis are not physical ones, but those of a spiritual and more permanent sort. She has only herself to look to; the man who is secure enough in himself to accept a woman who wishes to pursue her own career is indeed a *rara avis* in Cukor's cinema.

Like Frank Capra's heroes, who have to prove their moxie by picking themselves up after a shattering public humiliation, Cukor's heroines have to exhibit the strength of character to go on living after their foundations have crumbled around them. (Part of the problem is that the foundations on which they depend usually appear in the form of men of very little substance.) It is at this point that they really test their capacity for both financial and spiritual self-sufficiency. One of the earliest examples of this testing process can be seen in *Our Betters,* the last film Cukor made with Constance Bennett at RKO in the early Thirties. Bennett plays a wealthy expatriate who weds an English peer only to find that he has married her for her money. Soon after their marriage he leaves her to live with the woman he really loves, taking most of Bennett's fortune with him. Pearl (Bennett) now has to gold-dig a rich American (Minor Watson) in order to live in the expensive manner to which she has grown accustomed. The experience leaves her more than a little cynical, but also determined to prove that she can make it on her own, even if her methods are less than noble. The following exchange between Pearl and a guest at one of her parties summarises her attitude:

Guest: It's wonderful how you have made your way.
Pearl: Shall I tell you how I've done it? By force of character, wit, unscrupulousness, and push.

Sometimes push is the only attribute with which a woman can advance herself, but it may be enough. In *It Should Happen to You,* Gladys Glover (Judy Holliday), a woman from a small town in upstate New York without any special talents, comes to the big city to become a "somebody". After a couple of years she is still a "nobody", but one day she gets the bright idea to rent a huge billboard on Columbus Circle and have her name written across it in giant letters. When the soap company which usually rents the sign decides that they need it for their summer campaign, they make Gladys an offer—the Columbus Circle sign in exchange for having her name printed on six smaller signs throughout the city. Soon people begin to wonder about the mysterious Gladys Glover. She is invited to appear on a television show, "The People Speak", to tell her story in her own words. She is a big hit, and soon offers to appear on other shows begin to pour in. She gets herself an agent, and in a remarkably short time becomes a minor league celebrity advertising products as "the average American girl". During her exposure to the media world, however, she runs into the phoneyness seemingly inherent to that world, and with each success finds it more and more superficial. When she loses her boyfriend (Jack Lemmon), who has seen through the charade all along, she decides that the notoriety she has achieved is not what she wants after all.

Cukor recognises only too well that in trying to establish independence and individuality there is an enormous temptation to protect oneself from harsh realities by living in a fantasy world. In addition to

Gladys, the heroines in *Sylvia Scarlett, Camille, Keeper of the Flame, A Star Is Born, Travels with My Aunt* and *Love Among the Ruins* are all for a time immersed in make-believe worlds of their own creation. But for Cukor these dream worlds never last too long, because reality eventually penetrates the most elaborately constructed fantasies. Cukor fully expresses this idea in one of his more recent films, *Travels with My Aunt*. The protagonist in this film is Augusta Bertram (Maggie Smith), an eccentric woman, presumably in her seventies, and former member of an exclusive travelling brothel who, while she·takes every advantage of the present, also lives in a fantasy world concocted out of pleasant memories of her youth. Cukor endorses the value she places in her past. He himself enjoys telling of his experiences with Garbo, Tracy, and Hepburn, as Augusta enjoys telling her "nephew" (Alec McCowen) of her affair with Monsieur Visconti (Robert Stephens). But although, as Augusta suggests, it is our memories that let us know how well we have lived, a person with so many memories can become lost in them and lose touch with the present. For Cukor, and finally for Augusta, no matter how much we cherish the past, it is the present in which we must live.[22]

The importance of the fantasy-reality idea in Cukor's cinema is also underlined by the fact that so many of his heroines are thespians. The very nature of the profession suggests that they wish, at least in part, to bury their fears in a special kind of fantasy, a role in a play or film. For Cukor, acting may become a complete escape from reality and thus lead to disaster, as it does for both Norman Maine (James Mason) and Esther Blodgett (Judy Garland) in *A Star Is Born*; or, on the other hand, if the protagonist is able to separate fantasy and reality, it may work as a healthy emotional release, as it seems to for Julie Cavendish in *Royal Family*. But whatever profession they are in, Cukor's protagonists must eventually reconcile themselves to certain truths, no matter how painful, in order to survive. In *A Star Is Born*, Esther must face the truth about her husband. Although she marries Maine knowing that his career is on the downslide, she believes the power of her love is strong enough to redeem him. But near the end of the film when she finds him in "the drunk tank" of a local jail, indiscernible from the skid row bums that surround him, she realises, perhaps for the first time, the extent of his ailment and she is willing to sacrifice her career to help him. After his suicide she has to overcome another great obstacle, her own grief. Again, only after considerable personal struggle does she succeed. When she appears in front of the audience at the benefit affair at the conclusion of the movie, we see her as a

Maggie Smith
(centre) in
**TRAVELS WITH
MY AUNT (1972)**

complete human being: both a film star surrounded by the glamour
and tinsel and a person who has had to weather the severest agonies of
disappointment and despair. One of the most important concepts
embodied in Cukor's cinema is the idea that we have to accept
ourselves as we are before there can be any hope of establishing
lasting relationships with others. The director's female characters
learn that this is the first step toward real independence.

The maturing process Cukor's heroines go through can be observed by charting the development of their relationships with men.
Generally, at the outset of a film, Cukor's women find themselves
caught in an ill-fated marriage or engagement. One explanation for
their failure is that they commit themselves without a complete
knowledge of themselves or their spouses. It is only through the

course of the film, as the result of separation, divorce, death or disaster, that the protagonists are able to make essential discoveries about themselves in order to clear the way for a stronger reunion (*Tarnished Lady*), or a clean break through which they find a superior partner (*Pat and Mike*). In *The Philadelphia Story*, Tracy Lord (Katharine Hepburn), the scion of a wealthy Eastern family, is afraid to let down her defences and expose herself to the caprices of life. She is afraid to take chances, even though they might lead to greater happiness, because she knows they might also lead to greater pain. Divorced from her first husband, Dexter (Cary Grant), because she could not tolerate his drinking problem, she also feels superior to him as a consequence of his weakness and is now engaged to a caddish social climber, George Kittridge (John Howard), whose aggressiveness she mistakes for spiritual strength, but to whom she can also feel superior. Tracy feels safe in this situation even if it is less than she might secretly long for, but Cukor obviously objects to such smug complacency. As in *Holiday*, an earlier film also adapted from a Philip Barry play, there is a call here for passion, for a release. Tracy answers this call when, after being sharply criticised for her intolerance and coldness by both Dexter and her father, she gets very drunk at a party the night before her wedding. By the late evening she has left her *fiancé* and joined Mike (James Stewart), a reporter who has been sent by a gossip magazine to cover the wedding. In his company she releases the fires which Mike, an aspiring author, tells her are "banked down within her." Although Tracy has difficulty remembering her encounter with Mike the next morning, it is clear that she is a "new" person for the experience. When George, with his conventional moral leanings, learns of her fling, he considers calling off the wedding. Tracy, now realising that she cannot marry George, insists that their engagement must end, and in the last scene remarries Dexter, to whom she is best suited.

From only a sampling of Cukor's work it becomes clear that the director sees the male-female relationship as essentially a clash between the desire of the male to retain the nineteenth century imbalance between the sexes, and the equally fervent desire of the female to correct that imbalance and establish a new order of mutual equality. That Cukor's women wish to establish a new balance has been shown; that his male characters frequently feel threatened by this female assertion of independence can now demonstrated. Ironically, the men who most often display insecurity are those who are most overtly masculine. Acting according to their fears, they marry

Wallace Beery and Jean Harlow in DINNER AT EIGHT (1933)

women they consider to be their intellectual inferiors, women they think they can master. Hence Dan Packard (Wallace Beery) marries a comely young tart (Jean Harlow) that he, as he puts it, "picked out of the gutter", in *Dinner at Eight*, the same place Harry Brock (Broderick Crawford) claims he found Billie (Judy Holliday) in *Born Yesterday*. Barrie (Fredric March) marries Susan (Joan Crawford) in *Susan and God* because she is beautiful and brainless and Chet (Aldo Ray) marries likable but seemingly muddle-headed Florence (Judy Holliday) in *The Marrying Kind*. Packard and Brock are insensitive brutes whose energies are concentrated on expanding their already sizable fortunes and influence. As with everything else, they buy themselves a mate. Thinking that they own these women gives them a strong sense of superiority, but this comfort quickly evaporates when their women prove much more cunning than either bargained for. By the conclusions of *Dinner at Eight* and *Born Yesterday*, the two women are giving orders and the two men are left alone with their insecurities to search for another female, if they dare. The situation is much the same in *Susan and God*. At one point in the film, Barrie asks Susan, from whom he has been separated for months, "Whatever happened to the beautiful scatterbrain I married?" In a nutshell, she got smart and discovered that she had little room in her plans for a man who wanted her only in the role of adoring housewife to his king-of-the-castle husband. Near the end of the movie Susan is seized by the revelation that she has been a neglectful mother (she and Barrie have a teenage daughter) and returns home, presumably to stay. If she and Barrie are now to have a happy marriage (that they will seems improbable despite the movie's optimistic conclusion), they will both have to compromise their marital expectations; that is, Barrie must acknowledge that Susan has a mind of her own and will not accept being his vassal, and Susan must abandon her self-serving schemes and accept certain responsibilities incumbent on her as a wife and mother.

The Marrying Kind, released twelve years after *Susan and God*, expresses this idea much more clearly. The movie concerns a young, lower middle-class couple whose marriage collapses under the weight of life's misfortunes. Their first "big blow-up" comes when Chet gets drunk at a party at his brother-in-law's and pays too much attention to a buxom blonde. Next they lose a chance to win $2600 when they fail to "name that tune" for a radio game show. Then they are hit with a disaster which their marriage is not strong enough to withstand—the sudden death of their son. While Chet recovers in a sanitarium from an accident and the nervous breakdown that follows the child's death, Florence must carry the burden of maintaining their home. When Chet returns, their marriage goes from bad to worse because, despite the necessity of the arrangement, Chet resents the fact that his wife has taken over the "masculine" role of family provider. That Florence has rapidly matured to accept the responsibilities placed upon her complicates matters further. When Chet seeks to return her to the same position of dependence he assigned her and which she accepted when they were first married, she resists. That she has taken over the male role causes Chet to doubt his masculinity. Unfortunately, his conventionally middle-class view of the marriage relationship precludes him from seeing his marriage any other way, and Florence, a product of the same conventions, does not possess the depth of understanding necessary to calm Chet's fears.

Chet and Florence finally decide to get a divorce, and it is in Divorce Court, before a sympathetic judge (Madge Kennedy), that their story is told in flashback. Like *Susan and God*, *The Marrying Kind* ends

ADAM'S RIB (1949): Judy Holliday, Katharine Hepburn, Spencer Tracy

ambiguously. Chet and Florence decide to give their marriage another try, but we cannot be certain that their differences will be resolved. Their chance of success rests with Chet's being allowed to return gracefully to his position of family provider while at the same time acknowledging the importance of Florence's contribution to the family unit—a very delicate proposition for people whose station in life leaves them little room for delicacy.

In *The Marrying Kind*, Cukor suggests that the resolution of the conflict between husband and wife can only come about through the creation of a new order in which both share an equal, yet distinct, role in the marriage. This concept is still more fully stated in two movies Cukor made in the late Forties and early Fifties, *Adam's Rib* and *Pat and Mike*. They stand as his most complete statement of the concern which has dominated his cinema: what are the conditions necessary for a successful male-female relationship? In *Adam's Rib*, husband and wife, Adam (Spencer Tracy) and Amanda (Katharine Hepburn),

Courtroom tactics in ADAM'S RIB: Spencer Tracy and Hope Emerson

both lawyers, he with the district attorney, she in private practice, work against each other on a case involving a wife (Judy Holliday) who has assaulted her adulterous husband (Tom Ewell). Amanda bases her defence on the principle that women are discriminated against by the law; that is, if a man takes action to save his home, society looks favourably upon him, but if a woman does the same—as Amanda claims her client has done—society takes a negative view. In order to prove her point that women are the equals of men, she calls on three female witnesses: a brilliant scholar (Elizabeth Flourney), a construction foreman (Polly Moran), and a weightlifter in a circus (Hope Emerson). Adam, who views the case as a straightforward example of assault with intent to kill, is first amused, then confused, and finally outraged by his wife's courtroom tactics. The trial evolves into a case of one-upmanship as Adam and Amanda try to upstage and outduel each other. Their conflict spills over into their marriage, which soon becomes as competitive an arena as the courtroom.

Amanda wins her case in court, but Adam wins his point later when he confronts Amanda at her friend's (David Wayne) apartment the following evening. Their marriage, however, is not so satisfactorily resolved until the end of the film, when a few well-timed tears by Adam bring them back together.

At the beginning of the film, Adam and Amanda are involved in a free exchange of ideas, which Cukor regards as one of the necessary ingredients for a successful male-female relationship. But, when their courtroom rivalry flares, that dialogue breaks down and their marriage falls apart. Adam and Amanda re-establish a healthy dialogue at the close of the film while coming to some important new insights about the nature of their relationship. Their respective temperaments unite to form a complete unit with each considering and intelligently reacting to the idiosyncrasies, faults, and qualities of the other. Yet for Cukor the perfect marriage is not the blending of two complementary temperaments into one being, because this implies the repression of individuality the director finds to be an essential quality in his best characters. The husband must be able to pursue certain traditional male roles while at the same time his wife must be free to follow her ambitions.

The premise behind Adam and Amanda's relationship goes to the heart of the male-female conflict and thus to the heart of the director's cinema. For Cukor there is no steadfast line dividing the two sexes. We are all androgynous to a point, and it is in realising that the most masculine male possesses important female characteristics, and that the converse is also true, that we can begin to establish a true equality between the sexes. Molly Haskell writes of *Adam's Rib*:

> The film brilliantly counterpoints and reconciles two basic assumptions: (1) that there are certain "male" qualities—stability, stoicism, fairness, dullness—possessed by Tracy, and that there are certain "female" qualities—volatility, brilliance, intuition, duplicity—possessed by Hepburn; and (2) that each can, and must, exchange these qualities like trading cards. It is important for Hepburn to be ethical, just as it is important for Tracy to be able to concede defeat gracefully, and if she can be a bastard, he can fake tears. If each can do everything the other can do, just where, we begin to wonder, are the boundaries between male and female? The question mark is established most pointedly, and uncomfortably when, during the courtroom session, the faces of Holliday and Ewell are transposed, each becoming the other.[23]

Certain American films have dealt successfully with the marriage relationship, but no director has dealt with the subject as extensively and as intelligently as Cukor. *Adam's Rib* clearly testifies to the later half of the contention. That his work has been so unheralded would seem to be tied to the fact that women in films have all too seldom been taken seriously (Haskell's complaint), and to understand Cukor's cinema one must understand his heroines. But his unique perspective does not prevent him from seeing the full spectrum of the male-female relationship. In *Adam's Rib,* Cukor is not calling for role transformation, as his background in Thirties comedy might suggest, but for the end of any sort of role playing at all. The distinction is subtle but important. Cukor suggests that the sexes must shed themselves of the stereotypes and misconceptions which are in themselves roles and recognise that the best male-female relationships are to be had not by drawing lines between male and female behaviour, but in realising that if there are any lines they are nebulous. The fact that Spencer Tracy, an actor always thought to be the embodiment of virility, is the male through which Cukor demonstrates the similarity

Spencer Tracy and Katharine Hepburn in PAT AND MIKE (1952)

of the sexes, must be one of the most inspired examples of casting in the American cinema.

In *Pat and Mike,* Cukor's last Tracy-Hepburn film, Hepburn plays Pat Pemberton, a physical education teacher engaged to one of the cinema's great heels, Collier Weld (William Ching). In much the same mould as George Kittridge, Tracy's *fiancé* in *The Philadelphia Story,* Collier sees Pat as a "little woman" to his "big man". Pat instinctively rebels against this, and she postpones their wedding. She decides to put her considerable athletic skills to use and becomes a professional athlete. She goes to see Mike Conovan (Tracy) whom she met under somewhat unusual circumstances while playing in a golf tournament, and he becomes her manager-promoter. Although Mike subjects her to strict training rules which run against her independent spirit, the two form a close relationship. In contrast to Collier, Mike treats Pat without regard to her sex, but as a dedicated professional athlete. Pat flourishes under this arrangement. Significantly, her athletic successes are only spoiled when Collier watches her play. To Pat he symbolises the self-doubt she wishes to dispel by proving to herself that she can survive on her own talent. Naturally (for this is a Cukor film), she finally rids herself of him in much the same way Tracy frees herself from Kittridge.

Like *Adam's Rib, Pat and Mike* demonstrates that in addition to recognising all that is shared by the two sexes, there is a need for each of the protagonists to recognise the other possesses a distinct identity and that this identity has certain conditions which cannot be tread upon. Consequently, when Pat roughs up the thugs who were planning to rough up Mike, she tramples on his self-esteem, and he is infuriated by her interference. He tells her: "I like a he to be a he and a she to be a she." Mike, who knows that everything between them must be "five-oh, five-oh", nevertheless considers the handling of any physical threats his province. When Pat in effect proposes to him at the end of the film, she acknowledges this and clears the way for a successful relationship.

If *Adam's Rib* and *Pat and Mike* are Cukor's clearest statements on the requirements of the marriage relationship, they are only two representative films in a cinema that spans five decades. Significantly, this concern for balance within a marriage can be traced to his first solo directing effort, *Tarnished Lady,* which for all its stylistic faults suggests that only through intelligent compromise can the protagonists establish a successful relationship. The treatment of this theme has evolved through a variety of *genres* and a myriad of technical advancements; still its basic thrust remains the same and Cukor continues to look for ever more lucid ways of expressing it.

Now into his eighties, Cukor shows no inclination to retire. Why should he? In a profession which is supposed to be a "young man's game", Cukor's recent films are as in tune with what his audiences are thinking today as his early films were with the audiences of the Thirties. His best films transcend time barriers. Cukor's movies remain contemporary because the ideas behind them have not aged. In some instances, like *Adam's Rib,* perhaps his best film, he expresses ideas which are still ahead of their time. *Camille,* for another, is as fresh today as it was when it was released forty years ago, because the ideas and sentiments behind the film transcend historical period or studio convention.

Perhaps the key to the quality of Cukor's films is that the director has always concentrated on individuals, and on their attitudes toward themselves and those close to them. He treats all of his characters with equal understanding and sympathy. In *Holiday,* for example, although old man Seton (Henry Kolker) and his daughter Julia (Doris Nolan) are the villains of the film, Cukor is careful to point out that there exists a strong love between father and daughter, an understanding in its own way as strong as the love between Linda (Katharine Hepburn) and Johnny (Cary Grant), and consequently we feel a strange warmth towards these characters. Yet although he prefers to work on an intimate level, the intimacy does not detract from the force of his themes. Nor does it prevent him from seeing the questions raised in his films from two sides. If he sympathises with the female's quest for equality, he realises that female supremacy would be no improvement over its opposite. If he recognises that we must always be ready to face reality, he knows that we all need an occasional respite from it. If he sees the dangers of being caught in a romantic distortion of one's own past, he also perceives that the past is inextricably bound to the present. The ability to explain apparent contradiction, to untangle ostensible paradoxes, is perhaps Cukor's greatest skill as a director. It allows him to probe deeply into the human spirit without ever forgetting how complex that spirit is.

NOTES

[1]Richard Schickel, "Interview with George Cukor," *The Men Who Made the Movies* (New York: Atheneum, 1975), p. 165.

[2]Richard Overstreet, *Interviews with Film Directors,* ed. Andrew Sarris (New York: Avon, 1967), p. 118.

[3]Charles Higham, "George Cukor," *The London Magazine,* May 1965, pp. 61-2.

[4]Overstreet, p. 212.

[5]Richard Schickel, p. 172.

[6]Margaret Drabble, *The Garrick Year* (Middlesex, England: Penguin, 1966), p. 109.

[7]Penelope Houston, "Film Reviews: *A Star Is Born,*" *Sight and Sound,* Spring 1955, p. 194.

[8]Unpublished interview between George Cukor and author, Feb. 15, 1976.

[9]*Current Biography,* ed. Maxine Block (New York: H. W. Wilson, 1943), p. 156.

[10]*The Theatre,* Oct. 1925, p. 66.

[11]Paraphrased from an unpublished interview between Samson Raphaelson and Robert Carringer, August 1973. Transcript in the Archives of the University of Illinois at Urbana-Champaign.

[12]In his autobiography, *I Blow My Own Horn* (Garden City: Doubleday, 1957), p. 219, Jesse Lasky says he signed Cukor for Paramount at the suggestion of Rouben Mamoulian, who knew Cukor from the days he was directing the American Opera Company in Rochester. When I asked Cukor about this he called it "ridiculous" but he could not remember who specifically was responsible for bringing him to Paramount.

[13]This was a common practice during the first few years of sound. But the function of the "co-director", like that of the dialogue director, soon disappeared when beginners like Cukor and veterans like Milestone learned the essentials of sound technique. For *Virtuous Sin* Cukor's co-director was Louis Gasnier, a Frenchman who had led a distinguished career as a silent director in Hollywood. As the talkies approached his star began to fade, but at the time of *Virtuous Sin* he would have still probably been better known in the industry than Cukor. One of Gasnier's sound films, however, has recently become a popular favourite on college campuses. The film is *Reefer Madness.*

[14]Cukor and Stewart, of course, went on to bigger and better things, like *Holiday, Philadelphia Story,* and *Keeper of the Flame,* but Bankhead was never to make it big in Hollywood. Cukor has said that she lacked star quality, her eyes were strangely dull, and her smile did not radiate. I do not find this to be the case; more likely she flopped because she was mismanaged by Paramount. She needed to fashion her own mystique, but the studio kept trying to make her look like Garbo, Dietrich, or Shearer. Had Cukor's ability with actresses been as finely honed in 1931 as it was six years later when he directed Garbo in *Camille,* he might have been able to develop her considerable talent as he did Garbo's. But in 1931 his direction of her seems more closely tied to Paramount's indecision than his own intuition.

[15]Cukor, however, was frequently "loaned out" to other studios. He made *Sylvia Scarlett* (1935) at RKO, *Holiday* (1938) at Columbia, *Zaza* (1938) at Paramount, and *Winged Victory* (1944) at 20th Century-Fox.

[16]*Motion Picture,* Sept. 1936, p. 76.

[17]In one tabulation designed to measure the popular success of American film directors (Steven P. Hill, "The Popular Directors," *Films in Review,* Aug.-Sept. 1962, pp. 385-389), Cukor is ranked second only to Capra for the Thirties. He finishes nineteenth for the Forties, sixteenth for the Fifties, and second to William Wyler in the overall ranking.

[18]In fairness to Cukor, it should be pointed out that other major figures on *Gone with the Wind,* such as cinematographer Lee Garmes, left the production over differences with Selznick. The producer drove Cukor's replacement, Victor Fleming, to feign a nervous breakdown just so he could get a respite from Selznick's incessant meddling.

[19]The actual footage Cukor shot, nearly all of which remained in the film, is detailed by Gavin Lambert in his book, *GWTW: The Making of Gone with the Wind* (Boston: Little, Brown and Co., 1973, p. 118). Lambert credits Cukor with five per cent of the film, listing these scenes: "Mammy lacing up Scarlett for the barbecue, Rhett arriving at Aunt Pittypat's with the hat for Scarlett, Scarlett and Prissy delivering Melanie's baby, and Scarlett shooting the union deserter at Tara. The final 'authorship' of the opening porch scene, which was reshot three times, remains in doubt. It is probably a mixture of Cukor's second version and the Fleming retake."

[20]In an interview with John Gillett and David Robinson (*Sight and Sound,* Aug. 1964, p. 191), Cukor specifies some of the scenes that were removed: ". . .they made cuts, including some

charming songs; some very funny scenes between Judy Garland and James Mason, little episodes building up the relationship between them. There were scenes when they meet again when she is living in a very shabby boarding-house downtown in Los Angeles; a scene on the way to the film premiere, when she's so nervous, she jumps out of the car and is sick, all amongst oil derricks; and a scene I was very fond of when they play a love scene on the sound stage, with a live microphone going so the whole thing is played back to them."

[21]Molly Haskell, *From Reverence to Rape: The Treatment of Women in the Movies* (New York: Holt, Rinehart, and Winston, 1973), p. 25.

[22]In an excellent analysis of *Travels with My Aunt,* Jesse Brandt makes an interesting point about how this relates to Cukor as a film director: "Augusta must constantly relive (in her dreams) and retell the past to validate her present; to be more than 'just an old woman'. Without her past, Augusta would be robbed of the very substance of her life. Yet no matter how vital her memories may be, they are always pitted against the assumption that the present is all that should and can count. This is true for Cukor and other veteran directors as it is for Augusta." ("Adventures in Time and Space," *Movietone News,* 29 Sept. 1975, p. 31). Brandt might have added that Augusta's coming to grips with the present also implies that one can, in effect, be "re-born" at seventy-five as well as at any other age. Indeed, Cukor himself has seldom been busier directing films than in these last few years. In fact, he made *Travels with My Aunt* at age seventy-three after having directed only two films in the previous ten years.

[23]Haskell, p. 229.

George Cukor Filmography

Before coming to Hollywood, Cukor directed the following Broadway stage productions: ANTONIA (1925), THE GREAT GATSBY (1926), THE CONSTANT WIFE (1926), THE DARK (1927), HER CARDBOARD LOVER (1927), TRIGGER (1927), A FREE SOUL (1928), THE FURIES (1928), YOUNG LOVE (1928), and GYPSY (1929).

GRUMPY (1930). Cagey old lawyer solves mystery of a diamond robbery. *Sc:* Doris Anderson (the play by Horace Hodges and Thomas Wigney). *Ph:* David Abel. *Ed:* Cyril Gardner. *With* Cyril Maude (*"Grumpy" Bullivant*), Phillips Holmes *(Ernest Heron)*, Frances Dade *(Virginia)*, Paul Lukas (*Berci*), Halliwell Hobbes (*Ruddick*), Paul Cavanagh (*Jarvis*), Doris Luray (*Susan*), Olaf Hytten (*Kebble*), Robert Bolder (*Merridew*), Colin Kenny (*Dawson*). *Prod:* Paramount. 74m. (Co-directed with Cyril Gardner.)

THE VIRTUOUS SIN (1930). A beautiful woman sacrifices her virtue to save the life of her husband. *Sc:* Martin Brown, Louise Long (the play "The General" by Lajos Zilhay). *Ph:* David Abel. *Ed:* Otho Lovering. *With* Walter Huston (*Gen. Gregori Platoff*), Kay Francis (*Marya Ivanova*), Paul Cavanagh (*Captain Orloff*), Kennenth MacKenna (*Lieut. Victor Sablin*), Eric Kalkhurst (*Lieut. Glinka*), Oscar Apfel (*Major Ivanoff*), Gordon McLeod (*Col. Nikitin*), Victor Potel (*sentry*), Youcca Troubetzkoy (*Captain*), Jobyna Howland (*Alexandra*). *Prod:* Paramount. 80m. (Co-directed with Louis Gasnier.)

THE ROYAL FAMILY OF BROADWAY (1930). A fictional portrait of the Barrymores. *Sc:* Herman J. Mankiewicz, Gertrude Purcell (the play by Edna Ferber and George S. Kaufman). *Ph:* George Folsey. *Ed:* Edward Dmytryk. *With* Ina Claire (*Julia Cavendish*), Fredric March (*Tony Cavendish*), Mary Brian (*Gwen Cavendish*), Henrietta Crossman (*Fanny Cavendish*), Arnold Karff (*Oscar Wolfe*), Frank Conroy (*Gilmore Marshall*), Charles Starrett (*Perry Stewart*), Royal G. Stout (*Joe*), Elsie Edmonds (*Della*), Murray Alper (*McDermott*), Wesley Stark (*Hall boy*), Herschel Mayall (*Doctor*). *Prod:* Paramount. 82m. (Co-directed with Cyril Gardner.)

TARNISHED LADY (1931). Financial problems force a woman to marry for money. *Sc:* Donald Ogden Stewart. *Ph:* Larry Williams. *Ed:* Barney Rogan. *With* Tallulah Bankhead (*Nancy Courtney*), Clive Brook (*Norman Cravath*), Phoebe Foster (*Germaine Prentiss*), Alexander Kirkland (*DeWitt Taylor*), Osgood Perkins (*Ben Sterner*), Elizabeth Patterson (*Mrs. Courtney*). *Prod:* Paramount. 83m.

GIRLS ABOUT TOWN (1931). Gold-digger falls in love with customer. *Sc:* Raymond Griffith, Brian Marlow (a story by Zoë Akins). *Ph:* Ernest Haller. *With:* Kay Francis (*Wanda Howard*), Joel McCrea (*Jim Baker*), Lilyan Tashman (*Marie Bailey*), Eugene Pallette (*Benjamin Thomas*), Allan Dinehart (*Jerry Chase*), Lucille Webster Gleason (*Mrs. Benjamin Thomas*), Anderson Lawler (*Alex Howard*), Lucille Browne (*Edna*), George Barbier (*Webster*), Robert McWade (*Simms*), Louise Beavers (*Hattie*), Adrienne Ames (*Anne*), Hazel Howard (*Joy*), Claire Dodd (*Dot*), Patricia Caron (*Billie*), Judith Wood (*Winnie*). *Prod:* Paramount. 90m.

WHAT PRICE HOLLYWOOD? (1932). The rise and fall of a Hollywood actress. *Sc:* Jane Murfin, Ben Markson (adaptation by Gene Fowler and Rowland Brown of an Adela Roger St. Johns story). *Ph:* Charles Rosher. *Art dir:* Carroll Clark. *Ed:* Jack Kitchin. *Mus:* Max

Steiner. *With* Constance Bennett (*Mary Evans*), Lowell Sherman (*Maximilian Carey*), Neil Hamilton (*Lonny Borden*), Gregory Ratoff (*Julias Saxe*), Brooks Benedict (*Muto*), Louise Beavers (*Cassie*), Eddie Anderson (*James*). *Prod:* David O. Selznick for RKO. 87m.

A BILL OF DIVORCEMENT (1932). Father returns from an asylum after a long absence and finds things are not the way he left them. *Sc:* Howard Estabrook, Harry Wagstaff Gribble (the play by Clemence Dane). *Ph:* Sid Hickox. *Art dir:* Carroll Clark. *Ed:* Arthur Roberts. *Mus:* Max Steiner. *With* John Barrymore (*Hillary Fairchild*), Billie Burke (*Margaret Fairchild*), Katharine Hepburn (*Sydney Fairchild*), David Manners (*Kit Humphrey*), Henry Stephenson (*Dr. Alliot*), Elizabeth Patterson (*Aunt Hester*), Paul Cavanagh (*Gray Meredith*), Gayle Evers (*Bassett*), Bramwell Fletcher (*Gareth*). *Prod:* David O. Selznick for RKO. 80m.

ROCKABYE (1932). Romance between playwright and actress ends when playwright's wife arrives on the scene. *Sc:* Jane Murfin, Kubec Glasmon (the story Lucia Bronder). *Ph:* Charles Rosher. *Art dir:* Carroll Clark. *Ed:* George Hively. *Mus:* Max Steiner. *With* Constance Bennett (*Judy Carroll*), Joel McCrea (*Jake Pell*), Paul Lukas (*De Sola*), Walter Pidgeon (*Commissioner Howard*), Jobyna Howland (*Snooks*), Virginia Hammond (*Mrs. Pell*), Walter Catlett (*Dunn*), June Filmer (*Lilybet*), J. M. Kerrigan (*Dugan*), Clara Blandick (*Brida*). *Prod:* David O. Selznick for RKO. 71m.

OUR BETTERS (1933). Expatriate American woman uses her feminine wiles to rise in London society. *Sc:* Jane Murfin, Henry Wagstaff Gribble (the play by Somerset Maugham). *Ph:* Charles Rosher. *Art dir:* Van Nest Polglase and Hobe Erwin. *Ed:* Jack Kitchin. *Mus:* Max Steiner. *With* Constance Bennett (*Lady Pearl Grayston*), Violet Kemble Cooper (*the Duchess*), Phoebe Foster (*the Princess*), Charles Starrett (*Fleming Harvey*), Grant Mitchell (*Thornton Clay*), Gilbert Roland (*Pepi*), Anita Louise (*Bessie Saunders*), Minor Watson (*Arthur Fenwick*), Hugh Sinclair

(*Sir Harry Bleane*), Alan Mowbray (*Sir George Grayston*), Harold Entwhistle (*Pole*). *Prod:* David O. Selznick for RKO. 85m.

DINNER AT EIGHT (1933). Drama surrounds a dinner party. *Sc:* Herman J. Mankiewicz, Frances Marion (the play by Edna Ferber and George S. Kaufman). *Additional dialogue:* Donald Ogden Stewart. *Ph:* William Daniels. *Art dir:* Hobe Erwin and Fred Hope. *Ed:* Ben Lewis. *Mus:* William Axt. *With* Marie Dressler (*Carlotta Vance*), John Barrymore (*Larry Renault*), Wallace Beery (*Dan Packard*), Jean Harlow (*Kitty Packard*), Lionel Barrymore (*Oliver Jordan*), Lee Tracy (*Max Kane*), Edmund Lowe (*Dr. Wayne Talbot*), Billie Burke (*Millicent Jordan*), Madge Evans (*Paula Jordan*), Jean Hersholt (*Joe Stengel*), Karen Morley

Katharine Hepburn in LITTLE WOMEN, lower shot with Douglass Montgomery and Cukor

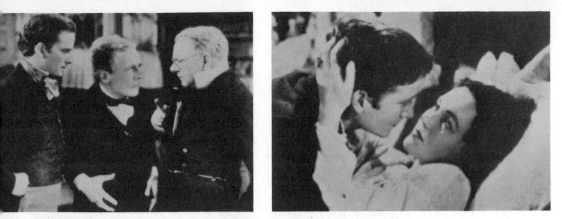

DAVID COPPERFIELD. Left, Frank Lawton, Roland Young and W. C. Fields. Right, Frank Lawton and Maureen O'Sullivan

(*Lucy Talbot*), Louise Closser Hale (*Hattie Loomis*), Phillips Holmes (*Ernest*), May Robson (*Mrs. Wendel*), Phoebe Foster (*Miss Alden*), Grant Mitchell (*Ed Loomis*), Elizabeth Patterson (*Miss Copeland*), Hilda Vaughn (*Tina*), Harry Beresford (*Fosdick*), Edwin Maxwell (*Mr. Fitch*), Anna Duncan (*Dora*). *Prod:* David O. Selznick for M-G-M. 110m.

LITTLE WOMEN (1933). Story of a New England family during the mid-19th century. *Sc:* Sarah Y. Mason, Victor Heerman (the novel by Louisa May Alcott). *Ph:* Henry Gerrard. *Art dir:* Van Nest Polglase. *Ed:* Jack Kitchin. *Mus:* Max Steiner. *With* Katharine Hepburn (*Jo*), Joan Bennett (*Amy*), Paul Lukas (*Fritz Bhaer*), Edna May Oliver (*Aunt March*), Jean Parker (*Beth*), Frances Dee (*Meg*), Henry Stephenson (*Mr. Laurence*), Douglass Montgomery (*Laurie*), John David Lodge (*Brooke*), Spring Byington (*Marmee*), Samuel S. Hinds (*Mr. March*), Mabel Colcord (*Hannah*), Marion Ballou (*Mrs. Kirke*), Nydia Westman (*Mamie*), Harry Beresford (*Dr. Bangs*). *Prod:* RKO. 117m.

DAVID COPPERFIELD (1935). Adaptation of Dickens's fictionalised autobiography. *Sc:* Howard Estabrook (adaptation by Hugh Walpole of the novel by Charles Dickens). *Ph:* Oliver Marsh. *Art dir:* Cedric Gibbons, Merrill Pye, Edwin B. Willis. *Ed:* Robert Kern. *Mus:* Herbert Stothart. *With* W. C. Fields (*Micawber*), Lionel Barrymore (*Dan Peggotty*), Maureen O'Sullivan (*Dora*), Madge Evans (*Agnes*), Edna May Oliver (*Aunt Betsey Trotman*), Lewis Stone (*Mr. Wickfield*), Frank Lawton (*David, the man*), Freddie Bartholomew (*David, the boy*), Elizabeth Allan (*Mrs. Copperfield*), Roland Young (*Uriah Heep*), Basil Rathbone (*Mr. Murdstone*), Elsa Lanchester (*Clickett*), Jessie Ralph (*Nurse Peggotty*), Violet Kemble-Cooper (*Jane Murdstone*), Harry Beresford (*Dr. Chillip*), Hugh Walpole (*Vicar*), Herbert Mundin (*Barkis*), John Buckler (*Ham*), Una O'Connor (*Mrs. Gummidge*), Lennox Pawle (*Mr. Dick*), Renee Gadd (*Janet*), Jean Cadell (*Mrs. Micawber*), Fay Chaldecott (*Little Emily, the child*), Marilyn Knowlden (*Agnes, the child*), Florine McKinney (*Little Emily, the woman*), Hugh Williams (*Steerforth*), Mabel Colcord (*Mary Ann*), Ivan Simpson (*Littmer*). *Prod:* David O. Selznick for M-G-M. 135m.

SYLVIA SCARLETT (1936). The adventures of a young woman who disguises herself as a man. *Sc:* Gladys Unger, John Collier, Mortimer Offner (the

Katharine Hepburn and Natalie Paley in SYLVIA SCARLETT

128

novel by Compton MacKenzie). *Ph:*
Joseph August. *Art dir:* Van Nest Pol-
gase, Sturges Carné. *Ed:* Jane Loring.
Mus: Roy Webb. *With* Katharine Hep-
burn (*Sylvia Scarlett*), Cary Grant (*Jimmy
Monkley*), Brian Aherne (*Michael Fane*),
Edmund Gwenn (*Henry Scarlett*), Natalie
Paley (*Lily*), Dennie Moore (*Maudie Tilt*),
Lennox Pawle (*drunk*). *Prod:* Pandro S.
Berman for RKO. 90m.

ROMEO AND JULIET (1936). Shake-
speare's star-crossed lovers. *Sc:* Talbot
Jennings (the play by William Shake-
speare). *Ph:* William Daniels. *Art dir:*
Cedric Gibbons, Oliver Messel, Fredric
Hope, Edwin B. Willis. *Ed:* Margaret
Booth. *Mus:* Herbert Stothart. *With*
Norman Shearer (*Juliet*), Leslie Howard
(*Romeo*), John Barrymore (*Mercutio*),
Edna May Oliver (*nurse to Juliet*), Basil
Rathbone (*Tybalt*), Andy Devine (*Peter*),
Henry Kolker (*Friar Laurence*), Reginald
Denny (*Benvolio*), C. Aubrey Smith
(*Capulet*), Violet Kemble-Cooper (*Lady
Capulet*), Robert Warwick (*Montague*),
Virginia Hammond (*Lady Montague*),
Ralph Forbes (*Paris*), Conway Tearle (*Es-
calus*), Maurice Murphy (*Balthasar*).*Prod:*
Irving Thalberg for M-G-M. 140m.

CAMILLE (1936). The tragic history of a
Paris demimondaine. *Sc:* Zoë Akins,
Frances Marion and James Hilton (the
play and novel by Alexandre Dumas).
Ph: William Daniels, Karl Freund. *Art
dir:* Cedric Gibbons, Fredric Hope,
Edwin B. Willis. *Ed:* Margaret Booth.
Mus: Herbert Stothart. *With* Greta Garbo
(*Marguerite*), Robert Taylor (*Armand*),
Lionel Barrymore (*Monsieur Duval*),
Elizabeth Allan (*Nichette*), Jessie Ralph
(*Nanine*), Henry Daniell (*Baron de Var-
ville*), Lenore Ulric (*Olympe*), Laura Hope
Crews (*Prudence*), Rex O'Malley (*Gaston*),
Russell Hardie (*Gustave*), E. E. Clive
(*Saint Gaudens*), Douglas Walton (*Henri*),
Jean Brodel (*Marie Jeanette*), Marion Bal-
lou (*Corinne*), June Wilkins (*Louise*), Elsie
Esmonds (*Madame Duval*), Fritz Leiber,
Jr. (*Valentin*). *Prod:* Irving Thalberg for
M-G-M. 108m.

HOLIDAY (1938). A free-spirited
young woman seizes her chance for happiness when her sister unwittingly pre-

Greta Garbo and Henry
Daniell in CAMILLE

sents her with the opportunity. *Sc:*
Donald Ogden Stewart, Sidney
Buchman (the play by Philip Barry). *Ph:*
Franz Planer. *Art dir:* Stephen Goosson,
Lionel Banks. *Ed:* Otto Meyer, Al Clark.
Mus: Morris Stoloff. *With* Katharine
Hepburn (*Linda Seton*), Cary Grant
(*Johnny Case*), Doris Nolan (*Julia Seton*),
Lew Ayres (*Ned Seton*), Edward Everett
Horton (*Nick Potter*), Henry Kolker (*Ed-
ward Seton*), Binnie Barnes (*Laura Cram*),
Jean Dixon (*Susan Potter*), Henry Daniell
(*Seton Cram*). *Prod:* Everett Riskin for
Columbia. 93m.

ZAZA (1938). Romance between chorus
girl and wealthy Parisian. *Sc:* Zoë Akins
(the play by Pierre Berton and Charles
Simon). *Ph:* Charles Lang, Jr. *Art dir:*
Hans Dreier, Robert Usher. *Ed:* Edward
Dmytryk. *Mus:* Frederick Hollander,
Frank Loesser. *With* Claudette Colbert
(*Zaza*), Herbert Marshall (*Dufresne*), Bert
Lahr (*Cascart*), Genevieve Tobin
(*Florianne*), Constance Collier (*Nathalie*),
Walter Catlett (*Malardot*), Rex O'Malley
(*Bussey*), Helen Westley (*Anais*), Rex
Evans (*Michelin*), Robert C. Fischer
(*Pierre*), Ernest Cossart (*Marechand*),
Dorothy Tree (*Madame Dufresne*), Monty
Woolley (*Fouget*), Maurice Murphy
(*Henri*), Ann Todd (*Tote*), Frank Puglia
(*Rug dealer*), Janet Waldo (*Simone*), Alex-
ander Leftwich (*Laron*), Fredrika Brown
(*Pierre's wife*), Olive Tell (*Jeanne Liseron*),
John Sutton (*First swain*), Michael Brooks
(*Dandy*), Philip Warren (*Dandy*), Maud
Hume (*Woman*), Alice Keating (*Maid*).
Prod: Albert Lewin for Paramount. 80m.

**Left, Rosalind Russell in THE WOMEN
Right, Joan Crawford in SUSAN AND GOD**

THE WOMEN (1939). Wife loses husband to temptress and schemes to win him back. *Sc:* Anita Loos, Jane Murfin (the play by Clare Boothe). *Ph:* Oliver T. Marsh, Joseph Ruttenberg. *Art dir:* Cedric Gibbons, Wade B. Rubottom. *Ed:* Robert J. Kern. *Mus:* Edward Ward, David Snell. *With* Norma Shearer (*Mrs. Stephen Haines, "Mary"*), Joan Crawford (*Crystal Allen*), Rosalind Russell (*Mrs. Howard Fowler, "Sylvia"*), Mary Boland (*The Countess De Lave, "Flora"*), Paulette Goddard (*Miriam Aarons*), Phyllis Povah (*Mrs. Phelps Potter, "Edith"*), Joan Fontaine (*Mrs. John Day, "Peggy"*), Virginia Weidler (*Little Mary*), Lucile Watson (*Mrs. Morehead*), Marjorie Main (*Lucy*), Virginia Grey (*Pat*), Ruth Hussey (*Miss Watts*), Muriel Hutchison (*Jane*), Florence Nash (*Nancy Blake*), Hedda Hopper (*Dolly de Peyster*), Dennie Moore (*Olga*), Cora Witherspoon (*Mrs. Van Adams*), Mary Cecil (*Maggie*), Mary Beth Hughes (*Miss Trimmerback*), Ann Morriss (*Exercise instructress*). *Prod:* Hunt Stromberg for M-G-M. 134m.

SUSAN AND GOD (1940). Headstrong wife learns family responsibility while chauvinistic husband learns to respect her selfhood. *Sc:* Anita Loos (the play by Rachel Crothers). *Ph:* Robert Planck. *Art dir:* Cedric Gibbons, Randall Duell. *Ed:* William H. Terhune. *Mus:* Herbert Stothart. *With* Joan Crawford (*Susan*), Fredric March (*Barrie*), Ruth Hussey (*Charlotte*), John Carroll (*Clyde*), Rita Hayworth (*Leonora*), Nigel Bruce (*"Hutchie"*), Bruce Cabot (*Michael*), Rose

Hobart (*Irene*), Constance Collier (*Lady Wigstaff*), Rita Quigley (*Blossom*), Gloria De Haven (*Enid*), Richard O. Carne (*Bob*), Norma Mitchell (*Paige*), Marjorie Main (*Mary*), Aldrich Bowker (*Patrick*). *Prod:* Hunt Stromberg for M-G-M. 115m.

THE PHILADELPHIA STORY (1940). Ex-husband breaks up ill-conceived

**THE PHILADELPHIA STORY:
Cukor directing James
Stewart and Ruth Hussey**

engagement between former wife and ambitious social climber. *Sc:* Donald Ogden Stewart (the play by Philip Barry). *Ph:* Joseph Ruttenberg. *Art dir:* Cedric Gibbons, Wade B. Rubottom. *Ed:* Frank Sullivan. *Mus:* Franz Waxman. *With* Katharine Hepburn (*Tracy Lord*), Cary Grant (*C. K. Dexter Haven*), James Stewart (*Macaulay Connor*), Ruth Hussey (*Elizabeth Imbrie*), John Howard (*George Kittridge*), Roland Young (*Uncle Willie*), John Halliday (*Seth Lord*), Mary Nash (*Margaret Lord*), Virginia Weider (*Dinah Lord*), Henry Daniell (*Sidney Kidd*), Lionel Pape (*Edward*), Rex Evans (*Thomas*). *Prod:* Joseph L. Mankiewicz for M-G-M. 111m.

A WOMAN'S FACE (1941). Woman falls in love with the plastic surgeon who corrects both her physical and spiritual disfigurement. *Sc:* Donald Ogden Stewart, Elliot Paul (play "Il Etait Une Fois" by Francis de Croisset). *Ph:* Robert Planck. *Art dir:* Cedric Gibbons, Wade B. Rubottom. *Ed:* Frank Sullivan. *Mus:* Bronislau Kaper. *With* Joan Crawford (*Anna Holm*), Melvyn Douglas (*Dr. Gustav Segert*), Conrad Veidt (*Torsten Barring*), Ona Munson (*Vera Segert*), Reginald Owen (*Bernard Dalvik*), Albert Basserman (*Consul Magnus Barring*), Marjorie Main (*Emma Kristiansdotter*), Connie Gilchrist (*Christina Dalvik*), Donald Meek (*Herman Rundvik*), Richard Nichols (*Lars-Eric*), Henry Daniell (*Public Prosecutor*), Charles Quigley (*Eric*), Gwili

A WOMAN'S FACE: Melvyn Douglas and Joan Crawford

Andre (*Gusta*), Clifford Brooks (*Wickman*), George Zucco (*Defense lawyer*), Henry Kolker (*Judge*), Robert Warwick (*Associate Judge*), Gilbert Emery (*Associate Judge*), William Farnum (*Court Attendant*), Sarah Padden (*Police Matron*). *Prod:* Victor Saville for M-G-M. 105m.

TWO-FACED WOMAN (1941). Romance between publisher and ski instructress goes awry when he returns to the city. *Sc:* S. N. Behrman, Salka Viertel, George Oppenheimer (suggested by a play by Ludwig Fulda). *Ph:* Joseph Ruttenberg. *Art dir:* Cedric Gibbons, Daniel B. Cathcart. *Ed:* George Boemler. *Mus:* Bronislau Kaper. *With* Greta Garbo (*Karin*), Melvyn Douglas (*Larry Blake*), Constance Bennett (*Griselda Vaughn*), Roland Young (*Q. Q. Miller*), Robert Sterling (*Dick Williams*), Ruth Gordon (*Miss Ellis*), Frances Carson (*Miss Dunbar*). *Prod:* Gottfried Reinhardt for M-G-M. 95m.

HER CARDBOARD LOVER (1942). Romance between woman and man she hires to impersonate her lover. *Sc:* John Collier, Anthony Veiller, William H. Wright, Jacques Deval (the play by Jacques Deval). *Ph:* Harry Stradling, Robert Planck. *Art dir:* Cedric Gibbons, Randall Duell. *Ed:* Robert J. Kern. *Mus:* Franz Waxman. *Song:* "I Dare You" by Burton Lane and Ralph Freed. *With* Norma Shearer (*Consuelo Croydon*), Robert Taylor (*Terry Trindale*), George Sanders (*Tony Barling*), Frank McHugh (*Chappie Champagne*), Elizabeth Patterson (*Eve*), Chill Wills (*Judge*). *Prod:* J. Walter Ruben for M-G-M. 90m.

KEEPER OF THE FLAME (1942). Reporter discovers that national hero was really a fascist conspirator. *Sc:* Donald Ogden Stewart (the novel by I. A. R. Wylie). *Ph:* William Daniels. *Art dir:* Cedric Gibbons, Lyle Wheeler. *Ed:* James E. Newcombe. *Mus:* Bronislau Kaper. *With* Spencer Tracy (*Steven O'Malley*), Katharine Hepburn (*Christine Forrest*), Richard Whorf (*Clive Kerndon*), Margaret Wycherly (*Mrs. Forrest*), Forrest Tucker (*Geoffrey Midford*), Horace McNally (*Freddie Ridges*), Percy Kilbride (*Orion Peabody), Audrey Christie (Jane Harding), Darryl Hickman (Jeb Rickards), Frank Craven (Dr. Fielding), Donald Meek (Mr. Arbuthnot), Howard da Silva (Jason Rickards), William Newell (Piggot). Prod: Victor Saville for M-G-M. 100m.

GASLIGHT (1944). Husband schemes to drive his wife insane so that he can recover precious jewels she unknowingly possesses. Sc: John Van Druten, Walter Reisch, John L. Balderston (the play "Angel Street" by Patrick Hamilton). Ph: Joseph Ruttenberg. Art dir: Cedric Gibbons, William Ferrari. Ed: Ralph E. Winters. Mus: Bronislau Kaper. With Charles Boyer (Gregory Anton), Ingrid Bergman (Paula Alquist), Joseph Cotten (Brian Cameron), Angela Lansbury (Nancy), Dame May Whitty (Miss Thwaites), Barbara Everest (Elizabeth), Emil Rameau (Maestro Guardi), Edmund Breed (General Huddleston), Halliwell Hobbes (Mr. Mufflin), Tom Stevenson (Williams), Heather Thatcher (Lady Dalroy), Lawrence Grossmith (Lord Dalroy), Jakob Gimpel (Pianist). Prod: Arthur Hornblow for M-G-M. 114m.

WINGED VICTORY (1944). Drama concerning the sober effects of war on a group of enthusiastic young soldiers. Sc: Moss Hart (his play). Ph: Glen MacWilliams. Art dir: Lyle Wheeler, Lewis Creber. Ed: Barbara McLean. Mus: David Rose. With Lon McAllister (Frankie Davis), Jeanne Crain (Helen), Edmond O'Brien (Irving Miller), Judy Holliday (Ruth Miller), Mark Daniels (Alan Ross), Jo-Carroll Dennison (Dorothy Ross), Don Taylor (Danny "Pinky" Scariano), Lee J. Cobb (Doctor), Peter Lind Hayes (O'Brian), Alan Baxter (Major Halper), Red Buttons (Whitey), Barry Nelson (Bobby Grills), Rune Hultman (Dave Anderson), Gary Merrill (Capt. McIntyre), Karl Malden (Adams), George Humbert (Mr. Scariano), Richard Hogan (Jimmy Gardner), George Reeves (Lt. Thompson), George Petrie (Barker), Alfred Ryder (Milhauser), Martin Ritt (Gleason). Prod: Darryl F. Zanuck for Twentieth Century-Fox. 110m.

A DOUBLE LIFE (1947). Actor playing Othello becomes so obsessed with his role that he cannot distinguish his stage character from his own life. Sc: Ruth Gordon and Garson Kanin. Ph: Milton Krasner. Art dir: Bernard Herzbrun, Harvey Gillett. Ed: Robert Parrish. Mus: Miklos Rozsa. With Ronald Colman (Anthony John), Signe Hasso (Brita), Edmond O'Brien (Bill Friend), Shelley Winters (Pat Kroll), Ray Collins (Victor Donlan), Philip Loeb (Max Lasker), Millard Mitchell (Al Cooley), Joe Sawyer (Pete Bonner), Charles La Torre (Stellini), Whit Bissell (Dr. Stauffer), John Drew Colt (stage manager), Peter Thompson (asst. stage manager), Elizabeth Dunne (Gladys), Alan Emiston (Rex), Art Smith, Sid Tomack (wigmakers), Wilton Graff (Dr. Mervin), Harlan Briggs (Oscar Bernard), Claire Carleton (waitress), Betsy Blair, Janet Warren, Marjory Woodworth (girls in wig shop). Prod: Michael Kanin for Universal. 103m.

EDWARD, MY SON (1948). Business man rationalises his unscrupulous methods by claiming that he is doing it all for his son. Sc: Donald Ogden Stewart (the play by Robert Morley and Noel Langley). Ph: Frederick A. Young. Art dir: Alfred Junge. Ed: Raymond Poulton. Mus: John Woolridge. With Spencer Tracy (Arnold Boult), Deborah Kerr (Evelyn Boult), Ian Hunter (Dr. Leary Woodhope), James Donald (Brouthon), Mervyn Johns (Harry Simpkin), Leueen MacGrath (Eileen Perrin), Felix Aylmer (Mr. Hanray), Walter Fitzgerald (Mr. Kedner), Harriette Johns (Phyllis Mayden), Clement McCallin (Sgt. Kenyon), Tilsa Page (Betty Foxley), Ernest Jay (detective), Colin Gordon (Ellerby). Prod: Edwin H. Knopf for M-G-M. 112m.

ADAM'S RIB (1949). Husband and wife lawyer team work against each other in an attempted murder case. Sc: Ruth Gordon and Garson Kanin. Ph: George J. Folsey. Art dir: Cedric Gibbons, William Ferrari. Ed: George Boemler. Mus: Miklos Rozsa. Song: "Farewell, Amanda" by Cole Porter. With Spencer Tracy (Adam Bonner), Katharine Hepburn (Amanda Bonner), Judy Holliday (Doris

Attinger), Tom Ewell (*Warren Attinger*), David Wayne (*Kip Lurie*), Jean Hagen (*Beryl Caighn*), Hope Emerson (*Olympia La Pere*), Clarence Kolb (*Judge Reiser*), Will Wright (*Judge Marcasson*), Elizabeth Flourney (*Dr. Margaret Brodeigh*), Polly Moran (*Mrs. McGrath*), Emerson Treacy (*Jules Fridde*). *Prod:* Lawrence Weingarten for M-G-M. 102m.

A LIFE OF HER OWN (1950). The rise and fall of a fashion model. *Sc:* Isobel Lennart. *Ph:* George Folsey. *Art dir:* Cedric Gibbons, Arthur Lonergan. *Ed:* George White. *Mus:* Bronislau Kaper. *With* Lana Turner (*Lily Brannel Jones*), Ray Milland (*Steve Harleigh*), Tom Ewell (*Tom Caraway*), Ann Dvorak (*Mary Ashlon*), Barry Sullivan (*Lee Gerrance*), Louis Calhern (*Jim Leversoe*), Jean Hagen (*Maggie Collins*), Margaret Phillips (*Nora Harleigh*), Phyllis Kirk (*Jerry*), Sara Hayden (*Smitty*), Hermes Pan (*speciality dancer*). *Prod:* Voldemar Vetluguin for M-G-M. 108m.

BORN YESTERDAY (1950). Not-so-dumb blonde outsmarts junk magnate with whom she has been living and runs off with newspaper reporter. *Sc:* Albert Mannheimer [and Garson Kanin, uncredited] (the play by Garson Kanin). *Ph:* Joseph Walker. *Production Design:* Harry Horner. *Ed:* Charles Nelson. *Mus:* Frederick Hollander. *With* Judy Holliday (*Billie Dawn*), William Holden (*Paul Verrall*), Broderick Crawford (*Harry Brock*), Howard St. John (*Jim Devery*), Frank Otto (*Eddie*), Larry Oliver (*Congressman Hodges*), Barbara Brown (*Mrs. Hodges*), Grandon Rhodes (*Sanborn*), Claire Carleton (*Helen*). *Prod:* S. Sylvan Simon for Columbia. 102m.

THE MODEL AND THE MARRIAGE BROKER (1951). Wise-cracking older woman plays cupid for two young lovers. *Sc*: Charles Brackett, Walter Reisch, Richard Breen. *Ph*: Milton Krasner. *Art dir*: Lyle Wheeler, John De Cuir. *Ed*: Robert Simpson. *Mus*: Cyril Mockridge. *With* Jeanne Crain (*Kitty Bennett*), Scott Brady (*Mat Hornbrook*), Thelma Ritter (*Mae Swazey*), Zero Mostel (*Wixted*), Michael O'Shea (*Doberman*), Helen Ford

(*Emmy Swazey*), Frank Fontaine (*Johannson*), Dennie Moore (*Mrs. Gingras*), John Alexander (*Mr. Perry*), Jay. C. Flippen (*Dan Chancellor*), Maude Prickett (*Delia Seaton*), Ken Christey (*Mr. Kuschner*), Jacqueline French (*Miss Perry*), Edna Mae Wonacott (*Miss Perry*), June Hedin (*Miss Perry*), Shirley Mills (*Ina Kuschner*), Athalie Daniell (*Trudy*), Nancy Kulp (*Hazel*), Bunny Bishop (*Alice*), Dennis Ross (*Joe*), Tommy Noonan (*young clerk*), Eve March (*Miss Eddy*). *Prod:* Charles Brackett for Twentieth Century-Fox. 103m.

THE MARRYING KIND (1951). The death of their first-born severely strains the marriage of a lower-middle-class couple. *Sc:* Ruth Gordon and Garson Kanin. *Ph:* Joseph Walker. *Art dir:* John Meehan. *Ed:* Charles Nelson. *Mus:* Hugh Friedhofer. *With* Judy Holliday (*Florence Keefer*), Aldo Ray (*Chet Keefer*), Madge Kennedy (*Judge Carroll*), Sheila Bond (*Jean Shipley*), John Alexander (*Howard Shipley*), Rex Williams (*George Bastian*), Phyllis Povah (*Mrs. Derringer*), Mickey Shaughnessy (*Pat Bundy*), Peggy Cass (*Emily Bundy*), Griff Barnett (*Charlie*), Susan Hallaran (*Ellen*), Wallace Acton (*Newhouse*), Elsie Homes (*Marian*), Christie Olsen (*Joey, age 4*), Barry Curtis (*Joey, age 6*). *Prod:* Bert Granet for Columbia. 108m.

PAT AND MIKE (1952). Talented amateur athlete turns pro and falls in love with her manager. *Sc:* Ruth Gordon and Garson Kanin. *Ph:* William Daniels. *Art dir:* Cedric Gibbons, Urie McCleary. *Ed:* George Boemler. *Mus:* David Raksin. *With* Spencer Tracy (*Mike Conovan*), Katharine Hepburn (*Pat Pemberton*), Aldo Ray (*Davie Hucko*), William Ching (*Collier Weld*), Sammy White (*Barney Grau*), George Matthews (*Spec Cauley*), Loring Smith (*Mr. Beminger*), Phyllis Povah (*Mrs. Beminger*), Charles Buchinski [Bronson] (*Hank Tasling*), Jim Backus (*Charles Barry*), Frank Richards (*Sam Garsell*), Chuck Connors (*Police Captain*), Owen McGivency (*Harry McWade*), Joseph E. Bernard (*Gibby,*), Lou Lubin (*Walter*), Carl Switzer (*bus boy*), William Self (*Pat Pemberton's caddy*), Gussie

Moran, Don Budge, Frank Parker, Beverly Hanson, Babe Didrikson Zaharias, Alice Marble, Betty Hicks, Helen Dettweiler. *Prod:* Lawrence Weingarten for M-G-M. 95m.

THE ACTRESS (1953). A fledgling thespian convinces her conservative father to let her study acting in New York. *Sc:* Ruth Gordon (her play "Years Ago").*Ph:* Harold Rosson.*Art dir:* Cedric Gibbons, Arthur Lonergan. *Ed:* George Boemler. *Mus:* Bronislau Kaper. *With* Spencer Tracy (*Clinton Jones*), Jean Simmons (*Ruth Gordon Jones*), Teresa Wright (*Annie Jones*), Anthony Perkins (*Fred Whitmarsh*), Ian Wolfe (*Mr. Bagley*), Kay Williams (*Hazel Dawn*), Mary Wickes (*Emma Glavey),* Norma Jean Nilsson (*Anna*), Dawn Bender (*Katherine*). *Prod:* Lawrence Weingarten for M-G-M. 90m.

IT SHOULD HAPPEN TO YOU (1954). A nobody becomes a somebody when she advertises her name on a giant billboard in Columbus Circle. *Sc:* Garson Kanin, *Ph:* Charles Lang. *Art dir:* John Meehan.*Ed:* Charles Nelson.*Mus:* Frederick Hollander. *With* Judy Holliday (*Gladys Glover*), Peter Lawford (*Evan Adams*), Jack Lemmon (*Peter Sheppard*), Michael O'Shea (*Brad Clinton*), Vaughn Taylor (*Entrikin*), Connie Gilchrist (*Mrs. Riker*), Walter Klavun (*Bert Piazza*), Whit Bissell (*Robert Grau*), Arthur Gilmore (*Don Toddman*), Rex Evans (*Cooley*), Heywood Hale Broun (*Sour man*), Constance Bennett, Ilka Chase, Wendy Barrie, Melville Cooper (*TV panelists*). *Prod:* Fred Kohlmar for Columbia. 100m.

A STAR IS BORN (1954). The paths of two stars—one on the way up and the other on the way down—cross. *Sc:* Moss Hart (the screenplay of the 1937 film by Dorothy Parker, Alan Campbell, and Robert Carson based on a story by William Wellman and Robert Carson). *Ph:* Sam Leavitt. *Special colour advisor:* George Hoyningen-Huene. *Art dir:* Malcolm Bert [for the "Born in a Trunk" sequence, Irene Sharaff]. *Production Design:* Gene Allen. *Ed:*Folmar Blangsted. *Dance direction:* Richard Barstow. *Musical direction:* Ray Heindorf. *Songs:* Harold Arlen, Ira Gershwin; "Born in a Trunk" by Leonard Gershe. *With* Judy Garland (*Esther Blodgett/Vicki Lester*), James Mason (*Norman Maine*), Charles Bickford (*Oliver Niles*), Jack Carson (*Matt Libby*), Tommy Noonan (*Danny McGuire*), Irving Bacon (*Graves*), Lucy Marlow (*Lola Lavery*), Amanda Blake (*Susan*), James Brown (*Glen Williams*), Hazel Shermet (*Libby's secretary*), Lotus Bobb (*Miss Markham*). *Prod:* Sidney Luft for Warners Bros. 182m [cut to 140m]. Technicolor. CinemaScope.

BHOWANI JUNCTION (1956). An Anglo-Indian woman seeks to establish her own identity in rebel-torn India. *Sc:* Sonya Levien and Ivan Moffat (the novel by John Masters). *Ph:* Frederick A. Young. *Colour consultant:* George Hoyningen-Huene. *Art dir:* Gene Allen, John Howell. *Ed:* Frank Clark, George Boemler. *Mus:* Miklos Rosza. *With* Ava Gardner *(Victoria Jones),* Stewart Granger *(Col. Rodney Savage),* Bill Travers *(Patrick Taylor),* Lionel Jeffries *(Lt. Graham McDaniel),* Abraham Sofaer (*Surabhai*), Francis Matthews (*Ranjit Kasel*), Peter Illing (*Ghanshyam, "Davay"*), Freda Jackson (*the Sadani*), Edward Chapman (*Thomas Jones*), Alan Tilvera (*Ted Dunphy*), Marne Maitland (*Govindaswami*). *Prod:* Pandro S. Berman for M-G-M. 109m. Eastman Color. CinemaScope.

LES GIRLS (1957). The comic and romantic adventures of three dancers and their manager. *Sc:* John Patrick (a story by Vera Caspary). *Ph:* Robert Surtees. *Colour Co-ordination:* George Hoyningen-Huene. *Art dir:* William A. Horning, Gene Allen. *Ed:* Ferris Webster. *Music and lyrics:* Cole Porter. *Choreography:* Jack Cole. *With* Gene Kelly (*Barry Nichols*), Mitzi Gaynor (*Joy Henderson*), Kay Kendall (*Lady Sybil Wren*), Taina Elg (*Angele Ducros*), Jacques Bergerac (*Pierre Ducros*), Leslie Phillips (*Sir Gerald Wren*), Henry Daniell (*Judge*), Patrick Macnee (*Sir Percy*). *Prod:* Sol C. Siegel for M-G-M. 114m. Metrocolor. CinemaScope.

WILD IS THE WIND (1957). Rancher marries his late wife's sister and finds her to be much different from his first one. *Sc:* Arnold Schulman (a story by Vittorio Nino Novarese). *Ph:* Charles Lang Jr. *Art dir:* Hal Pereira, Tambi Larsen. *Ed:* Warren Low. *Mus:* Dimitri Tiomkin. *With* Anna Magnani (*Gloria*), Anthony Quinn (*Gino*), Anthony Franciosa (*Bene*), Dolores Hart (*Angie*), Joseph Calleia (*Alberto*), Lili Valenty (*Teresa*). *Prod:* Hal B. Wallis for Paramount. 110m. VistaVision.

HELLER IN PINK TIGHTS (1960). Theatrical troupe tours the Old West. *Sc:* Dudley Nichols, Walter Bernstein (a novel by Louis L'Amour). *Ph:* Harold Lipstein. *Colour Co-ordinator:* George Hoyningen-Huene. *Art dir:* Hal Pereira, Eugene Allen. *Ed:* Howard Smith. *Mus:* Daniel Amfitheatrof. *With* Anthony Quinn (*Tom Healy*), Sophia Loren (*Angela Rossini*), Eileen Heckart (*Lorna Hathaway*), Margaret O'Brien (*Della Southby*), Ramon Navarro (*De Leon*), Steve Forrest (*Mabry*), Edmund Lowe (*Manfred "Doc" Montague*), George Matthews (*Sam Pierce*), Frank Cordell (*Theodore*). *Prod:* Carlo Ponti and Marcello Girosi for Paramount. 100m. Technicolor.

LET'S MAKE LOVE (1960). Billionaire falls in love with voluptuous neophyte actress. *Sc:* Norman Krasna (additional material by Hal Kanter). *Ph:* Daniel L. Fapp. *Colour Co-ordinator:* George Hoyninger-Huene. *Art dir:* Lyle Wheeler, Gene Allen. *Ed:* David Bretherton. *Musical dir:* Lionel Newman, Earle H. Hagen. *Songs:* Sammy Cahn and James Van Heusen; "My Heart Belongs to Daddy" by Cole Porter. *With* Marilyn Monroe (*Amanda Pell*), Yves Montand (*Jean-Marc Clement*), Tony Randall (*Howard Coffman*), Frankie Vaughn (*Tony Danton*), Wilfred Hyde-White (*John Wales*), David Burns (*Oliver Burton*), Michael David (*Dave Kerry*), Mara Lynn (*Lily Nyles*), Dennis King Jr. (*Abe Miller*), Milton Berle, Gene Kelly, and Bing Crosby (*as themselves*). *Prod:* Jerry Wald for Twentieth Century-Fox. 119m. De Luxe Colour. CinemaScope

THE CHAPMAN REPORT (1962). Investigation of sexual problems of a group of surburban housewives. *Sc:* Wyatt Cooper, Don M. Mankicwicz (adaptation by Grant Stuart and Gene Allen of the novel by Irving Wallace). *Ph:* Harold Lipstein. *Colour Co-ordination:* George Hoyningen-Huene. *Production Design:* Gene Allen. *Ed:* Robert Simpson. *With* Efrem Zimbalist Jr. (*Paul Radford*), Shelley Winters (*Sarah Garnell*), Jane Fonda (*Kathleen Barclay*), Claire Bloom (*Naomi Shields*), Glynis Johns (*Teresa Harnish*), Ray Danton (*Fred Linden*), Ty Hardin (*Ed Kaski*), Andrew Duggan (*Dr. George C. Chapman*), John Dehner (*Geoffrey Harnish*), Harold J. Stone (*Frank Garnell*), Corey Allen (*Wash Dillon*), Jennifer Howard (*Grace Waterton*), Chad Everett (*delivery boy*), Henry Daniell (*Dr. Jonas*), Cloris Leachman (*Miss Selby*). *Prod:* Richard D. Zanuck for Warner Bros. 125m. Technicolor.

MY FAIR LADY (1964). Musical adaptation of Bernard Shaw's play, "Pygmalion". *Sc:* Alan Jay Lerner (the musical comedy by Alan Jay Lerner and Frederick Lowe and the play "Pygmalion" by George Bernard Shaw). *Ph:* Harry Stradling. *Art dir:* Gene Allen. *Sets, Costumes and Production Design;* Cecil Beaton. *Ed:* William Ziegler. *Musical Dir:* Andre Previn. *Music and lyrics:* Frederick Loewe and Alan Jay Lerner. *With* Audrey Hepburn (*Eliza Doolittle*), Rex Harrison (*Prof. Henry Higgins*), Stanley Holloway (*Alfred P. Doolittle*), Wilfred Hyde-White (*Colonel Pickering*), Gladys Cooper (*Mrs. Higgins*), Jeremy Brett (*Freddie Eynsford-Hill*), Theodore Bikel (*Zoltan Karpathy*), Mona Washbourne (*Mrs. Pearce*), Isobel Elson (*Mrs. Eynsford-Hill*), John Holland (*Butler*), Henry Daniell (*Queen's chamberlain*), John Alderson (*Doolittle's friend*), John McLiam (*Doolittle's friend*). *Prod:* Jack L. Warner for Warner Bros. 170m. Technicolor. Super Panavision 70.

JUSTINE (1969). Romance and intrigue in modern day Alexandria. *Sc:* Lawrence B. Marcus (the four novels of the *Alexandria Quartet* by Lawrence Durrell). *Ph:* Leon Shamroy. *Art dir:* Jack Martin Smith, William Creber and Fred

Harpman. *Ed:* Rita Roland. *Mus:* Jerry
Goldsmith. *With* Anouk Aimée (*Justine*),
Dirk Bogarde (*Pursewarden*), Robert
Forster (*Narouz*), Anna Karina (*Melissa*),
Philippe Noiret (*Pombal*), Michael York
(*Darley*), John Vernon (*Nessim*), Jack Al-
bertson (*Cohen*), Cliff Gorman (*Toto*),
George Baker (*Mountolive*), Elaine
Church (*Liza*), Michael Constantine
(*Memlik Pasha*), Marcel Dalio (*French Con-
sul General*), Michael Dunn (*Mnemjian*),
Barry Morse (*Maskelyne*), Severn Darden
(*Balthazar*), Anapola Del Vando (*Mrs.
Serapamoun*), Abraham Sofaer (*proprie-
tor*), Peter Mamakos (*Kawass*), Stanley
Waxman (*Serapamoun*). *Prod:* Pandro S.
Berman for Twentieth Century-Fox.
116m. De Luxe Colour. Panavision.
(Cukor replaced Joseph Strick as the
director of the film.)
TRAVELS WITH MY AUNT (1972).
Staid London banker joins his aunt in a
trans-European adventure. *Sc:* Jay Al-
len, Hugh Wheeler (the novel by
Graham Greene). *Ph:* Douglas
Slocombe. *Production design:* John Box.
Ed: John Bloom. *Mus:* Tony Hatch. *With*
Maggie Smith (*Augusta*), Alec McCowen
(*Henry*), Lou Gossett (*Wordsworth*),
Robert Stephens (*Visconti*), Cindy Wil-
liams (*Tooley*), Jose Louis Lopez Vasquez
(*M. Dambreuse*), Valerie White (*Mme.
Dambreuse*), Corinne Marchand (*Louise*),
Raymond Gerone (*Mario*), Daniel Emil-
fork (*Hakim*), Robert Flemyng (*Crowder*),
Aldo Sanbrell (*Hakim's assistant*), David
Swift (*detective*), Antonio Pica (*elegant
man*), Charlie Bravo (*policeman*), Cass
Martin (*skipper of boat*), Olive Behrend
(*Madame in Messagero*), Javier Escriva
(*dancer in Messagero*). *Prod:* Robert Fryer,
James Cresson for M-G-M. 109m.
LOVE AMONG THE RUINS (1975).
An older woman is sued for breach of
promise by a young man and is defended
by a lawyer with whom she once had a
love affair. *Sc:* James Costigan. *Ph:*
Douglas Slocombe. *Art dir:* Carmen Dil-
lon. *Ed:* John F. Burnett. *Mus:* John
Barry. *With* Katharine Hepburn (*Jessica
Medicott*), Laurence Olivier (*Sir Arthur
Granville-Jones*), Colin Blakely (*J. F. De-
vine*), Richard Pearson (*Druve*), Joan

Sims (*Fanny Pratt*), Leigh Lawson (*Alfred
Pratt*), Gwen Nelson (*Hermione Davis*),
Robert Harris (*The Judge*), Peter Reeves
(*Malden*), John Blythe (*Tipstaff*), Arthur
Hewlett (*The Usher*), John Dunbar (*clerk
of the court*), Ian Sinclair (*Pratt's solicitor*).
Prod: Allan Davis for ABC Entertain-
ment. 120m.

THE BLUE BIRD (1976). A brother and
sister search for the Blue Bird of Happi-
ness. *Sc:* Hugh Whitmore, Alfred Hayes
(the play by Maurice Maeterlinck). *Ph:*
Ionas Gritaus, Freddie Young. *Art dir:*
Valery Urkevich. *Ed:* Ernest Walter,
Tatyana Shapiro. *Mus:* Andrei Petrov,
Irwin Kostal. *With* Elizabeth Taylor
(*Mother/Maternal Love/Witch/Light*),
Jane Fonda (*Night*), Cicely Tyson (*Cat*),
Ava Gardner (*Luxury*), Todd Lookinland
(*Tyttyl*), Patsy Kensit (*Mytyl*), Will Geer
(*Grandfather*), Mona Washbourne
(*Grandmother*), Robert Morley (*Father
Time*), Harry Andrews (*Oak*), George
Cole (*Dog*), Richard Pearson (*Bread*),
Nadejeda Pavlova (*The Blue Bird*), Mar-
gareta Terechova (*Milk*), Oleg Popov
(*The Clown*), Georgi Vitzin (*Sugar*),
Leonid Nevedomsky (*Father*), Valentine
Ganilaee Ganibalova (*Water*), Yevgeny
Scherbakov (*Fire*), Steven Warner,
Monique Kaufman, Russell Lewis, Grant
Bardsley and Ann Mannion (*Children of
the future*), Pheona McLellan (*Sick girl*).
Prod: Edward Lewis, Paul Maslansky for
Lenfilm Studios/Twentieth Century-
Fox. 97m. De Luxe Colour.

Other projects:

When Cukor first came to Hollywood
he worked as a dialogue director on two
films: *River of Romance* (1929) and *All
Quiet on the Western Front* (1930).
Cukor began a Lubitsch-produced
comedy, *One Hour with You* (1932), but
was removed after two weeks following
disagreements with the producer.
In 1939 Cukor spent several months
preparing for *Gone with the Wind* and
directed the film for three weeks before
being replaced by Victor Fleming.
Cukor directed *Desire Me* (1946) which
was extensively reshot by Mervyn LeRoy.

Cukor disowns the film.

Cukor completed *Song Without End* (1959) when Charles Vidor died after a month of shooting. Cukor did not claim a screen credit.

Something's Got to Give (1962) was abandoned after three weeks because of problems involving its star, Marilyn Monroe.

Between the completion of *My Fair Lady* (1964) and *Justine* (1969), Cukor was involved in a number of projects which, for a variety of reasons, did not get off the ground. These include:

Casanova's Homecoming to star Rex Harrison in a story of the renowned gentleman's later years, *Peter Pan* with Audrey Hepburn, and a film biography of Virginia Woolf.

Sources for the Cukor filmography: Tom Vallance, *International Film Guide 1977*, ed. Peter Cowie (London: Tantivy; New York: Barnes, 1976), pp. 41-47; Barbara Helen Battle, "George Cukor and the American Theatrical Film," Ph. D. dissertation, Columbia University, 1969; and the credits from the films themselves.

CLARENCE BROWN

If the phrase "Hollywood Professional" denotes a craftsman or workman who is more concerned with producing solid entertainment than with expressing his own personal preoccupations, then Clarence Brown comes closer to meeting the designation than either Capra or Cukor. Capra was too independent and too imaginative to have made anything as dreary as *The Gorgeous Hussy* (1936), Cukor was too sophisticated and too skilled with actors to make something as awkward as *Idiot's Delight* (1939); Brown was just enough of a "company man" to have made them both. In certain film to film comparisons Brown would not fare too well against either of the other two. *The Bitter Tea of General Yen* (1932) and *The Son-Daughter* (1932) are both films with an oriental setting which attempt to deal with oriental philosophy, but Capra's film must unquestionably be ranked the better of the two. When *Conquest* (1937) is placed alongside *Camille* (1936) (both films starring Greta Garbo), Brown's film seems stilted and stuffy in comparison. Even *Anna Karenina* (1935), another Brown-Garbo film, and much better than *Conquest,* does not equal Cukor's exquisite portrait of a woman doomed to destroy herself for love. In his reference book. "A Biographical Dictionary of the Cinema," David Thomson asserts that any attempt to elevate Brown to the pantheon of American film directors will inevitably fail if Brown is matched against Cukor.[1] On the basis of the examples I have given, Thomson's assertion would seem to be indisputable. On the other hand, one wonders whether if Cukor had directed silent films, he could have matched the expressionistic visual poetry of *Flesh and the Devil* (1927) or *Woman of Affairs* (1929); and clearly *National Velvet* (1944) and *The Yearling* (1946) both compare favourably with two of Cukor's best "family" films, *David Copperfield* (1934) and *Little Women* (1933). Similarly, *Intruder in the Dust* (1949) penetrates as far into the psyche of the common man as any of Capra's films. Who is the best director of the three? Certainly, Brown made more bad films than either Cukor or Capra. In fact, his entire output of the Thirties is virtually a critical blank. But to look at Brown's best work closely—his silent classics, his gentle and understanding portraits of the passage from adolescence to young adulthood, his incisive pre-1950 treatment of blacks and whites living together in the South, his incomparable individual moments in *Anna Christie* (1930), *A Free Soul* (1931), *Sadie McKee* (1934), *Ah, Wilderness* (1935), *Of Human Hearts* (1938), and *The Human Comedy* (1943)—is inevitably to come to the realisation that at his best Brown can compare favourably with any director in the American cinema.

Along with actor John Gilbert, Brown wrote the scenario for his first film, *The Great Redeemer* (1920), and another early work, *The Light in the Dark* (1922), but did not participate in the writing of any of his films thereafter. Consequently, he cannot be considered the author of his films in the European sense. But like Cukor, Brown made his influence felt in other equally important ways and his best films can be clearly distinguished as his own. He spent ten years as a silent director before moving into sound, and before that worked for five years as Maurice Tourneur's assistant. Although a silent director worked from a reasonably detailed scenario, since he directed the movements of the actors and the camera while a scene was in progress, he necessarily gave each scene his own definition. In other words, the scenario worked primarily as an outline from which the director filled in the relevant details. And, since silent films were pictures without words, everything rotated around the director's ability to communicate the story visually, something at which Brown was a master. In *Smouldering Fires* (1925), for example, the fact that Brown's female protagonist has entered into an ill-fated marriage with a man who does not love her is deftly suggested by the way Brown directs the wedding ceremony. First, he creates a disturbing effect by filming the bride and groom from the waist down as they kneel at the altar. The newlyweds then rise but the camera remains stationary so that we can only see their legs and feet. The groom's feet are fidgety. The wedding ring drops from his hand; he picks it up, drops it again, picks it up again.

Brown acquired his sense of visual style from his mentor, Maurice Tourneur, one of the first directors to explore the compositional possibilities of the cinema. Tourneur was a painter before he became a film-maker and was fascinated by the use of light to create tone and depth in a motion picture frame, a fascination Brown also acquired. Brown constantly sought new ways to use light, and he achieved some of the most stunning chiaroscuro effects to be found in the American cinema: the seduction scene in the garden and the duel in silhouette in *Flesh and the Devil* (1927), the heavy shadows surrounding Anna and Vronsky as they quarrel before attending the opera in *Anna*

Karenina, and the midnight ride to Vinson Gowrie's grave in *Intruder in the Dust* comprise only a few examples of Brown's genius.

In addition to seeking new ways to light his films, Brown sought to keep his camera as mobile as possible. His silent films are as noteworthy for the way in which the director moves his camera as for the way in which he composes his frames—for example, the bold opening of *Woman of Affairs,* where the camera follows Diana Merrick's reckless drive down a country road, or Dubrovsky's dramatic rescue of Mascha in *The Eagle* (1925). Striking examples of camera mobility are also to be found in his sound work: the opening of *A Free Soul* (1931), in which the camera moves from outside the Ashes' apartment into the living room, the tracking shot which reveals a sumptuous banquet table in *Anna Karenina* (1935), the spectacular horse race in *National Velvet* (1944), and Jody and Flag running through the forest in *The Yearling* (1946). Intertwined with his concern for a mobile camera is a preference for exterior and location shooting, a preference which extended through his career as a contract director for MGM in the Thirties and Forties when nearly everything the studio produced was recreated on sound stages. For his now "lost" epic, *The Trail of '98* (1929), a story about the Alaskan gold rush, the director went to a location just north of Denver at the Great Divide to recreate the Chilkoot Pass. The hardships Brown and his crew endured in making this film are legendary. Working at eleven thousand feet for five weeks, they battled temperatures that were nearly always below zero, sometimes falling to sixty below, and fierce winds that destroyed sets. Cameras had to be specially heated so that they would not freeze, but could not be made warm enough to prevent electrostatic flashes from registering on the negative. And despite precautions, several crew members were killed in accidents during filming. Twenty years later, for *The Yearling,* Brown went to the Everglades and locations in Florida where he had to deal with heat almost as pernicious as the cold of the Rockies.

Brown's *mise-en-scène* is in itself enough to provoke an interest in the director's career, but his films offer much more than brilliant technical feats. Less self-consciously than Capra, certainly, Brown nevertheless reveals thematic preoccupations that can be found consistently throughout his work. That he made fifty-one films in the space of thirty-two years demonstrates that he took considerable care with each of his productions, often directing only one or two films a year. Throughout his association with MGM, which lasted from 1927 till the end of his career in 1952, Brown had freedom to select his own stories. Occasionally, he bought story properties himself, as with *Of Human Hearts* and *The White Cliffs of Dover*. Furthermore, Brown (who had learned to edit under Tourneur) also supervised the editing of nearly all his films.

In terms of his thematic preoccupations, Brown's career divides itself more or less neatly into two phases. The first (and lesser known because it includes most of his silent career and therefore films not often seen) concerns the trials of female protagonists, women who often love not wisely but too well, and who after too many disappointments develop a fine hatred for the male sex, a hatred sometimes mitigated by the conclusion of the film and sometimes not. In all of the following films—*Smouldering Fires* (1924), *The Goose Woman* (1925), *Kiki* (1926), *Flesh and the Devil* (1927), *A Woman of Affairs* (1929)—all silent—and *Anna Christie* (1930), *Romance* (1930), *Inspiration* (1931), *A Free Soul* (1931), *Possessed* (1931), *Emma* (1932), *Letty Lynton* (1932), *Sadie McKee* (1934), *Chained* (1934), and *Anna Karenina* (1935)—the female protagonist is intelligent and high-spirited like Cukor's heroines. In fact, Brown might be considered Cukor's predecessor as the premier "woman's director" in Hollywood, not only because he was renowned for his handling of female stars, but because his early films also deal with the problems of the heroine rather than the hero. But, unlike Cukor, whose women cautiously guard their independence, Brown usually depicts female protagonists who become incautiously involved with men whose weaknesses destroy them, or nearly so. Such proves the case with the heroines of *Smouldering Fires, A Woman of Affairs, Sadie McKee* and *Anna Karenina,* all of whom fall in love with men who do not prove worthy of their trust. Brown's women, like Cukor's, have to struggle against social conventions in their effort to achieve happiness, conventions which prove so strong that they are seldom overcome. Events, usually male directed, seem to conspire against the director's heroines, a conspiracy that is crystallised in *The Son-Daughter* where a Chinese-American father agrees to sell his daughter to the highest bidder and destroys not only her happiness, but eventually his own life, in the name of a revolution in the homeland. In short, for Brown it is truly a grim world for an intellectual and free-spirited woman who seeks to live her own life, a world that ends in suicide for the heroines of *A Woman of Affairs* and *Anna Karenina,* and emotional suicide for many of the others. Yet intriguingly, while Brown's female protagonists frequently pursue romance, often self-destructively, one might detect in many of them an ill-concealed contempt for the male sex. This is best seen in *The Eagle* in which the Czarina, the one Brown woman who is really in a position of power, indulges her lusts by taking sexual favours from selected members of her palace guard in exchange for granting them military promotions; and in *Flesh and the Devil* where the female protagonist, this time ostensibly the villain of the story, moves from one wealthy lover to the next, meanwhile cleverly arranging events so that her new lover will kill the one she has grown tired of. Perhaps the key difference between the two directors, finally, is that Brown never works himself up to a sense of that delicate balance between male and female we find in Cukor's films like *Adam's Rib* and *Pat and Mike.*

Around 1935, a perceptible shift of emphasis in the subject matter of Brown's films can be discerned. Beginning with *Ah, Wilderness!* (1935), there is more marked interest within his films in various aspects of Americana. It is interesting to note that this occurred about the same time Cukor began to replace Brown as Hollywood's foremost director of female stars. After 1935, it was Cukor more often than Brown whom Garbo, Shearer, Crawford and other of M-G-M's leading ladies sought to direct their films. It should also be pointed out, however, that Brown's strong interest in Americana actually goes back well before 1935. In 1921, he co-directed with Maurice Tourneur *The Last of the Mohicans*, still considered to be the best film adaptation of Cooper's novel. And in 1928 when he had several properties to select from, he chose to make *The Trail of '98* rather than something more consistent with the drift of his current work. But after 1935 his interest in native American subjects intensified and he made a series of films on various phases of American history—the pilgrims' crossing in *Plymouth Adventure* (1952), the Civil War in *Of Human Hearts* (1938), the career of Thomas Edison in *Edison, the Man* (1939)—and on various American epochs—the administration of Andrew Jackson in *The Gorgeous Hussy* (1936), the turn of the century in *Ah, Wilderness!*, World War Two in *The Human Comedy* (1943). Like others who have dealt with Americana, such as Henry King and John Ford, Brown takes substantial liberties at times with the facts of the histories he dramatised. But in his better, more enduring films such as *The Yearling* and *Intruder in the Dust*, the director could be unflinchingly honest in his understanding of the realities of time and place.

Strong female characters appear in nearly all these films—in *The Gorgeous Hussy*, Brown deals (though not very effectively) with the rise and fall of a 19th century feminist; but it is not on the female mind on which Brown focuses here, but on youth on the verge of young adulthood. Richard in *Ah, Wilderness*, Homer in *The Human Comedy*, Chick in *Intruder in the Dust* are all in their middle teens; Velvet Brown in *National Velvet* is thirteen, Jody in *The Yearling* twelve. These characters are all moving out of childhood and adolescence into a new, expanded sense of maturity in which they have to come to grips with certain realities that have been kept from them as children. The director's young protagonists ask hard questions and expect honest answers, and in each case a parent or a close relative, generally laconic and forthright, points them in the right direction.

The genuine sympathy and understanding Brown demonstrated for the problems his young heroes face reflected itself in the skill with which he handled young actors; so much so that, in effect, while Cukor was usurping Brown's former title as Hollywood's premier woman's director, Brown established himself as the foremost director of young actors. As a director of silent films, Brown often worked with neophyte film actors who under his guidance developed into major stars. Greta Garbo and Louise Dresser are two examples. In the early Thirties Brown continued to develop new talent; Clark Gable, for instance, received his "big break" in *A Free Soul*. But more often, as the Thirties wore on, Brown worked with established stars such as Garbo, Norma Shearer, Joan Crawford and Helen Hayes. Their films were primarily showcases for their screen personas. Brown saw it as his function to enhance these personas, and in doing so made the star the justification for the film rather than merely an integral part of it. Consequently, Brown's own position as the person responsible for the quality of the production diminished, and so in a sense did his identity as film director. It is not surprising, then, that the quality of Brown's work reaches its nadir during the Thirties when he guided the course of expensive, often ostentatious "star vehicles" like *Wife versus Secretary* or *Conquest*. Perhaps we ought to view Brown's shift after 1935 to films involving young actors in the lead roles as an effort to regain his artistic integrity: when directing young actors like Elizabeth Taylor or Claude Jarman, he was working with "raw material" which he could fashion to fit his needs. He had no responsibilities to the young actors' screen personas other than what he himself dictated. And so it is indeed the case that Brown's best sound films—*Ah, Wilderness, National Velvet, The Yearling* and *Intruder in the Dust*—all involve young heroes played by actors who had little or no screen experience.

In the characters these young actors portray, Brown identified what he saw as the best qualities of the American spirit: a constructive

**Spring Byington, Bonita Granville, Frank Albertson,
Eric Linden and Lionel Barrymore in AH, WILDERNESS! (1935)**

curiosity, strong ambition, an indomitable will, an intuitive grasp of
the difference between right and wrong, and a certain healthy
ingenuousness. The willingness to dare against long odds, to fight for
what they believe to be right, to combat ignorance, all qualities which
Brown highlighted in his female protagonists can also be found in his
youthful heroes. And if one thing can be said for all of Brown's
protagonists it is that they never turn their back on a good fight: Diana
battles moribund social conventions in *A Woman of Affairs* as commit-
tedly as Velvet trains the Pi for the Grand National in *National Velvet*.

★   ★   ★

Clarence Brown was born in Clinton, Massachusetts, on May 10,
1890. His father was a loom-repairer and his mother a weaver. His

family moved freely about the country until Brown was eleven, when they settled in Knoxville, Tennessee, where Brown's father managed a cotton mill. Brown, like Capra, proved something of a child prodigy, and at fifteen received special permission to enter the University of Tennessee. Four years later he graduated with two degrees, in electrical and mechanical engineering. The elder Brown wanted his son to join him in the cotton business, but the new graduate had taken a passionate interest in automobiles and became a top mechanic for a company based in Moline, Illinois. In the course of his work Brown moved extensively throughout the country, and, as with Capra, his travels gave him an insight into the American people that he would later apply to his work. In 1912 Brown established his own automobile dealership in Birmingham, Alabama, and soon built a thriving concern. While in Birmingham, he became fascinated by nickelodeons. He was particularly impressed by the films which came from Peerless Studios where Maurice Tourneur was the mainstay. After observing the development of motion pictures for several years, Brown finally decided to become involved in the new industry. He sold his automobile company and travelled to Fort Lee, New Jersey, where Peerless was located, to see Tourneur. On his way to visit the director he heard that Tourneur had just fired an assistant and needed a new one. Brown found the director on location and immediately offered his services. Tourneur inquired as to his experience; Brown admitted he had none, but impressed the director with his eagerness to learn. Tourneur was intrigued. Perhaps he saw in Brown the same burning ambition and curiosity that had brought himself to films. In any case, he needed a new assistant, and the automobile dealer was hired at a salary of $30 a week.

Brown remained with Tourneur for five years, during which he became the director's confidant and *protégé*. Even now Brown refers to Tourneur with genuine reverence and attributes to his mentor a great deal of credit for his own success. Within a few months after starting his new job, Brown became Tourneur's editor and also wrote titles. Tourneur did not like shooting exteriors because of the vagaries in lighting conditions, so soon Brown also began to function, in effect, as a second unit director filming the open air scenes with his own cameraman and crew.

When war broke out, he joined the Army's new air corps where he became a flying cadet and later a flying instructor. When the war ended, he rejoined Tourneur and in 1920 directed his first film, *The Great Redeemer*, in which a convicted murderer "gets religion" (significantly enough, by the virtue of some clever lighting) at the eleventh hour and goes to his execution a happy man. Brown filmed the story with his own "second unit" crew. Despite everyone's relative inexperience or perhaps because of it, *The Great Redeemer* enjoyed considerable success. Brown, however, did not immediately venture out on his own, but remained with Tourneur to co-direct two more films—*The Last of the Mohicans* (of which Brown actually shot three-quarters, because Tourneur became ill during filming) and *Foolish Matrons* (1921)—for which he received co-direction billing but none of the credit for the film's artistry. But if film reviewers did not yet recognise Brown's particular talents, those within the industry did and in 1922 Brown finally split with Tourneur to make *Light in the Dark* with Hope Hampton for First National. In the film Brown tried to innovate a new colour process. His experiment intrigued reviewers but because of technical difficulties did not catch on with other film-makers. By the spring of 1923, Carl Laemmle of Universal Pictures was sufficiently impressed with Brown's work to sign him to a five-picture contract that called for the director to receive $12,500 per film.

In two years Brown completed four successful features for Laemmle—*The Acquittal* (1923), a courtroom drama with a scenario by Jules Furthman; *The Signal Tower* (1924), a drama about railroad life; *Butterfly* (1924), a romantic melodrama; and the fourth, *Smouldering Fires*, which is the first of his films that can be readily seen today. It demonstrates just how well the young director had absorbed both Tourneur's imaginative cinematic style and penchant for symbolism. The opening scene in which Brown cleverly outlines the nature of the film's heroine, Jane Vale (Pauline Frederick), illustrates the skill and seeming ease with which the director was able to communicate ideas visually. He begins with a close-up of Jane's feet tapping the floor; her shoes are styleless like those of a man. Quick fade to her hand pounding a desk; her sleeve looks to be that of a man's garment. Then a full shot (the first time we actually see her) as she issues orders to the men who manage her clothing factory. She is wearing a jacket and tie and her hair is tightly bundled in the back. All that Brown wishes us to know about Jane at this point is revealed—that she is a woman devoid of any obvious feminine charms who acts with the authority of a man, and commands the same respect that any executive in her position would.

The plot of *Smouldering Fires* is a conventional love triangle with an interesting twist: the heroine is not a beautiful young starlet but a middle aged woman who is the owner and president of a thriving clothing company. Brown does not attempt to artificially enhance Frederick's physical attractiveness, but in fact chooses to accentuate her rather formless figure and plain face. As the opening scene further suggests, Jane is a career woman who would appear to have no romantic interest in men and actually has a thinly veiled contempt for them. One day, however, she encounters an ambitious young employee, Rob (Malcolm McGregor), and becomes infatuated with him. She elevates the young man to a position on the managing board of the factory. Although intrigued with her, the ingenuous new manager is unaware of the depth of Jane's feeling for him. Their "affair" soon becomes a joke among factory employees. Rob gets into a fight with one of the workers and heatedly announces to everyone that he and Jane are planning to be married. When Jane learns of his announcement Rob decides that it would now only be "honourable" to marry her. After their engagement, Jane's beautiful young sister, Dorothy (Laura La Plante), comes home from college. For Rob it is love at first sight. After a little resistance, Dorothy soon falls in love with him, too. Neither, however, has the courage to tell Jane of their mutual love. Rob and Jane are married, but Dorothy and Rob's affection for each other does not diminish. Jane eventually learns of her sister's love for her husband, and in a gesture of altruism gives him up to her.

In this film, as in all his best work, Brown uses recurring symbols and images to create a certain resonance and establish a distinct tempo. Here, for instance, two "threads" are drawn throughout the film. Consider firstly Jane's wardrobe. She dresses like a man and also acts like one. After she falls foolishly in love with Rob, she makes a considerable effort to alter her appearance; she begins to wear heavy make-up and flapper dresses and acts like the proverbial schoolgirl. At the conclusion she is dressed tastefully as a mature woman might be, and so her final action suggests newly acquired wisdom and compassion, as well as an expanded sense of herself as a woman. Secondly, consider the way in which Brown composes his film during several key scenes. When Dorothy first arrives home from Brwyn Mawr, Brown sets her off in a single shot and Rob and Jane in a two-shot. When the three of them go to the park together Brown changes his composition and sets Jane off in a single shot and Rob and Dorothy are now together in the two-shot to suggest the way in which the triangle has evolved; that is, Rob's affections are with Dorothy and Jane is, in effect, now alone again. Furthermore, since the story is a love triangle, Brown also concentrates on three shots of protagonists. In fact by viewing only selected frames one could easily chart the course of their relationship. In the middle of the film, for instance, Dorothy and Jane playfully split a "wish-bone" as Rob looks on while standing between them. The camera fades out before the winner can be determined.

Like many complex works, *Smouldering Fires* lends itself to varying interpretations. Ostensibly, it seems that Brown means to suggest that Jane was merely a fool who deceived herself into believing that a handsome young man could really find her attractive. The fact that she is cast as the prototypical castrating female at the opening might also lend to the conclusion that her unhappy marriage is in essence a punishment for her unconventional life-style; that is, if she had been like her sister, a conventional upper-middle class female, she might have once found herself an attractive husband and thus precluded the lonely existence she now seems likely to endure. On the other hand, the film lends itself to another, more "modern" interpretation. Despite the unflattering—that is, unfeminine—portrait of Jane at the opening, there lies behind this profile a respect for her considerable business abilities. As Jane herself points out, she has significantly expanded the small business she inherited from her father. Further-more, her unfortunate union with Rob might be seen to be as much a product of the fact that she is cruelly misled by him as of her own obtuseness. If so, Rob then becomes the villain. Even though he realises that Jane's vision is clouded by her love for him, he continues to deceive her. Equally, Dorothy might have enlightened Jane, but does not do so ostensibly for fear of spoiling her happiness. Finally, though the film ends with Jane giving up Rob to her sister, one cannot help being pleased with her decision. After all, even if Jane refuses to see it, her relationship with Rob was doomed from the first, not because she has lost her youth—as Dorothy believes—but because Rob is a vacuous young bore with about as much backbone as a jellyfish. Clearly, he is much better suited to Dorothy who is nearly as conventional and dull as he is.

In *The Goose Woman*, Brown's next film and his last for Universal, the protagonist is, again, not a beautiful nymph but an older woman; this time an ugly old hag, the Goose Woman, Mary Holmes (Louise Dresser). Once a celebrated opera star who called herself Mari De Nardi, she had a love affair that led to an illegitimate child. In the process of giving birth, she lost her magnificent voice and so quickly fell to ruin. Now she lives in a dilapidated shack and tends her geese.

Occasionally, she is visited by her son, Gerald (Jack Pickford), whom
she holds responsible for her ill-fortune. Gerald is engaged to an
actress in town who is also pursued by another man. When this man is
murdered (coincidentally near Mary's shack), Gerald becomes the
prime suspect. Mary is the district attorney's only eye-witness to the
crime. He promises to transform her once again into a beautiful
woman if she will tell the jury what she saw on the night of the
murder; she accepts his offer, thinking that her testimony will return
her to the limelight. She makes up a story that inadvertently clinches
the case against her son. When she learns what she has done, she
confesses to the district attorney that she has been lying. But the
prosecutor, who has her sworn statement and an air-tight case, does
not choose to believe her, attributing her about-face to a mother's
instinct to protect her son. The real murderer, however, comes forth
and confesses, and Gerald is released. Mary, Gerald, and his *fiancée*
are happily re-united.

The film received high praise from contemporary critics. They
were also generous in their praise of Brown's direction as well they
might have been. *The Goose Woman* reveals a director completely in
command of his craft and, although the story falters at the end, it is
difficult to find fault with Brown's direction at any point. Even the
most captious of silent film critics, Paul Rotha, was impressed by the
film, or at least a large segment of it: "During the first portion," he
writes, "while Miss Dresser played the drink-sodden prima donna,
Clarence Brown's direction was remarkable. He made her live in the
filthiest squalor with gin bottle and geese, and at night she would
hunch up her back over her precious book of press-cuttings, to read
over the reports of her glorious days."[2]

Brown demonstrates here, as he does in *Smouldering Fires,* a keen
eye for detail. The sets in this film all have an air of authenticity,
especially Mary's tumbledown shack. And, as Rotha suggests, Brown
makes no compromises in his effort to portray Mary as a pathetic
alcoholic harridan: her hair is in complete disarray, her eyes are
sunken, her clothes hopelessly tattered, and her thoughts embittered.
In one of the film's most forceful scenes, Brown communicates the
depth of this woman's despair by focusing on a key detail. Mary still
has one cylinder recording of herself in her prime. She plays it over
and over to revive old memories of the grand days of her youth.
Gerald visits her one day and, not realising the value of the recording,
accidentally knocks it off the table. Mary is grief-stricken for a
moment and then savagely reviles her son. Her last link to the past has
literally been smashed into small pieces.

Intriguingly, Brown practises a cinematic style in this film directly antithetical to the standard master to medium shot to close-up method of filming a scene. As noted in the opening scene of *Smouldering Fires*, he instead prefers to begin with a close-up on a limb—a hand or foot, for example—then move to a medium shot and lastly to a master. During the scene in which Gerald is interrogated by detective Kelly (George Nichols), for instance, Brown begins with a close-up of two hands cracking a nut (a clever visual metaphor for the interrogation process), then to a medium shot of the anguished and worried suspect, and finally to a full shot of Kelly. This scene also provides an excellent example of how a silent film director can visually create the impression of sound. Here, Brown cuts rapidly between one detective filing his finger nails, another dropping coins into his palm, another chewing gum, Kelly cracking nuts, and water dripping from a faucet.

Following *The Goose Woman,* Brown signed a contract with producer Joseph Schenck to direct Rudolph Valentino's next film—*The Eagle*. At the time, however, Valentino's popularity was on the wane. He had not appeared in a successful film since *Blood and Sand* in 1922. That Schenck entrusted Brown with this assignment, with both Valentino's career and a large production budget at stake, may be seen as an indication of the respect the director commanded within the industry. Indeed, *The Eagle* proved to be a great hit, and re-established Valentino as the screen's pre-eminent male star. More than this, it is also often considered to be Valentino's finest film and the best example of his considerable talents as a film actor.

In *The Eagle*, he plays a Robin Hood figure, Dubrovsky, a soldier on the run from the powers that be because he has refused to respond to the sexual advances of the Czarina (Louise Dresser), an older woman with a taste for young officers. After he escapes the Czarina's clutches, he returns home to find that his father has been cheated out of his estate by a nefarious landowner, Kyrilla Troekouroff (James Marcus). With the help of some loyal peasants, Dubrovsky wreaks havoc on the wealthy landowners in the area and the scoundrel Kyrilla. He infiltrates his enemy's home by posing as a French tutor, but soon falls in love with his pupil—Kyrilla's daughter, Mascha (Vilma Banky)—and his love for her stops him from taking full revenge on her father. Eventually, the Czarina's soldiers catch up with Dubrovsky and take him into custody. Just before he is to be executed, however, the Czarina relents and pardons him. He and Mascha, who were married while Dubrovsky was in prison, ride off in a carriage together as the Czarina looks on enviously, her newest favourite by her side.

As befits a Valentino vehicle, Brown charged his film with eroti-
cism. The opening sequence, for instance, which involves the Czarina's attempt to seduce Dubrovsky, is made all the more intriguing by
the fact that the Czarina, an older woman, hardly beautiful and
somewhat rotund, seethes with passion for the young officer, while
he, the dashing, strikingly handsome lieutenant, wants nothing to do
with her even though she promises him a generalship in return for
sexual favours. At one point, Dubrovsky kneels to kiss the Czarina's
hand; he starts to rise, but she pushes him down, firmly caressing his
head with her hand, her eyes alight with a look of ecstasy. And, of
course, there are the almost obligatory scenes with Valentino astride a
horse, which Brown plays for all their latent Freudian symbolism,
including the spectacular rescue of the heroine after her carriage
horses go berserk.

Throughout Brown's career, there are moments when the director
seems to self-consciously acknowledge the silliness of the material
with which he sometimes has had to deal. Nowhere can this be better
observed than in *The Eagle*. The entire film can be seen as a canny
parody of Valentino himself and the entire swashbuckling genre. In
fact, the film appears to be structured along the lines of a comic opera.
Hans Kraly, Lubitsch's favourite silent film scenarist, freely fashioned
his screenplay from Pushkin's novella, "Dubrovsky". The provocative
Czarina, among other aspects of the film, is purely a Kraly creation.
Adrian, who was now just beginning his illustrious career, designed
the costumes, and the legendary William Cameron Menzies the
stupendous, if hardly Russian-seeming, sets. Kevin Brownlow finds
Menzies' artwork to be "obtrusive" and "out of character" with the
subject matter, and the Adrian costumes "merely fancy dress".[3] But
how perfectly in character they are if the film is seen as a thinly veiled
spoof of Hollywood's own pretentiousness. That Brown and Kraly
have set their story in a sort of mythical present provides a good clue
as to the intent of the film. It is difficult to imagine how this very
amusing flight into the best sort of film fantasy could have been made
better had Menzies, for example, chosen to design an authentic
Russian setting. Certainly he could have if Brown had wished him to,
but by giving Menzies, Adrian and Kraly's imagination full vent as
well as his own, Brown avoids the very pretentiousness that makes so
many of Hollywood's "historical" dramas objectionable.

In 1919, Brown bought the rights to a story entitled *The Unholy
Three* which he wanted to make with Tourneur. However, Tourneur
did not care for it and the film was not made at that time. Neverthe-

less, Brown held on to the story rights. In 1925 M-G-M became interested in the property and made Brown an offer which he refused, saying he wanted three times what they offered. Reluctantly, Irving Thalberg gave his approval to purchase the story at Brown's price, but vowed that the director would never work at his studio.[4] Thalberg, however, was too good a businessman and film producer to hold a grudge for too long, at least not in the face of Brown's rapidly increasing status. Brown had now directed four very successful films for three different studios over the past several years, and in the process had acquired the enviable reputation of a director who could produce first-rate films and also stay within budget. By the spring of 1926, Thalberg conveniently forgot his promise and signed Brown to a two film contract, the first of a series of contracts that kept the director at M-G-M for the remaining twenty-six years of his career except for a single loan-out to Fox for *The Rains Came* (1939).

Brown's strong interest in the dramatic uses of light has been noted. Perhaps the best single example of his lighting and compositional skills is *Flesh and the Devil*. Credit for his achievement in this film needs to be shared with two other artists: William Daniels, long recognised as one of Hollywood's finest cinematographers, who in 1928 was as young and eager to experiment as Brown; and Greta Garbo, without question the most photogenic and charismatic actress in film and at the time a fast developing M-G-M contract star. Together they fashioned one of the American cinema's most stunningly visual films.[5] *Flesh and the Devil* contains far fewer titles than usually found in American silent films. Its expressionistic uses of chiaroscuro and silhouette suggest that Brown was influenced by the "foreign invasion". He did not, however, merely duplicate European technique, rather he absorbed the best of it, shaped it to his own *mise-en-scène* and adapted it to the strong linear narrative structure of the American silent cinema.

Once again Brown found himself working with an ostensibly trite storyline—Hermann Sudermann's romantic novel *The Undying Past*—about a demonic seductress who comes between the life-long friendship of two noblemen. Yet by virtue of his cinematic bravura, a bent for focusing on the more unusual aspects of the story and, perhaps most important, his recognition of Garbo's incomparable screen presence, Brown created a film that transcends the stereotypes with which it deals.

Several seduction scenes in the film have deservedly attained near-legendary status. The most familiar occurs early in the film

during a party soon after Leo (John Gilbert) and Felicitas (Garbo) have
met. In the course of the evening their love-at-first-sight relationship
quickly blossoms. Now, as she will throughout, Felicitas commands
their fate. When they step out into the garden, it is the woman who
leads and the man who follows. As their relationship grows more
passionate Brown switches almost exclusively to close-ups in contrast
to medium shots earlier. When Leo lights Felicitas's cigarette (in the
Twenties a sure clue to her questionable moral character), she does
not merely put it to her lips, she embraces it, and the light from the
match sets their faces aglow. Fade out. . .the two lovers are now lying
together on a settee. Both seem exhausted—the implications of their
dishevelled appearance need not be elaborated. In contrast to the
cool setting in the garden, Brown has moved the lovers inside a
sweltering room suffused with cigarette smoke and inundated with
pillows. And significantly, Felicitas has her hand not merely around
Leo's neck but firmly about his jugular, a touch which as well as any
other suggests the way Brown uplifts his material through the careful
manipulation of detail.

The two lovers are interrupted suddenly by the return of Felicitas's
husband, Count Von Rhaden (Marc MacDermott). As he stands in
the doorway, Von Rhaden stretches his hand out toward the two
lovers visually blocking Felicitas from the picture, just as he wishes he
could block her out of his mind, and then tightens his hand into a
clenched fist. The ensuing confrontation results in a duel. As men-
tioned earlier, Brown was inspired to film the duel in silhouette. The
starkness of the scene set in the cool early morning light most
effectively counterpoints the life and death challenge and also
contrasts sharply with the passionate nature of the previous scene. In
an interview with Kevin Brownlow, Brown vividly recalls the action at
this point: "The two men start back to back, then they walk out of the
picture. There are two bursts of smoke from each side of the screen.
We dissolve out to a shot over Garbo's shoulder as she tries on a black
hat in a millinery shop. In her hand is a handkerchief with a black
border. She has a slight smile on her face. That's how we told who was
shot—without a subtitle or any other sort of explanation."[6] In the

"The light from a match sets their faces aglow":
Greta Garbo and John Gilbert in FLESH AND THE DEVIL (1927)

wake of Von Rhaden's death Leo has to leave the country to avoid a
trial. He instructs his best friend, Ulrich (Lars Hanson), to look after
Felicitas while he is away.

It is raining very hard when Ulrich goes to see Felicitas. He finds
her in a sleeveless dress, and is instantly mesmerised by her, as Leo
was. Felicitas turns away from him and leans her head against the
window, her reflection cast in the glass (one of the many instances her
image is reflected in this film), highlighting both her duplicity and
narcissism. While Ulrich offers her spiritual support and advice her
eyes are closed, but when he concludes by telling her that his "purse is
Leo's", her eyes light up. She turns from the window toward Ulrich
and, for a split second, certainly long enough for Ulrich to absorb,
that enveloping, deeply sensual glance of a practised demi-mondaine
radiates from her eyes. She reaches for a cigarette, almost as if she
were beginning a well-rehearsed routine. Ulrich attempts to light a
match but nervously bungles it. He has lost his composure as
suddenly as she has begun to show a sexual interest in him.

When Leo returns from exile, ecstatic at the thought of seeing

**Barbara Kent, John Gilbert, Greta Garbo and
Lars Hanson in FLESH AND THE DEVIL**

Ulrich and Leo embrace at the end of FLESH AND THE DEVIL

Felicitas again, he discovers that his "faithful" lover and his best friend are now married. However, his friendship with Ulrich is such that he does not wish to come between his friend and his new wife. But without Leo's companionship, Ulrich veritably withers. When the two are finally re-united, Leo finds Ulrich immersed in shadows in a room otherwise drenched in sunlight, morosely playing a magnificent pipe organ. Soon the two renew their old friendship. Felicitas arrives to join the reunion and together the three toast their mutual friendship. Ulrich's glass breaks (a striking example of Brown's penchant for symbolism) and as he tends to his finger, Leo and Felicitas exchange a fateful glance. Again, they become lovers.

After a brief tryst they decide to run away together. But just before they leave Ulrich returns. Ignorant of the situation between his wife and his friend, he greets Felicitas warmly and presents her with a stunning diamond bracelet. Although he does not realise it, he has done the one thing that might prevent her from cuckolding him. She kisses the jewelled ornament and embraces Ulrich in her only sincere expression of affection for him in the film. After her husband retires for the evening, Felicitas agonises over whether she should stay with Ulrich or leave with Leo, staring at her new bracelet as if it could provide the answer. It does. She tells Leo that she cannot leave Ulrich and "all this". It suddenly becomes clear to Leo how destructive and futile his involvement with Felicitas has been: it has destroyed his relationship with the one true love of his life—Ulrich. He grabs her neck with both hands, his expression twisted with hate, and throws her on the bed to strangle her, but before he can complete the murder Ulrich walks in. His entrance and the manner in which Brown films it is reminiscent of Von Rhaden's timely entrance earlier in the film. Together with the two seduction scenes, this further instance of parallel but distinct actions within the film provides another example of how Brown gives resonance and depth to his work.

For their duel, Ulrich and Leo return to the place of their boyhood adventures, an island where they had long ago become "blood" brothers. Ulrich's sister begs Felicitas to stop them. The seductress vacillates. But when Hertha (Barbara Kent) starts to pray, Felicitas goes into a frenzy as if the power of Hertha's prayers has jolted her (one of the many suggestions of mysticism in this film). On her way to the island across the frozen lake, she falls through the ice. The moment she falls, Ulrich drops his gun (Leo has refused to raise his). The two men rush toward each other and embrace and the last bubbles rise to the surface at the spot where Felicitas has met her death.

Soon after he completed *The Trail of '98*, his second film for M-G-M, Brown's contract with the studio expired. It was rumored that the director had received offers from several producers for considerably more money that M-G-M was presently paying him. There were even discussions about establishing his own producing unit with United Artists. Thalberg, however, apparently had no intention of losing the director who had made a fortune for the studio on *Flesh and the Devil* and had recently been selected by his peers as one of the ten best directors in Hollywood. This time he made the director an offer he could not refuse. In the summer of 1927 Brown signed a new contract with M-G-M that "Motion Picture Classic" called "the finest held by any director in motion pictures, and that does not except the high-powered foreigners."[7] Among other things, the agreement reputedly raised his salary to $6000 per week and "stipulated that he may choose his own stories and players."[8]

Brown's first decision upon signing the new agreement was to reunite Garbo and Gilbert in an adaptation of Michael Arlen's sensational best seller, *The Green Hat,* about a "shameless, shamefaced lady . . . who must meet men on their own ground always," which he entitled *A Woman of Affairs.*[9] What the film lacks of Arlen's sardonic wit it compensates for in Brown's cinematic acumen, and on the whole stands as an excellent interpretation of the novel.

The opening scene tells us a great deal about the film's heroine, Diana Merrick (Garbo), and her relationship with her lover, Neville Holderness (Gilbert). Diana and Neville are motoring along a country road. That Diana is driving, and not Neville, immediately implies which of the two dominates the relationship, and for a Twenties audience reveals Diana to be one of those "new" women, independent and high-spirited. In order to avoid a hay cart Diana swings her car sharply, sending it across a brook and over the heads of some workmen who are digging a ditch alongside the road. Recklessness and daring are thus added as traits of her character. Likewise, the following scene outlines the character of her twin brother, Jeffrey (Douglas Fairbanks Jr.). It begins with a shot of a silver tray on which are placed a bottle of seltzer water and a glass of scotch. We see a hand on the bottle; it pushes down on the tap and the water sprays out. The first burst misses the glass, then goes in; the last squirt spills over the top. By the breezey, routine manner in which Jeffrey squirts the water, it becomes clear that he drinks frequently; the careless way he pours the drink points to poor reflexes: in short, an alcoholic. Finally, a hand reaches out for the drink and pulls it away from the camera. Like the opening of *Smouldering Fires,* in which we learn about Jane Vale through a selective view of her extremities before we actually get a full shot of her, Brown sketches Jeffrey's personality through an action of his hands before we see anything else of him.

Like nearly all of Brown's romantic films, *A Woman of Affairs* rotates on an intertwining series of triangular relationships: Diana is in love with Neville, who eventually marries another woman, Constance (Dorothy Sebastian); David Furness (John Mack Brown), who has been friends with Neville and Diana since childhood, adores Diana; the sickly Jeffrey idolises the athletic, wholesome David. Consequently, the movie is rife with Brown's favourite set-up, the three shot, which is arranged in nearly every possible manner in the course

**Greta Garbo, John Gilbert, Lewis Stone, Douglas Fairbanks Jr.
and Hobart Bosworth in WOMAN OF AFFAIRS (1929)**

of this film and, as it does in all of the director's work, serves
cinematically as a way of giving depth to a two-dimensional image,
and dramatically as a way of suggesting the characters' emotional
relationship to one another. In the central relationship between
Diana and Neville, it is the heroine who seeks to control the action. At
the beginning of the film it is clearly Diana, not Neville, who instigates
their first plan to elope. Their dreams, however, are waylaid when
Neville's father, a pillar of the sort of pre-war morality which Diana
rebels against, learns of the planned elopement. Sir Morton (Hobart
Bosworth) sets Neville down in his study and gives the boy a forceful
lecture on family responsibility. The scene begins with Neville, tall
and erect, determined to resist his father's entreaties, but ends (after a
fade out, fade in) with him sitting, elbows on the table and his head
bowed. His father, however, in a high-angle shot that peers down on
his pathetic, beaten son, still stands. Again, the camera eye explains all
that has transpired. Neville is sent off to Egypt on a diplomatic
assignment and Diana marries David on the rebound.

One of the most intriguing aspects of Brown's early work is the unexpected presence of the bizarre or the perverse: the marriage ceremony in *Smouldering Fires,* the attempted seduction of Dubrovsky by the Czarina in *The Eagle,* Felicitas in *Flesh and the Devil* rotating the chalice cup so that her lips might touch the same spot Leo's have. An equally strange incident takes place in this film during David and Diana's wedding night. To assuage the censors, much that was *risqué* about Arlen's novel was eliminated from the screenplay, but this fascinating scene is not in *The Green Hat* though it well might have been had it occurred to Arlen. The star athlete and hero of his generation, David is very nervous as Diana coolly awaits him in their wedding bed. David has long idolised Diana without any hope of marrying her and, now that they are wed, he seems unsure as to how he should behave. Still in his suit, he comes to the bedside and tentatively puts his arms around his new wife. But before he can get any further, Brown cuts to a close-up of a hand (the symbolic hand of fate, no doubt) rapping at the door. David looks up anxiously.

David in the three shot with the detectives:
John Mack Brown in WOMAN OF AFFAIRS

Gripped with fear, he walks to the door, the camera dollying along with him. He opens the door to form a three shot with the two men who are standing outside. The camera now closes in on David as some rice from the wedding slips out of his hand like sand out of a time piece. His dream has ended. Diana, who is playing with the light over the bed, remains unaware of this new twist of fate. She watches as one of the detectives fixes a pair of handcuffs (which now loom inordinately large in the foreground of the frame) on the groom. Unable to bear the disgrace, David bolts from the two men, heads straight for the window, and leaps to his death."[10]

An inquest is held during which Diana lies to the investigator, telling him that "David died—for decency" in order to preserve her brother's idealistic image of her deceased husband, and so leaves it to society to interpret her enigmatic remark to her disadvantage. Like Jane Vale, Diana sacrifices her own happiness to protect that of a sibling. Only Hugh (Lewis Stone), a long-time family friend, knows the truth: that David had accumulated a great many debts and the police finally caught up with him. Diana leaves England for Europe where her many love affairs with the continent's most notorious playboys make her a fixture in the society columns. Eventually, Diana meets Neville again, who is now engaged to be married, and they spend the night together.

In Arlen's novel, Diana and Neville's tryst leads to a stillborn child and Diana's subsequent near-fatal illness, but in the film the reasons for the heroine's ill-health are kept vague. Diana, however, recovers and returns to England. In the meantime, Neville begins to drink heavily. He visits Hugh, unaware that Diana is upstairs. "She is killing me," he tells his friend, "as surely as she killed David Furness." But the truth is that Neville, an insensitive, waffling coward who does not have the courage to defy bogus social conventions, has nearly ruined Diana. Only when Hugh tells Neville the real reasons behind David's death and of Diana's selflessness in taking the blame for it does he begin to return her love. Together Diana and Neville decide to run away to South America. Diana, however, goes to see Neville's father one last time at his request. When he refers to her dead husband in an effort to convince her to leave his son one last time, Neville, who has just arrived, interrupts him and tells his father the truth about the circumstances of David's death. Diana is deeply hurt that Neville has broken her secret and, by doing so, violated her integrity. "You have taken from me the only gracious thing I've ever done," she tells him. Although they leave together, Diana sends Neville back to his wife under the pretence that Constance is pregnant. Discovering her duplicity, Neville, his father and Hugh pursue Diana. They find her car wrecked against a tree. It is an ending, unfortunately, as enigmatic and unsatisfying on film as it is as literature.

The talkie revolution hit Hollywood while Brown was working on *A Woman of Affairs,* and the director remembers having a great deal of trouble controlling John Gilbert's performance. Gilbert—at the time, Hollywood's leading romantic male star—was, like everyone else, unsure about his future. Unfortunately for Gilbert, a good speaking voice was required, not hamming. He had one, but primitive early sound of equipment only picked up the high tones in his voice while losing the lows, and so in his early talkies the actor sounded unnaturally high-pitched. Audiences snickered and his popularity plummeted. After several unsuccessful films, M-G-M paid off his enormous contract, signed ironically just before the arrival of sound, and Gilbert was forced to retire.[11] Garbo, however, proved somewhat cagier and luckier, carefully choosing the right vehicle, Eugene O'Neill's play "Anna Christie," and the right director, Clarence Brown, before making her sound film debut.

Brown had already directed a minor film, *Navy Blues,* as a way of familiarising himself with the workings of sound. Since he had two college degrees in engineering, in this respect he was much better prepared for the transition than most. In *Anna Christie,* his manipulation of sound is both confident and innovative. The sounds of the wharfside—the haunting echo of a ship's horn, the clack of feet walking a plank from ship to shore—are all convincingly caught. That Garbo and the other actors seem to be at ease and thoroughly absorbed in their roles, and not self-consciously aware of the presence of the microphone, may perhaps be another reflection of Brown's confidence.

It was not really the mechanical problems posed by sound, problems that seriously impaired the work of some other directors, that account for the decline in the quality of Brown's work in this decade, but rather the sudden importance attached to the spoken word: words could convey what the camera had done so poetically before, so now the expressive use of the camera, Brown might have reasoned, was no longer necessary. I am not suggesting that Brown's talent for lighting and composition suddenly disappeared, but that gradually through the Thirties the stylistic and creative flair of his silent work became less evident.

In *Anna Christie* Brown continued to pursue those things that make his silent work so interesting. Despite the fact that the camera had to be kept in glass-encased booths, Brown sought mobility and freedom wherever possible, as during the carnival sequence where he places a camera in a rollercoaster car to follow Matt (Charles Bickford) and Anna (Garbo) on their ride. The story and its preoccupations also share a close continuity with the director's previous work. Eugene O'Neill's Anna, like Brown's other female protagonists, is a woman whose independence has been forged out of having to fend for herself since early womanhood. Her father, Chris (George Marion), a sailor, who like so many of Brown's male protagonists is unwilling to accept his responsibilities to others, leaves his daughter with relatives on a farm in Minnesota. Anna hates her life there, and when she gets the chance runs away. Unable to find employment, she turns to prostitution. She appears at the opening of the film at the wharf, hoping to stay with her father who lives on the coal barge he captains. He welcomes her, naively assuming that because of her midwest upbringing she is a paradigm of feminine virtue, and takes her out to sea with him. One night during a bad storm, they pick up a young sailor, Matt, whose ship has been wrecked. Anna and Matt fall in love, but the old man does not want his daughter to marry a sailor, knowing only too well what poor husbands they make, and a struggle ensues between Chris and Matt for control of Anna. In a scene that is dominated by Brown's favourite composition, the three shot, the struggle between the two men climaxes when Matt announces his intention to marry Anna and the old man refuses to give his blessing. Each grabs one of Anna's arms. Matt orders her to come with him; Chris orders her to stay with him on the barge. Anna does not want any part of either of them under these circumstances. She does not intend to be any man's vassal: "Nobody owns me, see," she tells them, "excepting myself. I'll do what I please and no man, I don't give a damn who he is, can tell me what to do." In her rage she goes on to confess her ignominious past, and ends by declaring her hate for all men, a declaration that echoes throughout many of Brown's early films. Both Chris and Matt are dumbfounded; their naive conception of her as a lily-white virgin is shattered, and their reaction is to desert her. But after going into town and getting drunk, her father and Matt return and the three are reconciled. A three shot with Anna with her arms around Matt and her father, a shot very much like the closing of both *Smouldering Fires* and *The Goose Woman*, concludes this most effective final sequence.

For the most part, *Anna Christie* is very much like Brown's silent

George F. Marion and Greta Garbo in ANNA CHRISTIE (1930)

work in terms of quality and style, and so seemed to promise well for the future. Unfortunately, however, Brown's subsequent work in the Thirties shows a marked artistic decline. Perhaps he simply lost his appetite for taking risks. After all, by the early Thirties he was comfortably ensconced at the biggest, most prestigious studio in Hollywood, and to direct a standard star vehicle for someone like Brown, with his command of the technical side of his art, would have been a breeze. Or perhaps the director was just not careful enough in selecting his material. In his silent films Brown could take the tritest plots and turn them into fine films, but he did not have to cope with absurd dialogue then—his camera spoke for him. The sort of admittedly self-conscious style of direction he employed as a silent film director, however, faded (although with important exceptions, like Hitchcock and Lang) during the Thirties with the advancement of sound. It was felt that since the dialogue could tell the story the camera should remain functional, that is "invisible". So Brown adopted a more conservative cinematic style which served M-G-M very well but not the director's subsequent critical reputation. If he had sustained the same sort of dynamic *mise-en-scène* exhibited in his silent films throughout the Thirties, in all likelihood we would regard him as one of Hollywood's pantheon directors.

Several of Brown's films of the Thirties, however, stand well above the average Hollywood product of the period and are interesting in their own right. *A Free Soul*, for example, remains an intriguing film, among other reasons because it must be one of the most erotic of the decade. Norma Shearer, looking positively ravishing in Adrian's clinging, sleeveless, one-piece gowns, plays a sybarite out for sexual adventure; Clark Gable in his first important role plays the brute ready and willing to give it to her. As the daughter of a famous but now disintegrating alcoholic lawyer, Stephen Ashe (Lionel Barrymore), Jan Ashe (Shearer) falls in love with a man her father has saved from the gallows, Ace Wilfong (Gable). Her father, however, does not approve of Jan's alliance with a man "mixed up in everything from opium to white slavery," so she makes a bargain with him: she will leave Ace if he will stop drinking. Stephen agrees. They embark on a three month camping trip together, but as soon as he gets the chance, Stephen goes back to the bottle. Jan returns to Ace only to find the gangster bitter over the fact that she had left him without a word. He still wants her, though, only this time on his terms. He lays it on the line for her (as only Gable could); "That's why you came back, because you had to. And that's all marriage is—just two people who want to live together. You can call the rest just nothin'. You're through. You're mine and I want ya."

Jan is first attracted to Ace because he represents the opposite of everything she has grown tired of—the effeminate world of social respectability—but now she realises that she has strayed too far on her quest, and so decides to break once and for all with her gangster-lover. But Ace will have none of it, and holds her in his gambling den against her will. Jan's former boyfriend, the ever-faithful Dwight (Leslie Howard) intervenes, however, and kills Ace. When Dwight is put on trial for Ace's murder, Jan searches for her father, who has disappeared, so that he might defend Dwight. Stephen is discovered on skid row and appears at the last moment of Dwight's trial. He delivers a stirring closing statement in which he blames himself and the way he raised his daughter for Ace's murder. Upon finishing, he collapses—dead. Dwight is acquitted and he and Jan are re-united.

The film opens auspiciously with an intricate travelling shot which begins outside the window of the Ashes' apartment, moves inside and through it to Jan who, appropriately enough, asks her father for her "undies" and then steps out winsomely clad in same. Likewise, Stephen's climactic courtroom peroration, filmed in one take with multiple cameras, is also cleverly orchestrated. As he does in all his better films, Brown uses light throughout *A Free Soul* most effectively. A misty sunrise is beautifully captured during the camping sequence and demonstrates how well Brown works with a natural light source. Later in the film, in Ace's office when Dwight warns the gangster to leave Jan alone, the director demonstrates his equally sure mastery of studio sources. Here dark, sinister shadows are cast around the gangster's eyes by a bright, diffuse light that seems, oddly, to emanate from Ace's desk. But perhaps most intriguing is the alluring way in which Norma Shearer is lit. Never has she appeared to better advantage than under William Daniels' high-key light in this film. If nothing else, it can be said for Brown and his cinematographer that they were without equals in their respective abilities to make M-G-M's female stars appear at their most enchanting.

In much the same vein as *A Free Soul* is *Sadie McKee*, the best of the five films Brown made with Joan Crawford. Here the actress plays a small town denizen who runs away to New York with her lover, Tommy (Gene Raymond), to be married. The morning before they are to meet at city hall, however, Tommy runs off with a vaudeville singer and leaves Sadie alone in the metropolis to fend for herself. With the help of a friend, the embittered Sadie gets a job as a cocktail waitress in a nightclub. There she meets an alcoholic millionaire, Brennan (Edward Arnold), who becomes infatuated with her and proposes marriage. Tired of being manipulated by men, Sadie decides to do some manipulating of her own and accepts his proposal. But soon she grows weary of her sterile riches and decides to redeem herself by helping her husband to stop drinking. After she succeeds, she leaves him to look for Tommy, with whom she is still in love. Tommy, however, has long since hit the skids and is seriously ill. Sadie gets him to a hospital, where he dies by her side. She returns to her working class origins.

The film is at times as trite and well-worn as this plot outline suggests. Nevertheless, it is important for its incisive view of depression-era society. For example, the hash house where the two

Gene Raymond and Joan Crawford in SADIE McKEE (1934)

lovers have their first meal in New York carries just the right dreary, dismal sense of everyday reality with which Brown's Thirties audience could identify only too well. So might they also identify with the comfortless dollar-a-day hotel where Sadie and Tommy spend their first night in the city. Nor do things get any less depressing when Sadie goes to work as a cocktail waitress. The questionable nature of the nightclub is poignantly suggested by the off-colour conversation of the dancing girls as they prepare for the next show. The coarse conduct of the "maitre d' " (Akim Tamiroff) with his hyena-like laugh further reinforces our impression of the seediness of this establishment.

Like most of Brown's heroines, Sadie reaches a point where she becomes disgusted with the male sex: "I'm kind of sick of men," she tells her friend after Tommy has deserted her. That she marries Brennan in the face of strenuous objections is an expression of revenge on the male sex as well as self-hate. But so basically fine is

Sadie that revenge eventually converts to pity and she helps her husband conquer his disease. Alcoholics appear frequently in Brown's early cinema. (However, as the thematic bent of his work changes in the middle of the Thirties to a more optimistic and wholesome view of life, they virtually disappear.) They can be found in *The Goose Woman* (Mary Holmes), *A Woman of Affairs* (Jeffrey Merrick), *A Free Soul* (Stephen Ashe), and *Sadie McKee* (Brennan). In all these films Brown's depiction of the effects of alcoholism is unrelievedly stark and as realistic as one might find before such post-war works as Billy Wilder's *The Lost Weekend* (1945). In *Sadie McKee*, for instance, Edward Arnold's rendering of Brennan's unfortunate condition is most convincing, as when the millionaire comes home drunk one evening and has to be undressed by his manservant as if he were a helpless child, or later, during his cure, when he tries to steal a drink. In both instances Brown uses distorted camera perspectives to mirror Brennan's demented state of mind. Except for Mary Holmes, all are secondary characters. One might wish that Brown had devoted an entire film to the subject of alcoholism. Nevertheless, his unflinching but sympathetic treatment of the matter provides one further indication of how much more there is to the best of Brown's cinema than merely matinee idols and lavish production values.

For the next ten years following *Sadie McKee* Brown's work continued to be of an uneven quality: *Ah, Wilderness!* and *Of Human Hearts* are evocative in their realisation of particular aspects of the American heritage; *Anna Karenina* is poignant in its depiction of the life of Tolstoy's most renowned heroine; *Conquest* is ostentatious and over-bearing in its recreation of the romance between Napoleon and Marie Walewska; *Idiot's Delight* pretentious in its "cellophaned intellectuality" (as Graham Greene aptly put it); and *The Human Comedy* and *The White Cliffs of Dover* are mawkish portraits of families during wartime. In most of these films there are fine moments: the graduation exercises in *Ah Wilderness,* Anna and Vronsky's garden rendezvous in *Anna Karenina*, the grand ball in *Conquest*, the hash house dinner in *Idiot's Delight,* Ulysses before the mechanical man in the shop window in *The Human Comedy*. But, of course a single excellent scene or even several such scenes do not make an enduring film, although it may, as Pauline Kael has suggested, redeem the two hours invested in making the discovery.

After the maudliness and moralising of his late Thirties and early Forties work, Brown revitalised his career with *National Velvet,* a thoroughly engaging Cinderella story which, after the bogus senti-

Above, Greta Garbo and Fredric March in ANNA KARENINA (1935)

mentality of *Idiot's Delight*, *The Human Comedy*, and *White Cliffs of Dover*, must have seemed like a breath of fresh air to the director. The story of *National Velvet*, which Brown relates with a *joie de vivre* unparalleled in the American cinema, concerns the dream of a butcher's daughter, Velvet Brown (Elizabeth Taylor), to win the Grand National. Her chance to make her dream come true occurs when she wins a promising sorrel gelding, Pi, in a village raffle. With the expert assistance of a horse-wise young vagabond, Mi Taylor (Mickey Rooney), Velvet tirelessly trains the horse for the great race, and with the one hundred gold sovereigns her mother (Anne Revere) won for swimming the English Channel in her youth, enters Pi in the

**Right, Mickey Rooney and Elizabeth Taylor in
NATIONAL VELVET (1944)**

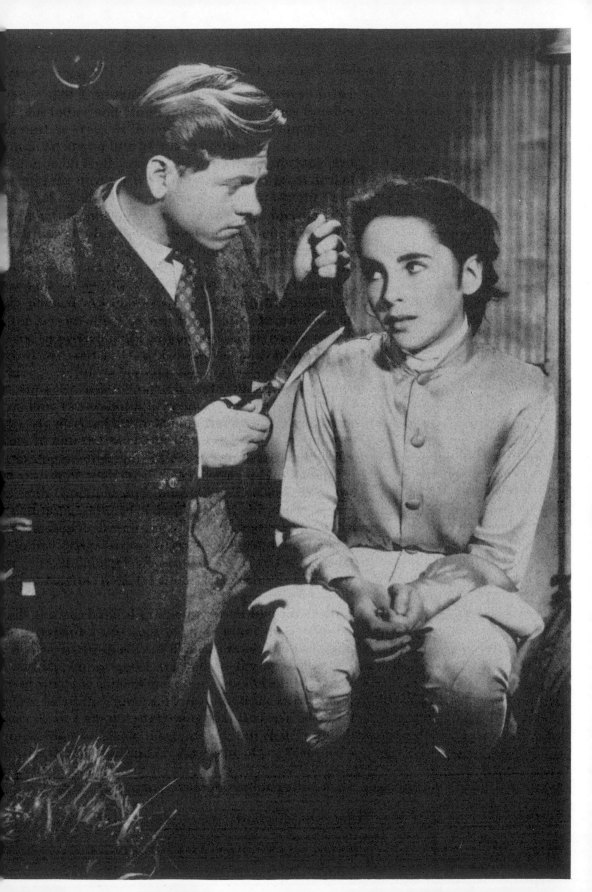

competition. On the eve of the race Velvet and Mi travel to Derby to find a jockey, but when they prove unsuccessful Velvet decides to ride the horse herself. In perhaps the most thrilling race ever put on film, she rides the gelding magnificently over the famous course and in a spectacular finish wins the race.

Brown's discovery of Elizabeth Taylor who appears briefly in *The White Cliffs of Dover,* and his use of her in this film, reflect the same understanding of star quality that established Greta Garbo as the first lady of the screen in the late Twenties. There is in *National Velvet* the conscious thrill, even now some thirty years later, of watching a new star, an original and important talent, being born, just as there is in watching Katharine Hepburn, for example, in *Bill of Divorcement.* It is an experience in itself as exciting as the film's climactic race.

Brown moves his camera more freely here than in any of his films since *Woman of Affairs,* and like the best of his silent work the film possesses a sure, fluid tempo that complements the story admirably. He also experiments extensively with new sources of light to illuminate colour film—overcast skies and interiors that seem to be lit by kerosene lamps—and exhibits a style of framing that recalls his early work in his use of natural objects like trees, fences, etc., to frame the action. As in many early Technicolor films, the sets are brightly coloured and rather lavishly decorated. That they carry little credence as a recreation of a "real" English village does not work against the film but for it. They serve to remind us that this is, after all, on one level, a fair story not unlike *The Wizard of Oz.* Counterpointing these sets is some beautiful exterior footage of Velvet and Mi training the Pi over the countryside, and, of course, the race itself (filmed, incidentally, not in England but on a Pasadena golf course). This union of stylised sets and exterior shooting accents the fact that, while a fairy tale, the film deals with some very real themes—the struggle of a young girl to make a dream come true and the important realisation that all things, even sudden fame, must be kept in perspective. Nor does Brown, even during the afterglow of Velvet's victory, try to sugar-coat the fact that hard adult realities await the young champion, as they do for every child. As the sagacious Mrs. Brown who once captured her own impossible dream tells her daughter, her "breathtaking piece of folly" needs to be an ambitious one for it will have to last her an entire lifetime.

The Yearling, Brown's next film, probes deeply into the lives of a frontier family residing in the wilds of Florida in the late 1870's. Like *National Velvet,* Brown directs this film with both exuberance and

Claude Jarman Jr. as Jody Baxter in THE YEARLING (1946)

clarity, but *The Yearling* is more contemplative and disturbing and is told with an unflinching eye for the realities of the setting. As this film so eloquently reveals, to move to the wilderness, as Penny Baxter (Gregory Peck) and his wife (Jane Wyman) do, is not to move to a new Eden, but to trade what is troublesome about the city for new hardships. The Baxters have to deal not only with the obvious difficulties presented by the wilderness and the vagaries of the weather, but with loneliness and the knowledge that death strikes especially swiftly on the frontier.

Like *National Velvet*, *The Yearling* concerns an adolescent's emergence into young adulthood. Here, again, there are three principal characters involved in the drama: Penny Baxter, who wants to give his son a chance to be a carefree boy and indulge in childish pleasures; his wife, who has seen three of her sons die in the wilderness and holds her love for her only remaining child in check; and the boy, Jody (Claude Jarman), a bright, sensitive child who shares his father's boundless love for nature and its creatures. At the outset Jody has two friends, Fodderwing (Donn Gift) and Oliver (Jeff York), but neither friendship lasts. Fodderwing, a melancholy and sickly boy who dreams poetically of flying, dies suddenly. Oliver, a sailor whom Jody idolises, marries and moves with his new bride to Boston. In the wake of Fodderwing's death and Oliver's departure, however, a near-disaster leads Jody to take a fawn, Flag, for a pet. When his father is bitten by a snake, he quickly shoots a doe, Flag's mother, and has Jody dig out its heart and kidneys. Then he wraps the organs around his leg to draw out the poison. Soon afterwards, Jody, with his father's permission, takes the fawn as a pet partly as a way of repaying its mother. The fawn becomes for the now otherwise friendless boy a cherished companion which he loves as sincerely and innocently as only a child can. But despite Jody's best efforts, Flag will not stay out of mischief and eventually so endangers the family's crops that it must be killed. There is a sad irony in the fact that such a lovely and graceful creature should cause so much harm but, as Jody learns, the order of man is not the order of nature, and to disrupt that order is to invite disaster. Ultimately, the fawn serves as a symbol for youthful dreams and ambitions that must finally and painfully be destroyed before ascendence to adulthood. In a spiritual sense Jody kills part of himself when he kills Flag, and there is sadness not only in the fawn's death but in the symbolic death of Jody's childhood innocence. As his father knows only too well, boys become men quickly in the wilderness.

In *The Yearling*, Brown characterises the spirit that built the country. In his next film, *Intruder in the Dust*, an adaptation of William Faulkner's novel about a black man suspected of murdering a white man in a southern town, he characterises that which has torn it apart. The film takes a penetrating look into the collective unconscious of the American South and its racial attitudes. To see this film is to see how much so many others dealing with the same subject owe to it, and how sadly they have failed to recapture the qualities Brown inspired. One need only play this film against *In the Heat of the Night* (1967), for example, heralded for its pioneering insights into racial prejudice, to recognise how shallow and lacking in truth the later film really is. Brown made his film without stars, filmed it entirely on location in Oxford, Mississippi, and used the townspeople both in important speaking roles and as extras. *Intruder in the Dust* is hardly a typical

M-G-M picture. One wonders if Brown had to collect a few accumulated debts for his long service to get the studio's backing for this film
he said he "had to make".

Brown's opening shots tell a great deal about what his story will
concern and how it will be approached. Here he opens on a church
steeple and then pans down slowly as an assembly of people file out
into the street. Immediately, the director anticipates the contradiction that will run like a strong undercurrent throughout this film:
how can people who profess to follow the teachings of Christ treat
their fellow men both of black skin and that of their own colour so
barbarously? Brown then cuts away to a panoramic view of the town
itself. Obviously he has not had his art director repaint the buildings
or pave the potholes, but has taken this town, the same one that
Faulkner used for the setting of his novel, as he found it. The
townspeople are simply standing around conversing as they would on
any Sunday in such a place, or getting their shoes shined, or doing
nothing at all. Only one who had stood against a lamp-post on Main
Street himself in a town like this one could have captured the
atmosphere as perfectly as Brown has here. But the conversation this
Sunday is a little more animated than usual: a white man belonging to
the county's most notorious family of "nigger" haters has been killed;
eye-witnesses report the murderer was a black man.

When the sheriff brings in the suspect, Lucas Beauchamp (Juano
Hernandez), a black known and despised for his aloofness and
unwillingness to kowtow to the social order of white superiority, the
townspeople grow excited at the prospect of a lynching. Just how
succinctly Brown can communicate important information in a
single well-composed frame is evidenced during Lucas's ride into
town: inside the sheriff's car, a shot from Lucas's perspective, in
which we can see his handcuffed hands hanging over the front seat,
but not his face, suggests the spectres of the many who have
preceded Lucas—the faceless, forgotten black people who have so
long been chained by southern whites. As Lucas is being escorted into
the county jail, he calls out to a young boy, Chick (Claude Jarman), to
contact his (the boy's) uncle, lawyer John Stevens (David Brian).
Chick, who is among the crowd that is watching Lucas being taken to
jail, is embarrassed that the prisoner has singled him out. He no more
wants to be associated with Lucas than any of the others, but when he
sees his uncle that afternoon he tells him of the prisoner's request.
The lawyer can see that Chick has been deeply disturbed by Lucas's
arrest and he tries to find out why. Chick then tells him (in flashback)

of how he and Alexander (Elzie Emanuel), one of his family's black servants, had gone hunting last winter; how he had fallen into a pond while on Lucas's land; and how Lucas had helped him out and taken him into his house so that he could dry his clothes and get something to eat. Chick felt he should pay Lucas, as a black man, for his courtesy, and so offered him money but Lucas wouldn't take it. "I was so awful ashamed," Chick tells his uncle. "I didn't know, what I didn't have sense enough to understand. He [Lucas] knew all the time, but I didn't, that I was his guest in his house."

Nevertheless, Chick still felt he owed a debt to Lucas and he was determined to pay it. He sent Lucas gifts, but Lucas matched each gift by sending another one back. Finally, Chick sent Lucas an expensive dress for his wife, and when he did not receive a gift in return, considered his debt repaid. But soon after, Chick learned that Lucas's wife had died before she could wear it. So today the still unpaid debt weighs heavily on Chick's mind. What the flashback elucidates, but what Chick himself cannot see, is that his conscience is being split between his desire to respect Lucas as a human being and his inclination to reject him as a too proud "nigger" who will not bend to the social order. Lucas's arrest has brought this internal conflict to the fore.

That night, Stevens and Chick go to visit the prisoner. On their way to the jail, they meet a typical town resident, Mr. Lilley (R. X. Williams). He and Stevens chat for a moment about the Vinson Gowrie murder with Lilley ending his remarks by offhandedly volunteering his service to the Gowries when the time comes to string up Lucas. "I expect they know they can depend on you, Mr. Lilley," Stevens responds. As he and Chick walk on, the lawyer comments on Mr. Lilley's attitude, a commentary that is peculiarly Faulknerian: "He [Mr. Lilley] has nothing against Lucas. He'll probably tell you that he likes him better than he likes a lot of white folks, and you'll believe it. All he requires is that Lucas act like a Negro which he believes is what must have happened: Lucas blew his top and murdered a white man. Now the white folks are going to take him out and burn him, no hard feelings on either side. In fact, Mr. Lilley will probably be the first to contribute cash money to Lucas's funeral, and the support of his widow and children if he had any."

But Lucas does not act as he is supposed to, nor does Chick. When the lawyer and the boy arrive in town, they find people gathered around the jail house, expectant and in high spirits. Stevens, who, like everyone else, assumes that Lucas is guilty, tells his client that the best

he can hope for is a change of venue and a merciful judge. Lucas
wants Stevens to do a "job" for him, but he will not tell the lawyer
exactly what he wants him to do or why, so Stevens refuses. Later,
Chick returns to the jail alone and asks Lucas what he wants done.
The vague kinship between Lucas and Chick is suggested in a number
of different ways throughout the film. In the last scene, for example,
Brown anticipates Chick's offer when he places the boy and the black
man together in the centre of a three shot with Stevens, the outsider,
as it were, on the edge of the frame. Lucas tells Chick that if he digs up
Vinson Gowrie's grave, he will find that the dead man was not killed
by his gun, a forty-one Colt. Chick is understandably reluctant—
Vinson is buried in the most dangerous section of the county, Beat
Nine, the Gowries' own stomping grounds—but he has that debt to
Lucas, and with the help of Alexander and an octogenarian, Miss
Habersham (Elizabeth Patterson), he sets about the task.

Their midnight venture is full of suspense. Here, as he does

**Charles Kemper (in vehicle) as Crawford Gowrie in
INTRUDER IN THE DUST (1949)**

throughout the film, Brown shuns standard Hollywood mood music and uses the sounds of the night—birds, crickets, and so on—to create tension. They dig up the coffin and find it's empty and return to town to tell their story to Stevens and the sheriff. Next morning all except Miss Habersham (who stays in the jailhouse to guard Lucas) go out to the grave site and finally discover Vinson's body in a hole of quicksand nearby. He was killed by a shot-gun, not by Lucas's pistol. Back at the sheriff's office the whole town is swept up in a carnival atmosphere: swing music blares from loudspeakers in the town square and large numbers of people, women with their babies among them, are gathered in groups laughing and talking, waiting for the hanging. But the mob is to be disappointed. On the basis of the new information, Lucas is freed, and the real murderer, Vinson's brother Crawford (Charles Kemper), is apprehended. Everyone goes home ashamed and uneasy. As Stevens tells his nephew, the people are not running away from Lucas or Crawford, but from themselves. But "it'll be alright," he explains to Chick, "as long as someone—you, Miss Habersham, and Alec and maybe me—or even as long as one of us, someone of us, doesn't run away." When Chick sees Lucas again it is clear that his long standing debt to the black man has been paid, and that now only a genuine friendship exists between them.

Upon its release, *Intruder in the Dust* was highly praised. Bosley Crowther wrote in the *New York Times:* "Producer-director Clarence Brown has made a brilliant, stirring film . . . Without the moment's hesitation, this corner, still shaking, proclaims that it is probably this year's pre-eminent picture and one of the great cinema dramas of our times."[12] Crowther's comments were indicative of the sort of response generated by the film. Even as captious a commentator as Marxist critic V. J. Jerome found something praiseworthy in this film that presents "a Negro as the central character, the hero of the drama."[13] Brown narrowly lost out to Carol Reed in the voting for the New York Critics best direction award for 1949. Typically, the film was ignored by the Academy of Motion Picture Arts and Sciences, probably because its theme was still too sensitive to receive widespread popular support, but Brown did, however, win the British Academy's prize for best direction that year.

Ultimately for Brown, *Intruder in the Dust* proved a fitting climax to an illustrious, if sometimes inconsistent, career as a film director. That he made it at all suggests the genuine commitment he felt toward his art not only as a way of providing first-class entertainment, but as an outlet for himself and his own world view. Perhaps having devoted himself so completely to *Intruder in the Dust,* directing and producing it, Brown wore out the last of his creative energies. His last four films—*To Please a Lady* (1950), *Angels in the Outfield* (1951), *When In Rome* (1952) and *Plymouth Adventure* (1952)—are not up to the standard set by his late-forties work. And perhaps he left Hollywood in 1952 because he knew himself he had lost "it"—the ambition and drive and creativity to make new and better films. When he had been motivated to do his best work, few director, if any, were better.

NOTES

[1]David Thomson, *A Biographical Dictionary of the Cinema.* (London: Secker and Warburg), 1975.

[2]Paul Rotha, *The Film Till Now* (New York: Funk and Wagnalls, revised ed., 1949), p. 197.

[3]Kevin Brownlow, *The Parade's Gone By . . .* (New York: Knopf, 1968), p. 245.

[4]*The Unholy Three* was directed by Tod Browning and starred Lon Chaney. It was released in 1925 by M-G-M.

[5]Garbo had come to Hollywood the year before with her mentor Mauritz Stiller, and had already stirred great interest—especially with her last film *The Temptress*—but it was her performance here that established her screen persona. Together with Daniels, Brown gave the Swedish actress the "look" that became, in effect, her signature: the high-arched eyebrows, the wafer-thin lips, the high-key lighting that accented her angular features. Most importantly, Brown gave Garbo the freedom (and the visual accompaniment) to forge her own character, and in the case of *Flesh and the Devil* what may be the cinema's definitive portrait of a vamp. Garbo appreciated both Brown and Daniels. In fact, if both men are known outside of a small circle of film scholars and enthusiasts they are known as "Garbo's director" (Brown and Garbo did seven films together) and "Garbo's cameraman" (Daniels photographed nineteen of Garbo's twenty-three American films.)

[6]Brownlow, p. 149.

[7]Dorothy Manners, "Without Benefit of Close-Ups," *Motion Picture Classic* April 1928, p. 26.

[8]Manners, p. 78.

[9]Michael Arlen, *The Green Hat* (London: Collins, 1924), p. 309. The novel's reputation was such that the censors did not want the film to possess the title, *The Green Hat,* and so insisted that it be changed. When M-G-M honoured the request and altered the title to *A Woman of Affairs,* a title ostensibly far more risqué than *The Green Hat,* the censors inexplicably did not complain.

[10]In the novel, the reason David commits suicide on his wedding night is that he has syphilis. Obviously, that would not do for an explanation in the film. Arlen's contrivance is certainly more convincing than the film's but neither succeeds in suspending disbelief.

[11]Gilbert did star in *Queen Christina* with Garbo in 1934. Sound equipment had improved enough so that his voice now sounded normal. Unfortunately, although he gave a fine performance in the film, he did not recover his lost popularity.

[12]Bosley Crowther, "Intruder in the Dust" *The New York Times,* 23 Nov. 1949, p. 19.

[13]V. J. Jerome, *The Negro in Hollywood Films* (New York: Masses and Mainstream, 1950), p. 41.

Clarence Brown Filmography

THE GREAT REDEEMER (1920). Criminal sees the light while in prison. *Sc:* Jack Gilbert, Jules Furthman, Clarence Brown. *Ph:* Charles Van Enger. *With* House Peters, Marjorie Daw, Joseph Singleton, Jack MacDonald. *Prod:* Maurice Tourneur for Metro. 7,500 ft.

THE LAST OF THE MOHICANS (1920). Adventure during the French and Indian wars of pre-revolutionary America. *Sc:* Robert A. Dillon (the novel by James Fenimore Cooper). *Ph:* Philip R. DuBois, Charles Van Enger. *With* Barbara Bedford, Albert Roscoe, Wallace Beery. *Prod:* Maurice Tourneur for Associated Producers. 5,720 ft.

THE FOOLISH MATRONS (1921). Morality play involving the fate of three different women. *Sc:* Wyndham Gittens (the novel by Brian Donn-Byrne). *Ph:* Charles Van Enger, K. G. MacLean. *With* Hobart Bosworth (*Dr. Ian Fraser*), Doris May (*Georgie Wayne*), Mildred Manning (*Shelia Hopkins*), Kathleen Kirkham (*Annis Grand*), Betty Schade (*the mysterious woman*), Margaret McWade (*Mrs. Eugenia Sheridan*). *Prod:* Maurice Tourneur for Associated Producers. 6,544 feet. (Co-directed with Maurice Tourneur.)

THE LIGHT IN THE DARK (1922). Thief pursues a goblet that is thought to be the Holy Grail for the sake of his ailing girl friend. *Sc:* Clarence Brown, William Dudley Pelley (the story by William Dudley Pelley). *Ph:* Alfred Ortlieb, Ben Carré. *With* Hope Hampton (*Bessie*), E. K. Lincoln (*J. Warburton Ashe*), Lon Chaney (*Tony Pantelli*), Theresa Maxwell Conover (*Mrs. Templeton Orrin*), Dorothy Walter (*Mrs. Callerty*). *Prod:* First National. 7 reels. Colour sequence.

DON'T MARRY FOR MONEY (1923). Woman marries for money and lives to regret it. *Sc:* Hope Loring, Louis D. Lighton. *With* House Peters (*Peter Smith*), Rubye De Remer (*Marion Witney*), Aileen Pringle (*Edith Martin*), Cyril Chadwick (*Crane Martin*), Christine Mayo (*Rose Grahame*). *Prod:* B. F. Finneman for Weber and North. 6 reels.

THE ACQUITTAL (1923). A "whodunit". *Sc:* Jules Furthman (adapted from the Rita Weiman stage play by Raymond L. Schrock). *Continuity:* Jules Furthman, Dale Van Every. *Ph:* Silvano Balboni. *With* Claire Windsor (*Madeline Ames*), Norman Kerry (*Robert Armstrong*), Richard Travers (*Kenneth Winthrop*), Barbara Bedford (*Edith Craig*), Charles Wellesley (*Andrew Prentice*), Frederick Vroom (*Carter Ames*), Ben Deeley (*Butler*), Harry Mestagyer (*District Attorney*), Emmett King (*Minister*), Dot Farley *(Maid)*, Hayden Stevenson (*Taxi Driver*). *Prod:* Universal. 7 reels. [*The American Film Institute Catalog: Feature Films 1921-30* (New York: Bowker, 1971) also lists John Huston, Tom Reed, Tom Kilpatrick and Anthony Veiller as continuity writers for this film, impossible as this would seem.]

THE SIGNAL TOWER (1924). A psychological drama about railroad life. *Sc:* James O. Spearing (the story by Wadsworth Camp). *Ph:* Ben Reynolds. *With* Virginia Valli (*Sally*), Rockliffe Fellowes (*Dave*), Frankie Derro (*Sonny*), Wallace Beery (*Joe Standish*), James O. Barrows (*Old Bill*), J. Farrell MacDonald (*Pete*), Dot Farley (*Gertie*), Clarence Brown (*switch man*), Jitney (*the dog*). *Prod:* Universal. 7 reels.

BUTTERFLY (1924). Woman sacrifices her career and her one love for her sister. *Sc:* Olga Printzlau (the novel by Kathleen Norris). *Ph:* Ben Reynolds. *With* Laura La Plante (*Dora Collier*), Ruth Clifford (*Hilary Collier*), Kenneth Harlan (*Craig*

Spaulding), Norman Kerry (*Konrad Kronski*), Cesare Gravina (*Von Mandescheid*), Margaret Livingston (*Violet Van DeWort*). *Prod:* Universal. 8 reels.

SMOULDERING FIRES (1924). Business woman gives up her husband for the sake of her sister's happiness. *Sc:* Sada Cowan, Howard Higgin, Melville Brown. *Titles:* Dwinelle Benthall. *Ph:* Jackson Rose. *Art dir:* E. E. Sheeley. *Ed:* Edward Schroeder. *With* Pauline Frederick (*Jane Vale*), Laura La Plante (*Dorothy*), Malcolm McGregor (*Robert Elliot*), Tully Marshall (*Scotty*), Wanda Hawley (*Lucy*), Helen Lynch (*Kate Brown*), George Cooper (*Mugsy*). *Prod:* Universal. 8 reels.

THE GOOSE WOMAN (1925). Fallen opera star unwittingly makes her son the prime suspect in a murder. *Sc:* Melville Brown (the story by Rex Beach). *Titles:* Dwinelle Benthall. *Ph:* Milton Moore. *Art dir:* William R. Schmitt, E. E. Sheeley. *Ed:* Raymond F. Curtiss. *With* Louise Dresser (*Mary Holmes*), Jack Pickford (*Gerald Holmes*), Constance Bennett (*Hazel Woods*), James O. Barrows (*Jacob Riggs*), George Cooper (*reporter*), Gustave von Seyffertitz (*Vogel*), George Nichols (*detective*), Marc MacDermott (*Amos Etheridge*). *Prod:* Universal. 7,500 ft.

THE EAGLE (1925). Robin Hood bandit falls in love with his enemy's daughter. *Sc:* Hans Kraly (the novella "Dubrovsky" by Pushkin). *Titles:* George Marion Jr. *Ph:* George Barnes. *Art dir:* William Cameron Menzies. *Ed:* Hal C. Kern. *Costumes:* Adrian. *With* Rudolph Valentino (*Dubrovsky*), Vilma Banky (*Mascha*), Louise Dresser (*Czarina*), Albert Conti (*Kuschka*), James Marcus (*Krilla*), George Nichols (*Judge*), Carrie Clark Ward (*Aunt Aurelia*). *Prod:* John W. Considine for United Artists. 7 reels.

KIKI (1926). Comedy about ingenuous young actress who pursues swank theatrical manager. *Sc:* Hans Kraly (the play by David Belasco and André Picard). *Ph:* Oliver Marsh. *With* Norma Talmadge (*Kiki*), Ronald Colman (*Renal*), Gertrude Astor (*Paulette*), Marc MacDermott (*Baron Rapp*), George K. Arthur (*Adolphe*),

Frankie Darro (*Pierre*). *Prod:* Joseph Schenck for First National. 90m.

FLESH AND THE DEVIL (1927). Demonic temptress comes between the lifelong friendship of two noblemen. *Sc:* Benjamin F. Glazer (novel "The Undying Past" by Hermann Sudermann). *Titles:* Marian Ainslee. *Ph:* William Daniels. *Art dir:* Cedric Gibbons, Frederic Hope. *Ed:* Lloyd Nosler. *With* John Gilbert (*Leo*), Greta Garbo (*Felicitas*), Lars Hanson (*Ulrich*), Barbara Kent (*Hertha*), William Orlamond (*Uncle Kukowki*), George Fawcett (*Pastor Voss*), Eugenie Besserer (*Leo's mother*), Marc MacDermott (*Count Von Rhaden*), Marcelle Corday (*Minna*). *Prod:* Clarence Brown for M-G-M. 9 reels.

THE TRAIL OF '98 (1928). Gold fever draws fortune seekers to Alaska. *Sc:* Benjamin Glazer, Waldemar Young (the novel by Robert W. Service). *Titles:* Joe Farnham. *Ph:* John Seitz. *Art dir:* Cedric Gibbons, Merrill Pye. *Ed:* George Hively. *With* Dolores Del Rio (*Berna*), Ralph Forbes (*Larry*), Karl Dane (*Lars Peterson*), Harry Carey (*Jack Locasto*), Tully Marshall (*Salvation Jim*), George Cooper (*Summuel Foote*), Russell Simpson (*Old Swede*), Emily Fitzroy (*Mrs. Bulkey*), Cesare Gravina (*Grandfather*), Polly Moran (*Mrs. Peterson*). *Prod:* M-G-M. 127m.

WOMAN OF AFFAIRS (1929). Moribund social conventions thwart free-spirited woman. *Sc:* Bess Meredyth (novel "The Green Hat" by Michael Arlen). *Titles:* Marian Ainslee, Ruth Cummings. *Ph:* William Daniels. *Art dir:* Cedric Gibbons. *Ed:* Hugh Wynn. *With* Greta Garbo (*Diana*), John Gilbert (*Neville*), Lewis Stone (*Hugh*), John Mack Brown (*David*), Douglas Fairbanks Jr. (*Jeffrey*), Hobart Bosworth (*Sir Morton*), Dorothy Sebastian (*Constance*). *Prod:* M-G-M. 90m.

WONDER OF WOMEN (1929). Adulterous concert pianist comes to realise the depth of his love for his wife. *Sc:* Bess Meredyth (novel "Die Frau des Steffen Tromholt" by Hermann Sudermann). *Titles:* Marian Ainslee. *Ph:* Merritt B. Gerstad. *Art dir:* Cedric Gibbons. *Ed:*

William LeVanway. *With* Lewis Stone (*Stephen Tromolt*), Leila Hyams (*Karen*), Peggy Wood (*Brigitte*), Harry Myers (*Bruno Heim*), Sarah Padden (*Anna*), George Fawcett (*doctor*), Blanche Frederici (*housekeeper*), Wally Albright Jr. (*Wulle-Wulle*), Carmencita Johnson (*Lottie*). *Prod:* M-G-M. 11 reels.

NAVY BLUES (1929). Sailor falls in love with girl he meets in dance hall. *Sc:* J. C. Nugent, Elliott Nugent (adapted by Dale Van Every from a story by Raymond L. Schrock). *Ph:* Merritt Gerstad. *Art dir:* Cedric Gibbons. *Ed:* Hugh Wynn. *With* William Haines (*Kelly*), Anita Page (*Alice*), Karl Dane (*Swede*), J. C. Nugent (*Mr. Brown*), Edythe Chapman (*Mrs. Brown*), Gertrude Sutton (*Hilda*), Wade Boteler (*chief petty officer*). *Prod:* M-G-M. 9 reels.

ANNA CHRISTIE (1930). Drama on New York's wharfside. *Sc:* Frances Marion (the stage play by Eugene O'Neill). *Ph:* William Daniels. *Art dir:* Cedric Gibbons. *Ed:* Hugh Wynn. *With* Greta Garbo (*Anna*), Charles Bickford (*Matt*), George F. Marion (*Chris*), Marie Dressler (*Marthy*), James T. Mack (*Johnny, the harp*), Lee Phelps (*Larry*). *Prod:* M-G-M. 74m.

Greta Garbo and Gavin Gordon in ROMANCE

ROMANCE (1930). Student studying for the ministry falls in love with sybarite. *Sc:* Bess Meredyth, Edwin Justus Mayer (the stage play by Edward Sheldon). *Ph:* William Daniels. *Art dir:* Cedric Gibbons. *Ed:* Hugh Wynn. *With* Greta Garbo (*Rita Cavallini*), Lewis Stone (*Cornelius Van Tuyl*), Gavin Gordon (*Tom Armstrong*), Elliott Nugent (*Harry*), Florence Lake (*Susan Van Tuyl*), Clara Blandick (*Miss Armstrong*), Henry Armetta (*Beppo*). *Prod:* M-G-M. 76m.

INSPIRATION (1931). A jaded artist's model falls in love with a young university student. *Sc:* Gene Markey. *Ph:* William Daniels. *Art dir:* Cedric Gibbons. *Ed:* Conrad A. Nervig. *With* Greta Garbo (*Yvonne*), Robert Montgomery (*André*), Lewis Stone (*Delval*), Majorie Rambeau (*Lulu*), Judith Vosselli (*Odette*), Beryle Mercer (*Marthe*). *Prod:* M-G-M. 74m.

A FREE SOUL (1931). A bored sybarite finds more excitement than she bargained for when she becomes the mistress of a ruthless gangster. *Sc:* Becky Gardiner (the novel by Adela Rogers St. Johns). *Ph:* William Daniels. *Art dir:* Cedric Gibbons. *Ed:* Hugh Wynn. *With* Norma Shearer (*Jan Ashe*), Leslie Howard (*Dwight Winthrop*), Lionel Barrymore (*Stephen Ashe*), Clark Gable (*Ace Wilfong*), James Gleason (*Eddie*), Lucy Beaumont (*Grandma Ashe*). *Prod:* M-G-M. 91m.

POSSESSED (1931). Small-town girl goes to the big city and hooks up with a wealthy politician. *Sc:* Lenore Coffee (the play "Mirage" by Edgar Selwyn). *Ph:* Oliver Marsh. *With* Joan Crawford (*Marian*), Clark Gable (*Mark Whitney*), Wallace Ford (*Al Manning*), Skeets Gallagher (*Wally*). *Prod:* M-G-M. 76.

EMMA (1932). Nanny marries the master of the house despite family objections. *Sc:* Leonard Praskins (a story by Frances Marion). *Additional dialogue:* Zelda Sears. *Ph:* Oliver Marsh. *Art dir:* Cedric Gibbons. *Ed:* William LeVanway. *With* Marie Dressler (*Emma*), Richard Cromwell (*Ronnie*), Jean Hersholt (*Mr. Smith*), Myrna Loy (*Isabelle*), John Miljan (*district attorney*), Purnell B. Pratt (*Haskins*), Leila Bennett (*Matilda*), Barbara Kent (*Gypsy*). *Prod:* M-G-M. 72m.

**Myrna Loy, Marie Dressler
and players in EMMA**

LETTY LYNTON (1932). Beautiful New York socialite becomes involved with an international playboy and lives to reget it. *Sc:* John Meehan, Wanda Tuchock (the novel by Marie Belloc Lowndes). *Ph:* Oliver Marsh. *Art dir:* Cedric Gibbons. *Ed:* Conrad A. Nervig. *With* Joan Crawford (*Letty Lynton*), Nils Asther (*Emile Renaul*), Robert Montgomery (*Jerry Darrow*), Louise Closser Hale (*Miranda*), May Robson (*Mrs. Lynton*), Lewis Stone (*Haney*), Emma

**Lewis Stone and Helen Hayes
in THE SON-DAUGHTER**

Dunn (*Mrs. Darrow*), Walter Walker (*Mr. Darrow*). *Prod:* M-G-M. 84m.

THE SON-DAUGHTER (1932). A Chinese-American father sells his daughter to the highest bidder to raise money for a revolution in the homeland. *Sc:* John Goodrich, Claudine West, Leon Gordon (a play by George M. Scarborough and David Belasco). *Ph:* Oliver Marsh. *Art dir:* Cedric Gibbons. *Ed:* Margaret Booth. *Mus:* Herbert Stothart. *With* Helen Hayes (*Lien Wha*), Ramon Navarro (*Tom Lee*), Lewis Stone (*Dr. Dong Tong*), Warner Oland (*Ten Sha*), Ralph Morgan (*Tang Fou Hy*), Louise Closser Hale (*Toy Yah*), H. B. Warner (*Sin Kai*). *Prod:* M-G-M. 79m.

LOOKING FORWARD (1933). View of Depression as seen by lowly bookkeeper. *Sc:* Bess Meredyth, H. M. Harwood (play "Service" by C. L. Anthony). *Ph:* Oliver Marsh. *Art dir:* Cedric Gibbons. *Ed:* Hugh Wynn. *With* Lionel Barrymore (*Michael Benton*), Lewis Stone (*Gabriel Service*), Benita Hume (*Isobel Service*), Elizabeth Allan (*Caroline Service*), Phillips Holmes (*Michael Service*), Colin Clive (*Geoffrey Fielding*), Alec B. Francis (*Birkenshaw*), Doris Lloyd (*Mrs. Benton*), Halliwell Hobbes (*Mr. Felton*). *Prod:* Cosmopolitan for M-G-M. 82m.

NIGHT FLIGHT (1933). Aerial adventure of the first air mail flight from South America. *Sc:* Oliver H. P. Garrett (a story by Antoine de Saint-Exupéry). *Ph:* Oliver Marsh, Elmer Dyer, Charles Marshall. *Art dir:* Cedric Gibbons. *Ed:* Hal C. Kern. *With* John Barrymore (*Riviere*), Helen Hayes (*Madame Fabian*), Clark Gable (*Jules Fabian*), Lionel Barrymore (*Robineau*), Robert Montgomery (*Auguste Pellerin*), Myrna Loy (*Brazilian pilot's wife*), William Gargan (*Brazilian pilot*). *Prod:* M-G-M. 84m.

SADIE McKEE (1934). After being jilted by her fiancé, working girl has to fend for herself in the big city. *Sc:* John Meehan (a story Vina Delmar). *Ph:* Oliver Marsh. *Art dir:* Cedric Gibbons, Frederic Hope, Edwin B. Willis. *Ed:* Hugh Wynn. *With* Joan Crawford (*Sadie*), Gene Raymond (*Tommy*), Franchot Tone (*Michael*), Edward Arnold (*Brennan*), Esther Ralson (*Dolly*), Earl Oxford (*Stooge*), Jean Dixon (*Opal*), Leo Carroll (*Phelps*), Akim Tamiroff (*Riccori*), Zelda Sears (*Mrs. Craney*), Helen Ware (*Mrs. McKee*), Gene Austin and Cady and Coco (*cafe entertainers*). *Prod:* Lawrence Weingarten for M-G-M. 90m.

CHAINED (1934). Mistress leaves sugar daddy for rugged rancher. *Sc:* John Lee Mahin (story by Edgar Selwyn). *Ph:* George Folsey. *Art dir:* Cedric Gibbons, Alexander Toluboff, Edwin B. Willis. *Ed:* Robert J. Kern. *Mus:* Herbert Stothart. *With* Joan Crawford (*Diane Lovering*), Clark Gable (*Mike Bradley*), Otto Kruger (*Richard Field*), Stuart Erwin (*Johnnie Smith*), Una O'Connor (*Amy*), Marjorie Gateson (*Mrs. Field*), Akim Tamiroff (*Pablo*). *Prod:* Hunt Stromberg for M-G-M. 71m.

ANNA KARENINA (1935). Tolstoy's famous story of doomed romance between the unhappy wife of a politician and her soldier-lover. *Sc:* Clemence Dane, Salka Viertel, S. N. Behrman. *Ph:* William Daniels. *Art dir:* Cedric Gibbons, Frederic Hope, Edwin B. Willis. *Ed:* Robert J. Kern. *Mus:* Herbert Stothart. *With* Greta Garbo (*Anna Karenina*), Fredric March (*Vronsky*), Maureen O'Sullivan (*Kitty*), May Robson (*Countess Vronsky*), Constance Collier (*Countess Lidia*), Reginald Owen (*Stiva*), Freddie Bartholomew (*Sergei*), Basil Rathbone (*Alexei Karenin*), Phoebe Foster (*Dolly*), Reginald Denny (*Yashvin*), Gyles Isham (*Levin*). *Prod:* David O. Selznick for M-G-M. 95m.

AH WILDERNESS (1935). Sentimental recollection of family life in New England at the turn of the century. *Sc:* Francis Goodrich, Albert Hackett (from the stage play Eugene O'Neill). *Ph:* Clyde De Vinna. *Art dir:* Cedric Gibbons, William Horning. *Ed:* Frank E. Hull. *Mus:* Herbert Stothart. *With* Wallace Beery (*Sid*), Lionel Barrymore (*Nat*), Aline MacMahon (*Lily*), Eric Linden (*Richard*), Cecilia Parker (*Muriel*), Spring Byington (*Essie*), Mickey Rooney (*Tommy*), Charles Grapewin (*Mr. McComber*), Frank Albertson (*Arthur*), Edward Nugent (*Wint*),

Bonita Granville (*Mildred*), Helen Flint (*Belle*), Helen Freeman (*Miss Hawley*). *Prod:* Hunt Stromberg for M-G-M. 101m.

WIFE VERSUS SECRETARY (1936). Suspicious wife mistakenly believes her husband is having an affair with his secretary. *Sc:* Norman Krasna, John Lee Mahin, Alice Duer Miller (the story by Faith Baldwin). *Ph:* Ray June. *Art dir:* Cedric Gibbons, William Horning. *Ed:* Frank E. Hull. *Mus:* Herbert Stothart, Edward Ward. *With* Clark Gable (*Van*), Jean Harlow (*Whitey*), Myrna Loy (*Linda*), May Robson (*Mimi*), George Barbier (*Underwood*), James Stewart (*Dave*), Hobart Cavanaugh (*Joe*), Tom Dugan (*Finney*). *Prod:* Hunt Stromberg for M-G-M. 88m.

THE GORGEOUS HUSSY (1936). Inside the early nineteenth century American political scene. *Sc:* Ainsworth Morgan, Stephen Morehouse Avery (the book by Samuel Hopkins Adams). *Ph:* George Folsey. *Art dir:* Cedric Gibbons, William Horning, Edwin B. Willis. *Ed:* Blanche Sewell. *Mus:* Herbert Stothart. *With* Joan Crawford (*Peggy Eaton*), Robert Taylor ("*Bow*" *Timberlake*), Lionel Barrymore (*Andrew Jackson*), Franchot Tone (*John Eaton*), Melvyn Douglas (*John Randolph*), James Stewart ("*Rowdy*" *Dow*), Alison Skipworth (*Mrs. Beall*), Beulah Bondi (*Rachel Jackson*), Louis Calhern (*Sunderland*), Melville Cooper (*Cuthbert*), Sidney Toler (*Daniel Webster*), Gene Lockhart (*Mayor O'Neal*), Clara Blandick (*Louisa Abbott*). *Prod:* Joseph L. Mankiewicz for M-G-M. 102m.

CONQUEST (G.B.: MARIE WALEWSKA) (1937). Tragic romance of Napoleon and his mistress. *Sc:* Samuel Hoffenstein, Salka Viertel, S. N. Behrman (dramatisation by Helen Jerome of the novel by Waclaw Gasiorowski). *Ph:* Karl Freund. *Art dir:* Cedric Gibbons. *Ed:* Tom Held. *With* Greta Garbo (*Marie Walewska*), Charles Boyer (*Napoleon*), Reginald Owen (*Talleyrand*), Alan Marshall (*Capt. D'Ornano*), Henry Stephenson (*Count Walewska*), Leif Erickson (*Paul*), Dame May Whitty

(*Laetitia Bonaparte*), C. Henry Gordon (*Prince Poniatowski*), Marie Ouspenskaya (*Countess Pelagia*), Claude Gillingwater (*Stephen*), George Houston (*Marshall Duroc*). *Prod:* Bernard H. Hyman for M-G-M. 112m.

OF HUMAN HEARTS (1938). Minister and his family struggle with life in a small Ohio town in the middle of the nineteenth century. *Sc:* Bradbury Foote (story "Benefits Forgot" by Honoré Morrow). *Ph:* Clyde De Vinna. *Art dir:* Cedric Gibbons, Harry Oliver, Edwin B. Willis. *Ed:* Frank E. Hull. *Mus:* Herbert Stothart. *With* Walter Huston (*Ethan Wilkins*), James Stewart (*Jason Wilkins*), Gene Reynolds (*Jason Wilkins—as a child*), Beulah Bondi (*Mary Wilkins*), Guy Kibbee (*George Ames*), Charles Coburn (*Dr. Charles Shingle*), John Carradine (*President Lincoln*), Ann Rutherford (*Anne Hawks*), Leatrice Joy Gilbert (*Annie Hawks—as a child*), Charles Grapewin (*Jim Meaker*), Leona Roberts (*Sister Clark*), Gene Lockhart (*Quid*), Clem Bevans (*Elder Massey*), Arthur Aylesworth (*Rufus Inchpin*), Sterling Holloway (*Chauncey Ames*), Charles Peck (*Chauncey Ames—as a child*), Robert McWade (*Dr. Lupus Crumm*), Minor Watson (*Captain Griggs*). *Prod:* John W. Considine Jr. for M-G-M. 105m.

IDIOT'S DELIGHT (1939). A group of travellers are forced to stay in a European resort hotel during the outbreak of the Second World War. *Sc:* Robert E. Sherwood (his play). *Ph:* William Daniels. *Art dir:* Cedric Gibbons. *Ed:* Robert J. Kern. *Mus:* Herbert Stothart. *With* Norma Shearer (*Irene*), Clark Gable (*Harry*), Edward Arnold (*Achille Weber*), Charles Coburn (*Dr. Waldersee*), Joseph Schildkraut (*Capt. Kirvline*), Burgess Meredith (*Quillery*), Laura Hope Crews (*Madame Zuleika*), Skeets Gallagher (*Donald Navadel*), Peter Willes (*Mr. Cherry*), Pat Patterson (*Mrs. Cherry*), William Edmunds (*Dumpsty*). *Prod:* Hunt Stromberg for M-G-M. 100m.

THE RAINS CAME (1939). Natural disaster reshapes the lives of the people in an Indian city. *Sc:* Philip Dunne, Julien Josephson (the novel by Louis Bromfield). *Ph:* Arthur Miller. *Ed:* Barbara McLean. *Mus:* Alfred Newman. *With* Myrna Loy (*Lady Edwina Esketh*), Tyrone Power (*Major Rama Safti*), George Brent (*Tom Ransome*), Brenda Joyce (*Fern Simon*), Nigel Bruce (*Lord Esketh*), Maria Ouspenskaya (*Maharani*), Joseph Schildkraut (*Bannerjee*), Mary Nash (*Miss MacDaid*), Jane Darwell (*Aunt Phoebe*), Marjorie Rambeau (*Mrs. Simon*), Henry Travers (*Reverend Smiley*), H. B. Warner (*Maharjah*), Laura Hope Crews (*Lily Hoggett-Egbury*). *Prod:* Darryl F. Zanuck for 20th Century-Fox. 103m.

COME LIVE WITH ME (1941). Refugee marries writer in order to avoid deportation. *Sc:* Patterson McNutt (an original story by Virginia Van Upp). *Ph:* George Folsey. *Ed:* Frank E. Hull. *With* James Stewart (*Bill Smith*), Hedy Lamarr (*Johnny Jones*), Ian Hunter (*Barton Kendrick*), Verree Teasdale (*Diana Kendrick*), Donald Meek (*Joe Darsie*), Barton MacLane (*Barney Grogan*). *Prod:* Clarence Brown for M-G-M. 86m.

THEY MET IN BOMBAY (1941). Confidence man and beautiful jewel thief fall in love while pursuing precious gems. *Sc:* Edwin Justus Mayer, Anita Loos, Leon Gordon (story by John Kafka).

Rosalind Russell and Jessie Ralph in THEY MET IN BOMBAY

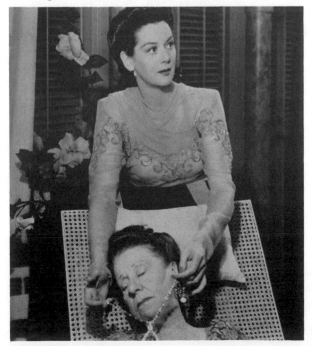

Ph: William Daniels. *Art dir:* Cedric Gibbons. *Ed:* Blanche Sewell. *With* Clark Gable (*Gerald Meldrick*), Rosalind Russell (*Anya Von Duren*), Peter Lorre (*Capt. Chang*), Jessie Ralph (*Duchess of Beltravers*), Reginald Owen (*General*), Matthew Boulton (*Inspector Cressney*). *Prod:* Hunt Stromberg for M-G-M. 86m.

THE HUMAN COMEDY (1943). A family has to come to grips with life during wartime. *Sc:* Howard Estabrook (the novel by William Saroyan). *Ph:* Harry Stradling. *Art dir:* Cedric Gibbons, Paul Groesse. *Ed:* Conrad A. Nervig. *Mus:* Herbert Stothart. *With* Mickey Rooney (*Homer*), Frank Morgan (*Willie Grogan*), James Craig (*Tom Spangler*), Marsha Hunt (*Diana*), Fay Bainter (*Mrs. Macauley*), Ray Collins *(Mr. Macauley)*, Van Johnson (*Marcus*), Donna Reed (*Bess*), Jack Jenkins (*Ulysses*), Dorothy Morris *(Mary)*. *Prod:* Clarence Brown for M-G-M. 118m.

WHITE CLIFFS OF DOVER (1944). American woman marries into English nobility. Her husband is killed in the First World War, her son in the second and she must stoically endure the sorrow of both. *Sc:* Claudine West, Jan Lustig, George Froeschel (poem "White Cliffs of Dover" by Alice Duer Miller). *Ph:* George Folsey. *Art dir:* Cedric Gibbons, Randall Duell. *Ed:* Robert J. Kern. *Mus:* Herbert Stothart. *With* Irene Dunne (*Susan Ashwood*), Alan Marshall (*Sir John Ashwood*), Frank Morgan (*Hiram Porter Dunn*), Roddy McDowall (*John Ashwood II as a boy*), Dame May Whitty (*Nanny*), C. Aubrey Smith (*Colonel*), Gladys Cooper (*Lady Ashwood*), Peter Lawford (*John Ashwood II*), Van Johnson (*Sam Bennett*), Elizabeth Taylor (*Betsy as a child*), June Lockhart (*Betsy*). *Prod:* Sidney Franklin for M-G-M. 126m.

NATIONAL VELVET (1944). Butcher's daughter captures impossible dream and wins the Grand National horse race. *Sc:* Theodore Reeves, Helen Deutsch (the novel by Enid Bagnold). *Ph:* Leonard Smith. *Art dir:* Cedric Gibbons, Urie McCleary. *Ed:* Robert J. Kern. *Mus:* Herbert Stothart. *With* Mickey Rooney (*Mi Taylor*), Donald Crisp (*Mr. Brown*), Elizabeth Taylor (*Velvet Brown*), Anne Revere (*Mrs. Brown*), Angela Lansbury (*Edwina*), Juanita Quigley (*Malvolia*), Jackie Jenkins (*Donald*), Arthur Treacher (*race patron*), Reginald Owen (*Farmer Ede*), Norma Varden (*Miss Sims*), Terry Kilburn (*Ted*), Arthur Shields (*Mr. Hallam*). *Prod:* Pandro S. Berman for M-G-M. 125m. Technicolor.

THE YEARLING (1946). Frontier family in the 1870's struggles to make a life for themselves in the wilds of Florida. *Sc:* Paul Osborn (the novel by Marjorie Kinnan Rawlings). *Ph:* Charles Rosher, Leonard Smith, Arthur Arling. *Art dir:* Cedric Gibbons, Paul Groesse. *Ed:* Harold F. Kress. *Mus:* Herbert Stothart. *With* Gregory Peck (*Pa Baxter*), Jane Wyman (*Ma Baxter*), Claude Jarman (*Jody Baxter*), Chill Wills (*Buck Forrester*), Clem Bevans (*Pa Forrester*), Margaret Wycherly (*Ma Forrester*), Henry Travers (*Mr. Boyles*), Forrest Tucker (*Lem Forrester*), Donn Gift (*Fodderwing*). *Prod:* Sidney Franklin for M-G-M. 134m. Technicolor.

SONG OF LOVE (1947). Film biography of 19th century German composer Robert Schumann and his wife, Clara. *Sc:* Ivan Tors, Irmgard Von Cube, Allen Vincent, Robert Ardrey (the play by Bernard Schubert and Mario Silva). *Ph:* Harry Stradling. *Art dir:* Cedric Gibbons, Hans Peters. *Ed:* Robert J. Kern. *Mus:* Bronislau Kaper. *With* Katharine Hepburn (*Clara Wieck Schumann*), Paul Hen-

Elizabeth Taylor and Roddy McDowall in THE WHITE CLIFFS OF DOVER

reid (*Robert Schumann*), Robert Walker (*Johannes Brahms*), Henry Daniell (*Franz Liszt*), Leo G. Carroll (*Prof. Wieck*), Else Janssen (*Bertha*), Gigi Perreau (*Julie*), "Tinker" Furlong (*Felix*), Anne Carter (*Marie*), Janine Perreau (*Eugenie*). *Prod:* Clarence Brown for M-G-M. 119m.

INTRUDER IN THE DUST (1949). Lynch mob forms when black man is accused of murdering a white man in a southern town. *Sc:* Ben Maddow (the novel by William Faulkner). *Ph:* Robert Surtees. *Art dir:* Cedric Gibbons, Randall Duell. *Ed:* Robert J. Kern. *Mus:* Adolph Deutsch. *With* David Brian (*John Gavin Stevens*), Claude Jarman Jr. (*Chick Mallison*), Juano Hernandez (*Lucas Beauchamp*), Porter Hall (*Nub Gowrie*), Elizabeth Patterson (*Miss Habersham*), Charles Kemper (*Crawford Gowrie*), Will Geer (*Sheriff Hampton*), David Clarke (*Vinson Gowrie*), Elizie Emanuel (*Aleck*). *Prod:* Clarence Brown for M-G-M. 87m.

TO PLEASE A LADY (1950). Racing car driver tames hard-nosed reporter who seeks to end his career. *Sc:* Barré Lyndon, Marge Decker. *Ph:* Harold Rosson. *Art dir:* Cedric Gibbons, James Basevi. *Ed:* Robert J. Kern. *Mus:* Bronislau Kaper. *With* Clark Gable (*Mike Brannan*), Barbara Stanwyck (*Regina Forbes*), Adolphe Menjou (*Gregg*), Will Geer (*Jack Mackay*), Roland Winters (*Dwight Barrington*), William C. McGraw (*Joie Chitwood*), Lela Bliss (*Regina's secretary*). *Prod:* Clarence Brown for M-G-M. 91m.

ANGELS IN THE OUTFIELD (G.B.: ANGELS AND THE PIRATES) (1951). Struggling baseball team gets some help from the heavens. *Sc:* Dorothy Kingsley, George Wells (a story by Richard Conlin). *Ph:* Paul C. Vogel. *Art dir:* Cedric Gibbons, Edward Carfagno. *Ed:* Robert J. Kern. *Mus:* Daniele Amfitheatrof. *With* Paul Douglas (*Guffy McGovern*), Janet Leigh (*Jennifer Paige*), Donna Corcoran (*Bridget White*), Keenan Wynn (*Fred Bayles*), Spring Byington (*Sister Edwitha*),

Ellen Corby (*Sister Veronica*), Bruce Bennett (*Saul Hellman*), Jeff Richards (*Dave Rothberg*), John Gallaudet (*Reynolds*), Lewis Stone (*Arnold F. Hapgood*). *Prod:* Clarence Brown for M-G-M. 102m.

IT'S A BIG COUNTRY (1951). Film anthology of the American way of life. Episode called LONE STAR. *Sc:* Dorothy Kingsley. *With* Gary Cooper. *Prod:* Dore Schary for M-G-M. 89m. (all episodes).

WHEN IN ROME (1952). Unregenerate criminal suddenly sees the light while passing through Rome. *Sc:* Charles Schnee, Dorothy Kingsley (a story by Robert Buckner). *Ph:* William Daniels. *Art dir:* Cedric Gibbons, Edward Carfagno. *Ed:* Robert J. Kern. *Mus:* Carmen Dragon. *With* Van Johnson (*Father John Halligan*), Paul Douglas (*Joe Brewster*), Joseph Calleia (*Aggiunto Bodulli*), Carlo Rizzo (*Antonio Silesto*), Tudor Owen (*Father McGinniss*), Dino Nardi (*Genoa Commissario*), Aldo Silvanti (*cabby*). *Prod:* Clarence Brown for M-G-M. 78m.

PLYMOUTH ADVENTURE (1952). Fictional history of Pilgrim crossing. *Sc:* Helen Deutsch (a novel by Ernest Gebler). *Ph:* William Daniels. *Art dir:* Cedric Gibbons, Urie McCleary. *Ed:* Robert J. Kern. *Mus:* Miklos Rosza. *With* Spencer Tracy (*Capt. Christopher Jones*), Gene Tierney (*Dorothy Bradford*), Van Johnson (*John Alden*), Leo Genn (*William Bradford*), Lloyd Bridges (*Coppin*), Dawn Addams (*Priscilla Mullins*), Barry Jones (*William Brewster*). *Prod:* Dore Schary for M-G-M. 104m. Technicolor.

Other Work

Brown produced THE SECRET GARDEN (1949) and NEVER LET ME GO (1953).

Sources for the Brown filmography: *The American Film Institute Catalog: Feature Films 1921-1930* (New York: Bowker, 1971), "Film Daily", "Variety", and the films themselves.

Bibliographies

FRANK CAPRA: SELECTED BIBLIOGRAPHY

Agee, James. "Comedy's Greatest Era." *Life,* 4 September 1949, pp. 70–88.

Bailey, G. "Why We (Should Not) Fight." *Take One,* September 1975, pp. 10–12.

Barsam, Richard. *Non-Fiction Film: A Critical History.* New York: Dutton, 1973.

Baskette, Kirtley. "Hollywood's New Miracle Man." *Photoplay,* December 1934, pp. 90–92.

Bergman, M. "The Telephone Company, the Nation and Perhaps the World." *Velvet Light Trap,* Winter 1971/72, p. 24.

Biberman, Herbert. "Frank Capra's Characters." *New Masses,* 8 July 1941, pp. 26–27.

"Bob Riskin Muses on 'Lost Horizon.' " *Variety,* 7 April 1937, p. 4.

Brady, Thomas. "Unrest in Hollywood." *New York Times,* 30 June 1946, sec. 2, p. 1.

Bressan, Arthur, and Moran, Michael. "Mr. Capra Goes to College." *Interview,* June 1972, pp. 25, 26, 30.

Capra, Frank. "Frank Capra Tells All." *New York Times,* 16 December 1934, sec. 11, p. 4.

———. "The Gag Man." In *Breaking into Movies,* edited by Charles Reed Jones. Unicorn Press, 1927.

———. "Mr. Capra (Humanist) Shares a Bow." *New York Times,* 19 April 1936, sec. 9, p. 4.

———. *The Name above the Title.* New York: Macmillan, 1971.

"Capra Corn." *Newsweek,* 18 December 1961, p. 97.

Childs, James. "Capra Today." *Film Comment,* November 1972, pp. 22–23.

Churchill, Douglas. "Capra and Points West." *New York Times,* 12 November 1939, sec. 9, p. 5.

Cohen, Harold. "Frank Capra." *Cinema Digest,* 10 April 1933, p. 12.

Collins, Frederick. "Hollywood Magician." *Liberty,* 18 May 1940.

"Columbia's Gem." *Time,* 8 August 1938, p. 35.

Corliss, Richard. "Capra and Riskin." *Film Comment,* November 1972, pp. 18–21.

———. *Talking Pictures: Screenwriters in the American Cinema.* New York: Penguin, 1975.

Crowther, Bosley. "Such Guys as Capra and Wellman." *New York Times,* 16 October 1938, sec. 9, p. 5.

Durgnat, Raymond. *The Crazy Mirror: Hollywood Comedy and the American Image.* New York: Horizon Press, 1969.

"Frank Capra." *Current Biography:* 1948. Ed. Anna Rothe. New York: H. W. Wilson, 1949, pp. 90–92.

"Frank Capra." *Positif.* No. 133, December 1971, pp. 1–89.

"Frank Capra: 'One Man, One Film.' " *Discussion* No. 3, The American Film Institute, 1971.

"Frank Capra's Secret." *Silver Screen,* January 1942, p. 35.

Glatzer, Richard, and Raeburn, John, eds. *Frank Capra: The Man and His Films.* Ann Arbor: University of Michigan Press, 1975.

Greene, Graham. *Graham Greene on Film: Collected Film Criticism.* New York: Simon and Schuster, 1972.

Griffith, Richard. *Frank Capra.* New Index Series, edited by Gavin Lambert, no. 3. London: British Film Institute, 1950.

Handzo, Stephen. "Under Capracorn." *Film Comment,* November 1972, pp. 8–14.

Harriman, M. C. "Mr. and Mrs. Frank Capra." *Ladies Home Journal,* April 1941, p. 35.

Hellman, Geoffrey. "Profiles: Thinker in Hollywood." *New Yorker,* 24 February 1940, pp. 23–28.

Hilton, James. *Lost Horizon.* New York: Morrow, 1933.

Houston, Penelope. "Mr. Deeds and Willie Stark." *Sight and Sound,* November 1950, pp. 276–79, 285.

Jacobs, Lewis. "More About Directors." *New York Times,* 27 October 1935, sec. 9, p. 4.

———. *Rise of the American Cinema.* 1939. Reprint. New York: Teacher's College Press, 1968.

Johnston, Alva. "Capra Shoots As He Pleases." *Saturday Evening Post,* 14 May 1938. p. 8.

Larkin, Rochelle. *Hail Columbia.* New Rochelle: Arlington House, 1975.

Mast, Gerald. *The Comic Mind.* New York: Bobbs-Merrill, 1973.

McBride, Joseph. "Coppola Inc." *American Film,* November 1975, pp. 13–17.

McCaffrey, Donald. *Four Great Comedians.* New York: A. S. Barnes, 1968.

Morris, Ruth. "Capra Foresees Satirical Cycle; Many Subjects 'Ripe for Ridicule.' " *Variety,* 2 February 1932, p. 2.

Nelson, J. "Mr. Smith Goes to Washington: Capra, Populism and Comic Strip Art." *Journal of Popular Film,* Summer 1974, pp. 245–55.

Pechter, William. *Twenty Four Times a Second: Films and Filmmakers.* New York: Harper and Row, 1971.

Poague, Leland. *The Cinema of Frank Capra: An Approach to Film Comedy.* New York: A. S. Barnes, 1975.

Richards, Jeffrey. *Visions of Yesterday.* London: Routledge and Kegan Paul, 1972.

Salemson, Harold. "Mr. Capra's Short Cuts to Utopia." *Penguin Film Review* No. 7. London: Penguin, 1948, pp. 25–34.

Sarris, Andrew. *The American Cinema: Director and Directions—1929–1968.* New York: Dutton, 1968.

Scherle, Victor, and Levy, William Turner. *The Films of Frank Capra.* Secaucus, N.J.: Citadel, 1977.

Schickel, Richard. *The Men Who Made the Movies.* New York: Atheneum, 1975.

Sklar, Robert. *Movie Made America: A Social History of American Movies.* New York: Random House, 1975.

Stuart, John. "Fine Italian Hand." *Colliers,* 17 August 1935. p. 13.

Thomas, Bob. *King Cohn: The Life and Times of Harry Cohn.* New York: G. P. Putnam, 1967.

Van Doren, Mark. *The Private Reader: Selected Articles and Reviews.* New York: Henry Holt, 1942.

Willis, Donald. *The Films of Frank Capra.* Metuchen, N.J.: Scarecrow Press, 1974.

GEORGE CUKOR: SELECTED BIBLIOGRAPHY

Arthur, R. A. "Hanging Out: The Russian Bluebird." *Esquire,* December 1975, p. 70.

Battle, Barbara Helen. "George Cukor and the American Theatrical Film." Ph.D. thesis, Columbia University, 1969.

Behlmer, Rudy, ed. *Memo from David O. Selznick,* New York: Avon, 1972.

Brandt, Jesse S. "By the Light of the RKO Moon." *Movietone News,* August 1974, pp. 1–6.
———. "Adventures in Time and Space." *Movietone News,* 29 September 1975, pp. 28–31.

Buscombe, E. "On Cukor." *Screen,* Autumn 1973, pp. 101–6.

Calendo, John. "Cukor on Cukor." *Interview,* December 1973, pp. 14, 15.

Carey, Gary. *Cukor and Co.: The Films of George Cukor and His Collaborators.* New York: Museum of Modern Art, 1971.

Clarens, Carlos. "Cukor and Justine." *Sight and Sound,* Spring 1969, p. 75.

Cutts, John. "The Philadelphia Story." *Films and Filming,* July 1962, p. 24.

Domarchais, Jean. *Cinema D'Aujourd'hui: George Cukor Vol. 33.* Paris: Edition Seghers, 1965.

Fritz, Bernardine S. "Our Cover Boy." *Script,* 2 December 1939, p. 18.

Gardner, Paul. "Spotlight on 'My Fair Lady' and Her Pygmalion." *New York Times,* 18 October 1964, sec. 2, p. 9.

"George Cukor." *Current Biography: 1943.* Ed. Maxine Block, New York: H. W. Wilson, 1944, pp. 156–57.

"George Cukor." *Who's Who in American Jewry: 1938–1939.* Ed. John Simons. New York: National News Assoc., p. 197.

Gillet, John, and Robinson, David. "Conversation with George Cukor." *Sight and Sound,* Autumn 1964, pp. 188–93.

Gow, Gordon. "The Quest for Realism." *Films and Filming,* December 1957, p. 13.

Haines, William. "A Bachelor's House." *Vogue,* 1 Nov. 1941, p. 89.

Harrison, Paul. "Famous Film Boss Tames High Strung Stars." *New York World Telegram,* 12 June 1936, p. 27.

Haskell, Molly. *From Reverence to Rape: The Treatment of Women in the Movies.* New York: Holt, Rinehart and Winston, 1973.

Higham, Charles. "George Cukor." *London Magazine,* May 1965, pp. 61–69.

Hill, Steven P. "Evaluating Directors." *Films in Review,* January 1961, pp. 7–13.
———. "The Popular Directors." *Films in Review,* August-September 1962 pp. 385–89.

Houston, Penelope. "Cukor and the Kanins." *Sight and Sound,* Spring 1955, pp. 186–91, 220.

189

———. "Film Reviews: 'A Star is Born.' " *Sight and Sound,* Spring 1955. pp. 194–95.

Lambert, Gavin. *On Cukor.* New York: Putnam, 1972.

———. *GWTW: The Making of Gone with the Wind.* Boston: Little and Brown, 1973.

Lasky, Jesse L., with Weldon, Don. *I Blow My Own Horn.* Garden City: Doubleday, 1957.

Mahin, John Lee. "A Writer's View of Directors." *Action,* March-April, 1975, p. 8.

McBride, J. "George Cukor: The Blue Bird." *Action,* November-December 1975, pp. 18–24.

"Men Behind the Stars: George Cukor, Director of 'Romeo and Juliet.' " *Motion Picture,* September 1936, p. 76.

Overstreet, Richard. "Interview with George Cukor." In *Interview with Film Directors,* edited by Andrew Sarris. New York: Avon, 1967, pp. 92–126.

Penfield, Cornelia. "Hollywood Helmsman: George Cukor." *Stage,* June 1936, pp. 60–64.

Phillips, Gene. "George Cukor: An Interview." *Film Comment,* Spring 1972, pp. 53–55.

Prouse, Derek. "Notes on Film Acting." *Sight and Sound,* Spring 1955, pp. 174–80.

Reid, John Howard. "So He Became a Ladies Man." *Films and Filming,* August 1960, p. 9.

———. "Women and Still More Women." *Films and Filming,* September 1960, p. 10.

Sarris, Andrew. *The American Cinema: Directors and Directions—1929–1968.* New York: Dutton, 1968.

Schickel, Richard. *The Men Who Made the Movies.* New York: Atheneum, 1975.

Seidenbaum, A. "Why They Let George Do It." *McCalls,* October 1964, pp. 189–90.

Small, Frank. "Filming the World's Greatest Love Story." *Photoplay,* September 1936, p. 46.

Theatre, July 1926, p. 35.

Tozzi, Romano V. "George Cukor: His Success Directing Women Has Obscured His Other Directorial Virtues." *Films in Review,* February 1958, pp. 53–54.

Tynan, Kenneth. "Genius and the Girls." *Holiday,* February 1961, p. 99.

CLARENCE BROWN: SELECTED BIBLIOGRAPHY

Brown, Clarence. "The Producer Must Be Boss." *Films in Review,* February 1951, p. 1.

Brownlow, Kevin. *The Parade's Gone By . . .* New York: Knopf, 1968.

"Clarence Brown Film Festival: Festival Notes." Ed. Ralph Allen et al. May 27–29, 1973. Knoxville: University of Tennessee, 1973.

"Clarence Brown May Leave M-G-M." *Moving Picture World,* 25 June 1927, p. 571.

Degenfelder, Pauline. "The Film Adaptation of Faulkner's 'Intruder in the Dust.' " *Literature Film Quarterly,* April 1973, pp. 138–48.

Everson, William. *American Silent Film.* New York: Oxford, 1978.

———. "Clarence Brown: A Survey of His Work." *Films in Review,* December 1973, pp. 577–89.

Fadiman, Regina. *Faulkner's 'Intruder in the Dust': Novel into Film.* Knoxville: University of Tennessee Press, 1978.

Gwin, Julia. " 'The Greatest Success of Joan Crawford and Clark Gable Is Yet to Come'—Says Director Clarence Brown." *Silver Screen,* December 1934, p. 26.

———. "The Inside Low Down." *Silver Screen,* May 1936, p. 34.

Jerome, V. J. *The Negro in Hollywood Films.* New York: Masses and Mainstream, 1950.

Manners, Dorothy. "Without Benefit of Close-Ups: Clarence Brown Never Displays His Temper." *Motion Picture Classic,* April 1928, pp. 26, 78.

McGilligan, Patrick. "Clarence Brown: Two Children's Movies." *Focus on Film,* Winter 1975, p. 34.

Norberg, Gunnar. "Men Behind the Stars: Clarence Brown, Director of Anna Karenina." *Motion Picture,* June 1936, p. 58.

Rotha, Paul. *The Film Till Now.* Rev. ed. New York: Funk and Wagnalls, 1949.

Shelton, John. "Life in the Raw." *Motion Picture Magazine,* January 1928, p. 28.

Thomson, David. *A Biographical Dictionary of the Cinema.* London: Secker and Warburg, 1975.

Tully, Jim. "Clarence Brown: An Estimate of the Foremost Exponent of the New School of Screen Directors." *Vanity Fair,* April 1928, pp. 79, 106.

Wagenknecht, Edward. *Movies in the Age of Innocence.* Norman: University of Oklahoma Press, 1962.

Weiner, Debra and McGilligan, Patrick. "Clarence Brown at 85." *Focus on Film,* Winter 1975, pp. 30–33.

Index
(to films cited in text)

Acquittal, The, 147, 180
Actress, The, 108, *109*, 133
Adam's Rib, 117, *117*, *118*, 131
Ah, Wilderness! *145*, 169, 184
American Madness, 33, 81
Angels in the Outfield, 187
Anna Christie, 163, *165*, 182
Anna Karenina, 139, 169, *170*, ⎩84
Arsenic and Old Lace, 84, *84*
Battle of Britain, The, 64, 85
Battle of China, The, 64, 68, 85
Battle of Russia, The, 64, 68, 85
Bhowani Junction, 133
Bill of Divorcement, A, 99, *99*, 126
Bitter Tea of General Yen, The, 31, 34, 81
Blue Bird, The, 105, 135
Born Yesterday, 115, 132
Broadway Bill, 82
Butterfly, 147, 180
Camille, 91, *93*, 94, 121, *128*, 128
Chained, 184
Chapman Report, The, 134
Come Live with Me, 185
Conquest, 169, 184
David Copperfield, 89, 100, 127, *127*
Dinner at Eight, 100, 115, *115*, 126
Dirigible, 81
Divide and Conquer, 64, 66, 84
Donovan Affair, The, 80
Don't Marry for Money, 180
Double Life, A, 101, 131
Eagle, The, 143, 151, 181
Edward, My Son, 101, 131
Emma, 182, *183*
Flesh and the Devil, 143, 153, *155, 156, 157,*
   181
Flight, 80
Forbidden, 31, 34, 81
For the Love of Mike, 24, 79
Free Soul, A, 166, 182
Fultah's Boarding House, 19
Gaslight, 101, *107*, 108, 131
Girls About Town, 98, 125
Gone with the Wind, 100

Goose Woman, The, 149, 181
Gorgeous Hussy, The, 143, 184
Great Redeemer, The, 146, 180
Grumpy, 97, 125
Heller in Pink Tights, 134
Her Cardboard Lover, 130
Here Comes the Groom, 75, 86
Hole in the Head, A, 76, 86
Holiday, 122, 128
Human Comedy, The, 169, 186
Idiot's Delight, 169, 185
Inspiration, 182
In the Heat of the Night, 174
Intruder in the Dust, 139, 174, *177*
It Happened One Night, 18, 36, *37, 38,* 82
It's a Big Country, 187
It's a Wonderful Life, 69, *71, 73,* 85
It Should Happen to You, 111, 133
Justine, 134
Keeper of the Flame, 130
Kiki, 181
Ladies of Leisure, 29, 80, *81*
Lady for a Day, 35, *35*, 36, 82
Last of the Mohicans, 180
Les Girls, 90, 133
Let's Make Love, 134
Letty Lynton, 183
Life of Her Own, A, 110, 132
Light in the Dark, 147, 180
Little Women, 100, *126*, 127
Long Pants, 20, *21*, 23, 79
Looking Forward, 183
Lost Horizon, 44, *46*, 82
Love Among the Ruins, 104, 135
Marrying Kind, The, 116, 132
Matinee Idol, The, 28, 79
Meet John Doe, 27, 58, *60, 62,* 84, *84*
Miracle Woman, The, 29, 81
Model and the Marriage Broker, The, 132
Mr. Deeds Goes to Town, 15, 39, *43*, 82
Mr. Smith Goes to Washington, 16, 19, 47,
   50, *51, 52, 53, 55,* 61, 65, 76, 83, *83*
My Fair Lady, 104, 134
National Velvet, 145, 169, *171*, 186

Navy Blues, 163, 182
Nazis Strike, The, 64, 67, 84
Night Flight, 183
Of Human Hearts, 169, 185
One Hour with You, 98
Our Betters, 111, 126
Pat and Mike, 108, *120,* 121, 132
Philadelphia Story, The, 114, 129
Platinum Blonde, 30, 81
Plymouth Adventure, 187
Pocketful of Miracles, A, 76, 86
Possessed, 182
Power of the Press, The, 80
Prelude to War, 64, 66, 84
Rain or Shine, 80
Rains Came, The, 185
Riding High, 75, 85
Rockabye, 126
Romance, 182, *182*
Romeo and Juliet, 128
Royal Family of Broadway, The, 98, 125
Sadie McKee, 167, *168,* 183
Say It with Sables, 80
Signal Tower, The, 147, 180
Smouldering Fires, 140, 147, 159, 181
Son-Daughter, The, 142, 183, *183*
Song of Love, 186
So This is Love, 79
Star Is Born, A, 92, *94,* 103, 104, 112, 133
State of the Union, 15, 74, 85
Strong Man, The, 20, 23, 79

Submarine, 80
Susan and God, 116, 129, *129*
Sylvia Scarlett, 127, *127*
Tarnished Lady, 98, 121, 125
That Certain Thing, 25, 79
They Met in Bombay, 185, *185*
To Please a Lady, 187
Trail of '98, The, 141, 181
Tramp, Tramp, Tramp, 22
Travels with My Aunt, 104, 112, *113,* 135
Two-faced Woman, 130
Unholy Three, The, 152
Virtuous Sin, The, 125
War Comes to America, 65, 85
Way of the Strong, The, 79
What Price Hollywood? 99, *109,* 125
When in Rome, 187
White Cliffs of Dover, The, 169, 186, *186*
Why We Fight series, The, 64, 84
Wife versus Secretary, 184
Wild is the Wind, 134
Winged Victory, 131
Woman of Affairs, A, 145, 159, *160, 161,* 181
Woman's Face, A, 130, *130*
Women, The, 101, 129, *129*
Wonder of Women, 181
Yearling, The, 141, 172, *173,* 186
You Can't Take It with You, 29, 49, 83
Younger Generation, The, 28, 34, 80
Zaza, 128